MEN IN PLACE

Men in Place

TRANS MASCULINITY, RACE,
AND SEXUALITY IN AMERICA

Miriam J. Abelson

 University of Minnesota Press
Minneapolis
London

Portions of chapter 5 were originally published as "'You Aren't from Around Here': Race, Masculinity, and Rural Transgender Men," *Gender, Place, and Culture* 23, no. 11 (2016): 1535–46; https://www.tandfonline.com/toc/cgpc20/current and "Dangerous Privilege: Trans Men, Masculinities, and Changing Perceptions of Safety," *Sociological Forum* 29, no. 3 (2014): 549–70.

Copyright 2019 by the Regents of the University of Minnesota

All rights reserved. No part of this publication may be reproduced, stored in a retrieval system, or transmitted, in any form or by any means, electronic, mechanical, photocopying, recording, or otherwise, without the prior written permission of the publisher.

Published by the University of Minnesota Press
111 Third Avenue South, Suite 290
Minneapolis, MN 55401-2520
http://www.upress.umn.edu

The University of Minnesota is an equal-opportunity educator and employer.

Library of Congress Cataloging-in-Publication Data
Names: Abelson, Miriam J., author.
Title: Men in place : trans masculinity, race, and sexuality in America / Miriam J. Abelson.
Description: Minneapolis : University of Minnesota Press, [2019] | Includes bibliographical references and index. |
Identifiers: LCCN 2018025293 (print) | ISBN 978-1-5179-0350-3 (hc) | ISBN 978-1-5179-0351-0 (pb)
Subjects: LCSH: Masculinity—United States. | Gender identity—United States.
Classification: LCC BF692.5 .A26 2019 (print) | DDC 155.3/32—dc23
LC record available at https://lccn.loc.gov/2018025293

To Shelley for, like, everything

Contents

	Introduction: "I Don't Have One Way to Be"	1
1	Masculinities in Space: Thugs, Rednecks, and Faggy Men	25
2	One Is Not Born a Man: Social Recognition and Situated Gendered Knowledges	59
3	"Strong When I Need to Be, Soft When I Need to Be": Situated Emotional Control and Masculinities	89
4	Geography of Violence: Spatial Fears and the Reproduction of Inequality	125
5	Institutional Contexts of Violence: Heterosexism and Cissexism in Everyday Spaces	155
	Conclusion: Contemporary Masculinities and Transgender Politics	193
	Acknowledgments	207
	Appendix A: Interviewee Demographics	211
	Appendix B: A Note on Methodology	215
	Notes	219
	Index	253

Introduction
"I DON'T HAVE ONE WAY TO BE"

What does it mean to be a man in America? Leo pondered this question as he sat at the kitchen table, recently cleared of dinner dishes, in his San Francisco apartment. The evening summer fog had crept in over the hills and settled above the streets, putting a chill in the air. At the start of the second decade of the twenty-first century, Leo's thoughts turned first to fear, even in the supposed progressive stronghold of the Bay Area. The recent killing of Oscar Grant, a young black man living in the Bay Area, by a transit police officer in the early hours of New Year's Day 2009 weighed heavily on Leo's mind:

> The consequences of being a black man was made even more relevant in my life when a young man named Oscar Grant was pulled off a train and shot in the back, and you know, I just easily see myself in that position being on a train coming from a party.... There was just this feeling of being on this crowded train and being pulled off because there was some kind of chaos and just resembling someone and to have that happen. It's just so tragic.

As a black man in his midthirties living in the same area, Leo could easily see Grant's fate as his own—pulled off a crowded train by police for fitting the description of a suspect and losing his life amid the chaos of New Year's revelry. The fear of being perceived by others as dangerous when in public spaces, by virtue of being a black man, was at the forefront of his mind. A big part of being a man meant watching himself when out in the world, never sure when he might become a target.

A few years later, Gavin pondered the same question as he sat in his office at the university where he had recently begun teaching. It was a late fall evening in his first semester living in a large city in the

Midwest Corn Belt state where he had spent most of his life. Frost was starting to form on the lawns surrounding the campus building, and the halls that had buzzed with students earlier in the day were now empty. As a white man in his late twenties, he was not worried about violence from the police like Leo. Yet upon reflection Gavin did notice that he watches himself in different spaces and shifts how he carries himself:

> I lower my voice sometimes when I'm going into auto part shops or whatever. Not in any conscious way. I just can feel this happening and recognizing that I'm doing it. Like, being hailed into this different version of masculinity or something. And I can tell that I move differently. And there have been times when I've said like [deep voice], "Thanks man," or something, and I'm like, "Who am I?"

His experience teaching courses in gender studies likely helped him interpret these interactions with other people in places like the auto parts stores.

> It's definitely not consciously this: "I don't want to be seen as gay." I think I usually feel like, going into auto parts stores in particular, I don't want to deal with the sort of scorn for people assuming that I don't know what I'm doing. I mean, I don't know what I'm doing. So it's also partly a compensation—if I seem more butch, maybe I won't have to deal.

Like Gavin, Leo also expressed himself differently depending on the situation. For instance, at work Leo changed his voice in order to enjoy camaraderie with the other men:

> At work I'm not going to use the funny high-pitched voice.... I work in a construction business, so it really is football, construction. Just kind of straight guy stuff, I guess, in its simplest form. They have a family, they have kids, they work, they support them. It really isn't too much that's going on. It's almost like a relief to go to work because it's almost so easy to get into that mode.

It was easy for Leo to fall into the expectations of this typically masculine space and the "straight guy stuff" that made up his interactions with coworkers, whereas Gavin was more uncomfortable in those kinds of spaces.

Leo and Gavin see themselves as different kinds of men. Gavin feels uncomfortable in "straight guy" spaces like the auto parts store, and Leo feels more at home in those spaces. Leo fears violence from the police as a black man, whereas Gavin, a white man, does not. Yet they both find themselves shifting and balancing their masculinity as they move through different contexts—not wanting to seem too feminine or gay in some settings but not wanting to be too masculine either. Another thing that Leo and Gavin have in common is that they are both trans men, in this case men who were assigned female at birth, raised as girls, and then transitioned to live as men.[1]

Despite their shared history of transition, Gavin identified as "mostly gay" and Leo as straight, though newly "bi-curious." Yet for both it was not just in straight guy spaces but also in queer or gay men's spaces that they shifted how they spoke and moved their bodies. Leo, who formerly identified as queer, was not into the "straight guy stuff" in every part of his life. In queer spaces, he expressed another aspect of himself:

> If I were to go to Pride or an all-queer event, then I could throw out my faggyness that I have and still be Leo and still be whole and all that. There's a time and a place that you allow certain things to come up.

In moving from his straight guy masculinity at work to being more effeminate in queer spaces, Leo expressed the whole range of himself. Even if he muted some of his more flamboyant side at work, he still felt that he was authentically himself. Gavin described being in gay male spaces versus the classroom where he teaches:

> Even though I feel more comfortable in gay male space, I feel myself pulled in a particular direction there too. I do more of the sort of gay gestures or speak in ways that are more gay in gay male space than I would in the classroom on a daily basis. . . . I think my movements are kind of like looser or my body moves more

in some ways. I sort of would like jut out my hip in some ways as part of talking.

Importantly, he did not say that anyone overtly pushed him to behave in a particular way but that he anticipated the possibility and then shifted his actions. Both Gavin and Leo felt pulled in different directions or to express particular parts of themselves, depending on the space.

Another trans man, Seth, a multiracial (black and white) twenty-three-year-old man living in urban Minnesota, summed up some of the tensions that underlie both Gavin's and Leo's stories:

> There are just general things about, you know, "What does it mean to be a man?" And having the relationships with some men that I do who are older than me, it's been eye-opening because it's like we're all trying to figure out what it means to be a man. Things that I thought were maybe more specific to me as a trans guy, it's actually that some of these things are just what it is to be a man. So I do fall into the stereotypes sometimes. Sometimes, I like stereotypical male things. Sometimes, I give in to the pressures of masculinity in America, and there are times where I feel more comfortable.

Seth had started living as a man about two years before I spoke with him. His was the final interview I conducted for a project that involved talking with over five dozen trans men in thirteen states across the U.S. West, South, and Midwest.[2] Seth's narrative mirrored one of the most consistent themes that emerged across the other men's stories: figuring out who he was as a man was an ongoing process, a process not unique to trans men. This process was complex and shifting for Seth, as it was for other interviewees. As his quote illustrates, this is a process he undertakes with a sense of larger standards for himself and other men, standards that line up at times with how he sees himself and, at other times, conflict with that self-image. Why did Seth "fall into stereotypes sometimes"? When did he "give in to the pressures of masculinity in America"? Where was he more comfortable?

The answer for Seth and the other men was that their expressions of masculinity and as men depended on the spaces and places they lived in and traveled through across their lives. Seth's own experiences illustrate the importance of context. Though he said being respectful and kind toward women was central to his identity, in sexual spaces he did not want to be seen as too much of a nice guy, because he thought women would not be attracted to him. He talked about how, as a man who is read as black, he tried to avoid dressing too "thuggish" when in public so that he would not become a target of the police or an object of fear to unknown women. In the context of public gender-segregated bathrooms, he feared violence against himself as a transgender person and, consequently, made sure to follow what he thought was typical behavior for men in that space. Visiting his white sister in a rural area of another state, he asked her why people were giving him strange looks, and she replied they were not used to seeing people of color in that town. The increased attention made him feel as if he did not belong as a man of color.

Seth's question about what it means to be a man in America was answered by another interviewee, Levi, who said, "I don't have one way to be. I have a bunch of ways, and I decide them situationally." Through the stories of sixty-six trans men living in the U.S. South, Midwest, and West, this book shows that men's experiences of gender, race, and sexuality are shaped by the various spaces they inhabit and move between throughout their lives. These spaces and places shape their masculinities and who they are as men. As the stories of Seth, Gavin, and Leo also show, race, sexuality, and class are tied up in these contexts. Their stories illustrate that something more complicated is happening in contemporary U.S. masculinity. Men do not want to be hypermasculine, but neither do they want to be too feminine. Instead, the ideal may be somewhere in between.

In the past few decades, feminist scholars have turned to the critical study of men and masculinities to understand the operation of patriarchal power and the ways men's behaviors and interactions constitute and support the systemic dominance of men over women. In the same period, transgender people have become more visible in U.S. society and transgender studies has expanded dramatically. The masculinities literature has mostly ignored the experiences of transgender men, and much of the research on transgender people has focused on trans people in urban areas on the East and West Coasts. Thus, it is crucial to move beyond these limitations to understand the full spectrum of transgender and masculine experiences. This book addresses these limitations by centering the stories of transgender men as men in three different regions and across urban, rural, and suburban spaces.

We learn from their stories that a sense of one's masculinity can change over time and is affected by shifts in life events. While a man might see his masculinity in a static way, the practices he engages in often shift depending on the spaces and places he finds himself. Indeed, we see that masculinities are tied up in relationship to others—spouses, potential sexual partners, parents, and other men in particular.

Further, the masculinities literature has long established that masculinities are patterns of practice but does not account for how individuals shift their practices, sometimes consciously but often in less than conscious ways based on the expectations of the situation. Trans men's stories offer a lens for seeing how the geographic context and institutional spaces where all men live their everyday lives shape these expectations. Men are pulled and sometimes pushed in everyday interactions to engage with these normative pressures. In most places and spaces, but certainly not all, I found the most common model for masculinity that emerged from interviewee's narratives was a Goldilocks masculinity.[3] This normative Goldilocks ideal prescribes an in-between masculinity that is not too masculine and not too feminine or effeminate and, in turn, shapes what people actually do in interaction. This masculine model is relational, meaning it is not just about how to be but about how or who not to be. One of the keys to this in-between ideal of contemporary U.S. masculinity is that men should be able to control their masculinity, such that they express it properly for the given situation and exert a spatially based control over their masculine expressions. Goldilocks masculinity is a hybrid masculinity, as it incorporates aspects of nonhegemonic masculinities to sustain the existing gender order amid challenges to its legitimacy. Inequalities persist under hybrid masculinities because they represent superficial rather than deep changes to contemporary dominating masculinities.

This chapter provides a foundation for the analysis that follows. It shows why any attempt to understand contemporary masculinities must engage in a deeply intersectional approach that compares men's experiences across multiple dimensions of space, such as region and urban and rural, as well as settings from public spaces to the home. The understanding that comes from this analysis expands our knowledge about masculinity, manhood, and the lives of transgender people, but more broadly, it tells us much about how inequalities of gender, race, sexuality, and class persist in the twenty-first century across a variety of spaces.

INTERSECTIONALITY

Emerging from the work of black and other women of color feminist scholars and activists, such as Kimberlé Crenshaw and Patricia Hill Collins, intersectional understandings of identity and social structure trouble white feminist notions that gender alone is a sufficient category of analysis.[4] Intersectionality has become something of a buzzword in both academic and popular feminist circles. According to Michael Hames-Garcia, it is often overused as an "umbrella for any and every theoretical contribution by a woman of color" or as a way to signal a feminist analysis that goes beyond analyzing gender alone.[5] That said, intersectional approaches generally share the idea that multiple social identities and positions are socially constructed, created, and perpetuated along with one another and are tied up with relations of both domination and privilege. Overall, these approaches share a nonadditive and complex understanding of power, identity, and social inequality.[6] They can be used to understand interlocking systems or matrices of domination, the inequality regimes of institutions, and how individuals cannot easily separate their many social identities of race, gender, sexuality, class, and other aspects of difference.[7]

I use Hames-Garcia's definition of multiplicity as my core understanding of the relationship between gender, sexuality, class, and race throughout this book. He defines multiplicity as "the mutual constitution and overlapping of simultaneously experienced and politically significant categories such as ability, citizenship, class, ethnicity, gender, race, religion, and sexuality."[8] This means all of these categories are constantly present, overlapping, and intermingling, even when one or another stands out more in a particular narrative or context. Though gender is often at the center of the analysis in *Men in Place*, I return regularly to the question of how sexuality, race, and class impact the social interactions I describe, whether these interconnections came from trans men's own reflections or by drawing on broader understandings of these linked dynamics.

The work of women of color feminist scholars has most influenced my analysis of gender, race, and sexuality as both interconnected with one another and shifting among regions and urban, rural, and suburban spaces. In particular, Evelyn Nakano Glenn's comparative regional approach in *Unequal Freedom* provides inspiration for viewing race, gender, and class as interconnected systems, not just individual traits or beliefs, that vary based on the regional conditions that shape local labor markets and citizenship rights, as well as resistance to inequality in those spaces.[9] Further, Chandra Talpade Mohanty's description in *Feminism without Borders* of her own experiences as a South Asian woman whose race was read differently in different U.S. regions, such as when she was seen as alternately Latinx or Native American by others on the street when she traveled in the U.S. Southwest, shows how the same individual is affected by different regional meanings of race and gender by moving between spaces.[10] These texts, among others by women of color feminist scholars, were both the inspiration for the project and the main frame I drew on to analyze the complexities of trans men's stories as they move across regions and urban, rural, and suburban spaces.[11] Using these frameworks demonstrates that geographic variation is as important to understanding the lives of men as knowing how men's lives differ from one another and are organized based on race, class, sexuality, and gender.

INEQUALITY IN INTERACTION

This book draws on a range of perspectives that explain how gender, race, class, and sexuality are produced and perpetuated, particularly in social interaction. Though each of these aspects of difference exist and intersect at individual, interactional, institutional, and structural levels, interaction is a key site where they are linked together, and it is the primary focus of *Men in Place*.[12] Race, gender, class, and sexuality cannot be reduced to one another and do not always work in the exact same ways. But they are each major forces in the social world, and the socially constructed nature of each has been extensively theorized across the social sciences and humanities. These theories' understandings of how race, gender, class, and sexuality are reproduced in interaction provide the foundation for this book's larger analysis.

Moments of racial and gender categorization, as well as the ways they shape interaction in everyday life, are important sites for the maintenance and re-creation of social inequality. Assigning race and gender to others in interaction, whether we get it right or not, sets the basis for the interaction that follows because that categorization carries with it a set of cultural scripts and ideas about race and gender. The importance of categorization is most clear when we have trouble categorizing someone else: often, the flow of the interaction slows or stops in these moments and, for most, must be resolved before the interaction can continue.[13]

Those resulting interactions, based on how one categorizes others, are where larger structures of racism and sexism play out. Candace West and Don Zimmerman's theory of "doing gender" illustrates that gender is formed in interaction and is an accomplishment or practice where individuals manage their behaviors in relation to normative expectations based on others' assumptions of them as men and women. These expectations of how men and women ought to behave vary between different spaces or contexts.[14] This does not mean that individuals always conform to what is expected of them; rather, it means that with every action, individuals are at risk of being held accountable by others for appropriately "manly" or "womanly" behavior, even when their practice does not meet normative standards. Importantly, individuals anticipate this risk, and this too shapes interaction.[15] For example, Gavin anticipates that if he goes against the expectations for how men are supposed to behave in the auto parts store, he may have to explain himself or face other potential consequences. This consideration of potential accountability does not fully determine his behavior but factors into what he does in the interaction. In a related vein, Judith Butler's work in *Gender Trouble* illustrates that the repetitive nature of this performance, doing, or practice of gender in interaction creates not only gender as we know it but heterosexuality as well.[16] Through Michael Omi and Howard Winant's foundational work in *Racial Formation*, we see that in the realm of everyday interaction race acts as a system of meaning masquerading as "common sense" that shapes the ways we categorize and then form ideas about and expectations of others.[17] Following Ruth Wilson Gilmore, I define racism as "the state-sanctioned or extralegal production and exploitation of group-differentiated vulnerability to premature death."[18] Race as a category not only inheres to and affects people who are racialized as black, Asian and Pacific Islander, Native American, or Latinx but also works in the formation of whiteness as a racialized category.[19] White or whiteness is an actively constructed racial identity, though it often remains unmarked, that confers power and material resources to white people.[20] Again, the salience of both race and gender as central forms of categorization in everyday interaction is clearly evident through examples of how interaction is disrupted and cannot easily move forward as a consequence of one person's inability to read the gender or race of another person.[21]

Sexuality scholars in both symbolic interactionist and queer traditions have also established that sexual difference and inequality are formed and play out in interaction. Despite some differences in their theoretical underpinnings, these perspectives both see sexual identity and the meaning of sexual desires and behaviors as historically constructed. The parallel emergence of these perspectives in the second half of the twentieth century is best exemplified through the early work of Mary McIntosh and Ken Plummer in sociology and the foundational work of Michel Foucault in queer approaches.[22] I utilize these perspectives in particular to highlight how the construction of heterosexuality as the normative standard of sexuality happens in interaction and rests on the perpetuation of a heterosexual/homosexual binary as a diffuse and diverse normalizing practice and power, which alternatively can be understood as compulsory heterosexuality.[23] Like racial, class, and gender subjugation, sexual subjugation is also created in discourse and reinforced through a range of disciplinary mechanisms. In interaction, individuals can be disciplined if they break the norms of the particular space. More important, the norms learned in domestic spaces and public settings, such as hospitals and schools, are internalized by individuals, and they actually engage in self-discipline.[24] Thus, sexuality, gender, and race are all reproduced in interaction through a variety of overlapping and interrelated mechanisms and processes.

Space, Place, and Inequality

The ways in which inequality in interaction is interconnected with space and place have been taken up unevenly in the social sciences and interdisciplinary fields of queer and transgender studies. Feminist and queer geographers demonstrate that space and place are simultaneously gendered, raced, classed, and sexualized.[25] Interactions happen in particular spaces and places. Gender, race, and sexuality each shape the meanings that people attach to space, how people shape the environment, and the ways they move in and through particular contexts. At the same time, the gendered and racialized subjectivities and identities created in particular spaces continue to shape the raced and gendered meanings of those spaces. Thus, there is a recursive effect and fluidity to the relation of gender, race, sexuality, and class to space.[26]

Sociologists of gender and sexuality often leave space and place unmarked in their understandings of social inequality, though some subfields, such as rural sociology, explicitly focus on space and place.[27] Space and place are at the center of scholarship on inequality in geography. As Tim Cresswell shows, people who deviate from the normative gendered, racial, classed, and sexual standards of particular spaces find themselves to be "out of place" in those spaces and are often punished for those transgressions.[28] Thus, this book is part of a larger effort to show how space and place are primary to understanding the production of inequality in interaction.

Space has been quite important, across a range of disciplines, to understanding the formations of sexual communities and identities. For example, sociologist Japonica Brown-Saracino's work shows how even small cities that share similar characteristics produce different lesbian and bisexual women's identity cultures.[29] Earlier queer writing tied the formation of lesbian and gay identities to urban spaces.[30] Jack Halberstam and others have argued that this notion produced a "metronormative" migration narrative from rural to urban, with the general charge for gender and sexual minorities to "get thee to a big city" in order to express queer and transgender selves.[31] More recent queer concerns with place have emerged as a challenge to the body of scholarship that tends to assume gay, lesbian, and transgender people flourish only in cities.[32] Mary Gray's ethnographic research on rural queers in Eastern Kentucky attests to the value of examining lesbian, gay, transgender, and queer stories outside urban centers. Gray documents the creative strategies used by rural queer youth to carve out queer spaces in small towns, such as doing drag shows at Wal-Mart.[33] Emily Kazyak's interviews with rural Midwest gays and lesbians also illustrate that individuals can develop sexual and gender identities in line with rural rather than urban spaces.[34] Further, E. Patrick Johnson's life histories of black gay men and same-gender-loving women in the South trace unique "quare" identities and particular racialized sexual knowledges across urban and rural spaces in the region commonly thought to be the most hostile for sexual minorities.[35]

The urban gay and lesbian communities that stand as the central place of queer and transgender life do not necessarily reflect the realities of many gender and sexual minority people of color. Though some queer theorists include race in their analysis, they tend to leave the unmarked queer subject as white. One way this commonly happens is by engaging in racial analysis only when examining texts featuring people of color, whereas their general analysis of sexuality or gender focuses on racially unmarked white subjects. Broadly speaking, queer of color scholarship integrates queer and women of color analyses, along with materialist approaches, to understand the complex workings of social life and relations of domination.[36]

While trans people are at the center of theorizing in queer theory and are treated frequently as objects of theory formation, they often face exclusion from the queer, lesbian, and gay spaces that have been the primary focuses of research in queer studies.[37] A small but growing literature on transgender geographies illustrates how trans people experience urban spaces differently from cisgender gay and lesbian people, including a higher incidence of harassment, and demonstrates that trans people's experiences differ between cities and other spaces.[38] Overall, rural trans men and those in urban areas outside the West Coast and the Northeast are often missing from the limited scholarship on trans people.[39] The approaches to space as developed by feminist, queer, and transgender geographers, along with the insights of rural sociology used in this book, are essential to getting at the complexity of trans men's lives. Thus, the critical focus on trans men in these places makes a crucial contribution to queer scholarship on space and place, as well as to the study of masculinities and trans men.

TRANS MEN AND MASCULINITIES

This book takes seriously the experience of trans men both as men and as transgender people. Some interviewees described themselves as men first and as transgender second; others, as transgender first; and still others, as equally both.[40] The experiences that are particular to trans men are men's experiences. Narratives of other particular groups of men, such as white men, disabled men, or young men, give us both insight into the larger category and understandings of the particularities of this group of men that may not generalize to all men. I do explore further what it means to be a man, but a central aim for this book is that readers will come away with a better understanding of the variety of trans men's lives as men. Trans men, due to their histories of being treated as women or girls for at least part of their life and the experience of transition, are often more capable than many cisgender men of articulating their experiences as men. Thus, this book focuses on trans men as a group of men who not only are often left out of masculinities scholarship but also may have particular insights into contemporary U.S. masculinities.[41]

The representation of transgender people in medical studies and media in Europe and the United States emerged in the early twentieth century, though people certainly challenged rigid gender binaries long before that. The academic and scientific study of transgender people has a troubled history. The medical and psychiatric discourses of the twentieth and twenty-first centuries have tended to frame transgender people as sometimes ill, deviant, and even menacing. Early writings by feminists such as Janice Raymond painted trans people as either agents or dupes of patriarchy and sociological studies, and others, such as those by Dwight Billings and Thomas Urban, viewed them as dupes of the medical–legal complex.[42] Feminists of Raymond's ilk have and continue to cause harm to transgender people.[43] In addition, trans people's lives and experiences have been objects for gender theory formation, as in the work of West and Zimmerman, as well as Butler.[44]

Newer scholarly efforts often by and for trans people work to address these past ills. Both the field of transgender studies and the use of *transgender* as an umbrella term for people whose gender varies from their sex assigned at birth or otherwise crosses established gender boundaries emerged in the United States in the 1990s. This emergence signaled a shift in which transgender people themselves were able to engage fully in scholarship about their lives and others began treating transgender people more as subjects than as objects.[45] One of the key features of the fast-growing field of transgender studies is that it is not just about transgender people or "transgender phenomena" but explicitly for the benefit of transgender people. Trans scholars, including Jay Prosser, Vivian Namaste, and Raewyn Connell, among many others, have roundly critiqued other gender and sexuality scholars for routinely theorizing from trans people's lives while often ignoring trans people's own understandings of themselves, as well as their material conditions.[46] This new field has begun to address its biases that center white, U.S. trans scholars and lives through the emergence of robust trans of color scholarship, including scholars such as micha cárdenas, C. Riley Snorton, and Jin Haritaworn.[47] Snorton, in particular in *Black on Both Sides*, exemplifies the potential to understand trans and blackness together in ways that remake understandings of race and gender.[48] *Men in Place*, while focusing on men and masculinity, shares a desire with this work to keep optics of sexuality, race, gender, and disability always at the forefront of analysis and to imagine new possibilities for expanding and rethinking possibilities for trans lives and analytics. The critical trans studies work of this book seeks to speak with instead of about trans communities—rather than merely draw forth trans people's understanding of themselves and their material conditions in order to generate new theoretical knowledge. This text combines approaches from transgender studies with critical scholarship on men and masculinities so as to fully recognize this group of men as transgender, as people who practice masculinities, and as men more broadly. It draws on an intersectional perspective, along with an understanding of the instability and fluidity of these categories, to show that trans men are men who have sometimes complicated gender identities and that the category of man is unstable and fluctuating.

Masculinities

While this book does contribute to understandings of inequality in interaction and to transgender studies, its primary contribution is to the field of critical masculinities studies. To analyze trans men's experiences of masculinity in interaction, I draw on the theories of masculinity and power associated with Raewyn Connell's work.[49] With an understanding of the socially constructed and relational nature of gender, Connell shows that masculinities play an important role in sustaining contemporary societies that are structured through gender, particularly the domination of men over women and some groups of men over others. According to Connell, masculinities are patterns of practice that "*refer* to male bodies (sometimes directly, sometimes symbolically and indirectly), but are not *determined* by male biology."[50] In other words, masculinities are practices associated with bodies assigned male at birth, but they are not always just the actual behaviors of men. These two concepts, patterns of practice associated with male bodies and what men do, are often treated as the same thing in scholarly writing.[51] This conflation of the two loses the nuance of Connell's definition and makes these social practices seem like natural extensions of bodies assigned male at birth. Yet scholars such as C. J. Pascoe, Jack Halberstam, and Kath Browne illustrate that women and people with bodies assigned female at birth also practice masculinities.[52] Thus, the lack of focus by masculinities scholars on masculinities practiced by women or transgender people means that the field evidences a cisgender and biologically essentialist bias.

To move away from these biases, men and masculinities need to be thought of as distinct but connected analytic concepts. Masculinities, as patterns of practice, can be enacted by people with various gender and sex embodiments or other aspects of social location (e.g., race, class, sexuality, ability); however, particular patterns of practice adhere more easily to some kinds of people. Compare, for example, a hip-hop masculinity as enacted by a young black man to the same masculinity as done by a white man. The joke of the white rapper shows that this particular style never adheres to white men's bodies as well as it does to black men's; instead, it slips off more easily because it is seen as inauthentic. Women and other people who are not men do masculinities, but those practices will likely be evaluated and seen differently by others based on how they categorize their sex, race, and so on. It can be difficult to define when women are practicing masculinities or when men are practicing femininities. This determination must be based on the social and historical context and by asking whether the practices are associated in that setting with male or female bodies, or if the association is contested and in flux. In line with these distinctions, trans masculinities are a subset of masculinities. I use this phrase to distinguish masculinities in general, which might be practiced by cisgender men, trans men, cis and trans women, and nonbinary people alike, from those that might be particular to trans men, though women and nonbinary people can practice trans masculinities as well.

While the wider field of men and masculinities research tends to leave out trans men as a group of men, scholarship that includes Henry Rubin's description of trans men as "always already men" and the recent special issue of the journal *NORMA* on trans masculinities consider trans men's experiences both as transgender people and as men.[53] Three themes that emerge from the most recent sociologically oriented research on trans men suggest that trans men are well versed in discussions of gender and sexuality, practice a variety of masculinities, and experience significant changes in interaction after transition that vary by differences in other identities or social positions.[54] Kristen Schilt's study of trans men in the workplace in California and Texas is an example of how trans men are treated differently at work based on whether others perceive them as men or women and that these workplace experiences vary based on race and other aspects of difference. Trans men's experiences in the workplace after transition illustrate that gender inequality, between men and women and for transgender people, persists in the twenty-first century.[55] Additionally, there has been growing research on partners of trans men, such as Carla Pfeffer's work on queer families, that demonstrates the family is a particularly important context in which to understand how gender transitions are relational.[56] Yet like much queer research, this field has tended to be geographically and racially limited, focusing on the lives of trans people in a few large cities on the East and West Coasts and on the experiences of white trans people.[57] In line with Vivian Namaste's call for research on trans people that shows how the construction of gender varies in different spaces, including region as a category of analysis, it is crucial to move this work across spaces and scales.[58]

The key insights of the critical study of masculinity drawing from Raewyn Connell's scholarship are that in a given time and place there are multiple masculinities, that there is a hierarchy of masculinities, and that at the top of that hierarchy is a hegemonic masculinity that serves to legitimate male dominance.[59] The idea of multiple masculinities, often marked by difference in race, sexuality, and class, implicitly signals something similar to an intersectional framework.[60] For example, Karen Pyke's work demonstrates that class differences among men affect the masculinities they practice between the contexts of work and family.[61] According to James Messerschmidt, hegemonic masculinity is "the culturally idealized form of masculinity in a given historical and social setting," and its most important feature is that it legitimates patriarchy.[62] As theorized by Connell, hegemonic masculinity is open to contestation and is not a static type, though in practice many researchers treat it as such.[63] Thus, rather than being associated with whatever form legitimates the dominance of men over women and some men over others in a particular time and place, it is more often thought of as a fixed and toxic type centered on traits such as violence, a lack of emotional expression, and control. In contrast, research has found that hegemonic masculinity varies historically, as in the changing meaning of manhood in the United States.[64] Hegemonic masculinity, as Connell and Messerschmidt have argued, also has local, regional, and global variants.[65]

The concept of hegemonic masculinity is so ubiquitous in scholarship on men and masculinities that it has many meanings, but as when hegemonic masculinity is portrayed as a fixed type, these uses often stray considerably from Connell's original ideas.[66] However, Demetrakis Demetriou shows that in Connell's understanding hegemonic masculinity is always defined against subordinated masculinities and femininities, without the capacity to incorporate them in the process of change.[67] This fixed notion of hegemonic masculinity has difficulty reconciling itself with observed changes to normative masculine ideals.[68] Thus, in the sense that Connell's concept is usually used, there is a hegemonic masculinity that is strictly defined against subordinated masculinities in a given time and place, but that hegemonic masculinity can be contested and changed. Demetriou instead proposes the concept of a hegemonic masculine bloc, which utilizes a more Gramscian meaning of hegemony, to think of hegemonic masculinity as incorporating or appropriating aspects of subordinated or marginalized masculinities in order to retain the gender order. This can be particularly insidious as a process of change, as Demetriou explains: "The hegemonic bloc changes in a very deceptive and unrecognizable way. It changes through negotiation, appropriation, and translation, through the transformation of what appears counter-hegemonic and progressive into an instrument of backwardness and patriarchal reproduction."[69] In other words, changes to masculinities may look substantial but can actually serve to mask the perpetuation of inequality.

Building on Demetriou's critique, C. J. Pascoe and Tristan Bridges argue that these softer and gentler hegemonic ideals are *hybrid masculinities*, where some subordinated or marginalized practices are taken up and incorporated into hegemonic ideals.[70] They describe three different possible explanations for this: that hybrid masculinities reflect local variations but not widespread changes to the global gender order (as Connell and Messerschmidt claim);[71] that they are a sign of decreasing homophobia (per Eric Anderson);[72] or (as Pascoe and Bridges argue) that they represent a change to the appearance of these masculinities but do not substantially effect the creation of gender inequality. In other words, the final explanation suggests that the incorporation of subordinated practices rather than the rejection of them may be a new way to produce gender inequality with a gentler face. In speaking to this debate, the crucial related questions become, where are hybrid masculinities emerging, and how does space figure into these contests among masculinities and filter into men's everyday practices?

Space and Masculinities

Masculinities are constructed in relation to space and place, and local through transnational levels are interconnected.[73] Rich feminist scholarship in the geography of masculinities has developed to examine this relationship between masculinities, place, and space. Though this area draws heavily from the sociology of masculinities, sociological and interdisciplinary masculinities literature tends to leave these geographic insights unexamined.[74] Connell and Messerschmidt, in their reevaluation of the concept of hegemonic masculinity, conclude that locally specific constructions of hegemonic masculinity have been an emergent theme of research on men and masculinities since the introduction of the concept.[75] In sociology, studies such as Shannon Bell and Yvonne Braun's research with environmental activists in Appalachia demonstrate that the regional hegemonic masculinity tied to coal mining prevents men from joining in environmental activism.[76] This is suggestive in seeing how regional industry shapes gender relations, but regions are not shaped by industry alone. For example, Sarah Crawley suggests that regional weather patterns affect female-assigned people's ability to practice masculinities through masculine gender displays, as when the heat and humidity in South Florida makes chest binding more difficult.[77] Scholars need to do more work to understand the multiple factors in the production of masculinities in different U.S. regions. Though there has been scholarship examining regional masculinities, there has been little comparative work between U.S. regions.[78] The comparative approach in this book addresses these gaps.

Throughout *Men in Place*, I demonstrate that rural and urban spatial distinctions are important for locally situated practices of masculinities but that individuals themselves are not static.[79] They are not fixed in one institution or spatial location throughout their life or even in the course of a typical day, and we must examine how gendered practices reflect moving between these locations. The spatial nature of masculinities and the contextual influences on gender, race, class, and sexuality in interaction point to the need to explore place as an important influence in gender relations when examining the lives of trans men.

THE STUDY

This book draws on interviews I completed with sixty-six trans men living in the U.S. West, Midwest, and Southeast across urban, rural, and suburban spaces. The first interviews took place on the West Coast, specifically California and Oregon. After seeing the importance of space and place in the early interviews, I expanded the study to the Southeast, including Georgia, Tennessee, Kentucky, North and South Carolina, and Florida. The final set of interviews took place in the Midwest, the literal and figurative middle of the United States, including Illinois, Indiana, Michigan, Ohio, Wisconsin, and Minnesota. Some interviews took place in major cities like San Francisco, Atlanta, Chicago, and Minneapolis; others, in medium-sized cities; and still others, in rural places known to few people besides the local population.

The interviews in each region cannot fully represent the nuance and difference of all places within each region, state, county or city. Yet interviewing men in a range of places allowed for a comparative analysis across the three regions and suburban, rural, and urban spaces. While this comparative approach may gloss over some differences within regions or between rural spaces, the analysis often relies more on interviewees' ideas about different places. These ideas are their geographic imaginaries, notions people and groups have about place and space that turn out to be quite meaningful for the reproduction of inequality in everyday life. It is important to note here that while my initial thinking about each region and of urban versus rural space started from official definitions, like those used by the U.S. census, the general sense of each region—West, South, and Midwest—was confirmed in trans men's narratives of their lives in these places. At the same time their experiences were particular to a specific place, interviewees' narratives of place contained a broader shared understanding of what ideas like "Midwest" or "city" meant. Regions can take on meaning and shape a sense of belonging due to shared ideas about the regional landscape, history, and literary and artistic production, and they did so among the interviewees.[80] As Katherine McKittrick demonstrates through an examination of black women's geographies, it is imperative to not just study maps or the physical features of spaces but also examine the ways they are imagined so that we do not fall into the trap of uncritically assuming that space "just is."[81]

At the time of interview, a little over half of the interviewees lived in urban places, a quarter in suburban, and the rest in rural or other nonmetropolitan settings—though some urban men had lived in rural places at some point in their lives and the other way around. About one-fifth of the interviewees identified as men of color, and the remainder, as primarily white. They ranged in age from nineteen to fifty-five years old and varied from just beginning their transition to having started twenty-two years before the interview. As I quote the interviewees throughout the book I try to give a sense of where they lived, though I am purposefully vague at times in order to maintain their confidentiality.

In most cases the interviews took place when I traveled to the areas where these men lived their day-to-day lives. The conversations took an open-ended approach; I encouraged them to tell the stories of their lives as men and to emphasize whatever was most important to them and their life. I used a modified grounded theory approach to code and analyze the interview transcripts. This method of analysis consists of starting from the interviews themselves and systematically reviewing them to see what themes and patterns emerge across the interviewee's stories, rather than just relying on what I or other researchers think might be important. At the same time, it is "modified" because I incorporated a few of those preconceived ideas that came from earlier research or theoretical ideas about masculinities and transgender men's experiences.[82] As a non-transgender-identified researcher, I emphasize the experiences and voices of the interviewees by including direct quotations from them throughout the book. These quotes are meant to illustrate various patterns that emerged across the interviews, though no single quote or single interviewee can stand in for all men, all trans men, or any other group of people. By looking across sixty-six men's experiences in depth, we learn something different from what we can through either a single memoir or a large survey about masculinities and space; about intersections of race, sexuality, class, and gender; or about transgender lives.

ORGANIZATION OF THE BOOK

Building on the intersectional lens on space, place, interaction, and inequality, chapter 1 intervenes in recent debates about the changing nature of U.S. masculinities through trans men's narratives of contemporary masculine ideals. After an overview of the histories of masculine ideals in the Midwest, South, and West, I sketch out the ideals that emerged in trans men's discussion of contemporary masculinity that fell on a continuum with hypermasculinity at one end and femininity or effeminacy at the other. Racialized hypermasculinities, such as the thug and the redneck, as well as hypereffeminacies, such as the faggy man, exist at the extremes of this continuum and operate as racial and sexual controlling images tied to particular spaces. These spatially inflected controlling images, which pose some men as excessive and out of control, become an image for most men to define themselves against. Instead, they strive to be a regular guy. The regular guy is not overtly macho, appears to be heterosexual but is not homophobic, and cares for and provides for his family. This is a middle-class white suburban ideal of normalcy, even if it exists across regions and urban and rural spaces. Goldilocks masculinity, not too masculine and not too feminine, is central to the regular guy. The prevalence of Goldilocks masculinity suggests that while there have been some surface changes to contemporary masculinities, it does not mean there have been substantive changes to the mechanisms that create systemic inequalities based on gender, race, sexuality, and class.

Chapter 2 focuses on the question, Who, exactly, is a man? Trans men's stories illustrate that inhabiting the social category of man is not based in biology, or even solely in one's identity or legal classification, but rather is a process tied to social recognition. This recognition as a man in everyday interaction provides a sense of authenticity but also carries the consequence of being treated differently by other people. Trans men's accounts of recognition suggest that for all men one is not born a man but rather becomes one again and again (and again) as they encounter the gendered, racialized, and sexual knowledges and related expectations of different social contexts. Thus, the social experience of being a man is a becoming that happens through recognition rather than a static or fixed trait.

Employing both sociological and interdisciplinary queer understandings of emotion and affect, chapter 3 demonstrates that the normative ideal for men in the contemporary United States is to be not too hard and not too soft. In practice this ideal means that from the public arena of politics to everyday life men should neither be emotionless nor show excessive emotion but instead be somewhere in between. Through an analysis of trans men's narratives of calm, crying, anger, aggression, and sexual urges, it is clear that the key to proper masculine emotion is for men to demonstrate control and rationality through expressing emotions that are appropriate in a given space. This control and spatially appropriate expression maps onto the in-between ideal of the regular guy and Goldilocks masculinity. Further, gendered, racialized, classed, and sexualized notions of emotion shape who does emotion properly and who does not. The idea of individual control of emotion valorizes a self-disciplining emotional subject who demonstrates contextually appropriate emotion and at the same time constructs its opposite—others who are less rational and unable to control themselves. This discourse of masculinity and emotion suggests that hypermasculine classed and racialized men, such as the thug and the redneck, cannot control violent emotions and that faggy men, as well as women, are overly emotional. Contextually appropriate emotion is central to being a regular guy and achieving a Goldilocks masculinity in contrast to classed, racialized, and sexualized others. Men who can express emotions that are "in place" in a given space are suitable citizens and holders of power.

One of the most persistent narratives of LGBT lives in the contemporary United States is that if queer and transgender people exist in rural spaces and regions, such as the South, they must lead incredibly difficult lives. At the center of this story is the idea that these spaces should be feared because they are inherently dangerous for queer and transgender people. Chapter 4 examines the relationship between fear, a powerful emotion shaped by space and place, and masculinities in the lives of trans men. Overall, this chapter adds a spatial dimension to understanding how fears operate and complicates narratives of queer and trans violence in rural and urban spaces. Trans men mapped their fears spatially, with a particular focus on how race and sexuality shape safety in rural spaces. Fears of violence operate as disciplinary mechanisms that keep existing social relations in place by encouraging men to enact conforming behaviors and to be complicit in sexism, racism, and other modes of domination. Some of the specific fears that interviewees expressed are particular to trans men, but these dynamics of fear and violence shape masculinities more broadly. Men's fears draw on racialized, classed, and sexualized controlling images, and spatially based fears affect the masculinities men engage in. This analysis demonstrates the importance of an intersectional approach to understanding the effects of fear and violence on men.

Chapter 5 applies the same framework on violence, fear, inequality, and space from chapter 4 to illustrate how particular features of two institutions, public bathrooms and medical contexts, promote specific patterns of social domination. As trans men's narratives illustrate, these institutions are important spaces where disciplinary power works through the enforcement of norms. Gender and sexuality—and to varying extents class, race, and ability—are particularly salient for trans men in these institutional spaces because the spaces are largely structured around these social categories. The chapter's two case studies show that these structural arrangements foster fear and violence that are produced in interaction; I suggest that these structural arrangements need to change in order to combat social inequality. Normative masculinities are reinforced through the structure of these contexts. The interactional rules of public gender-segregated bathrooms reproduce the link between homophobia and masculinity. Further, the structure of medical and psychiatric settings that gives authority to providers and makes patients vulnerable sets the stage for multiple experiences of violence for trans men. I call these types of spaces amplified sites, contexts structured in such a way that processes of categorization and norms of gender, sexuality, and race play out in heightened ways when people interact in the space. The effects produced in amplified sites carry out of these contexts and then reverberate or ripple across our social lives.

I conclude by returning to the larger questions about men's experiences of gender, race, and sexuality raised in the introduction by reconsidering the evidence provided throughout the book. The conclusion addresses wider discourses on contemporary understandings of social inequality, transgender politics, and masculinities. This discussion emphasizes that knowing how space and place shape everyday social interaction is necessary for understanding the continuing reproduction of social inequality in the contemporary United States and that this knowledge is crucial for projects of social justice that seek to dismantle this inequality. In this vein, I discuss the possibilities and pitfalls of contemporary trans politics that focus legal and political efforts on law-and-order tactics versus more transformative possibilities. Finally, I return to debates about the nature of contemporary hybrid masculinities to argue that they actually reinscribe gender, racial, and sexual inequality and that it is important to locate the spatial dimensions of hybrid masculinities in order to produce a sustained challenge to inequality.

In all, this book relies on trans men's narratives to show how space and place shape men's experience of race, gender, and sexuality in the contemporary United States. Due to the historical and continuing objectification of trans people in scholarship, I have often paused to reconsider whether I, as a non-trans-identified, gender-nonconforming woman, should continue this project at all. While I still have moments of ambivalence, the desires of the men I interviewed for their stories to be out in the world have kept this project going. Levi, a scholar and writer I interviewed early on, summed up this sentiment well when he said, "I encourage you, as much as you can, to get this stuff out there in as many formats as you can. That's our job. The world needs to hear in as many ways as possible." Even with the rapid increase of representation of trans people in recent years, from television shows to contentious public policy debates over bathrooms, the broad range of trans men's experiences is often absent. As a feminist researcher, my aim in this book is to center the interviewees' own interpretations of their lives in order to bring out the multiple voices of trans men. Further, I take the perspective that trans men give us crucial insight about men as a group because, quite simply, they are men.

1
Masculinities in Space
THUGS, REDNECKS, AND FAGGY MEN

From Michael Brown to Cliven Bundy, debates over the lives of racialized groups of men are central to the political and media landscape of the contemporary United States. In recent years, graphic video footage of police killings of black men such as Michael Brown—and its circulation on social media—has attracted public attention to the ongoing violence perpetrated by law enforcement against black men in urban spaces. This violence, as well as the militarized reactions to the protest movements that have risen up in response, illustrates that authorities and the public at large perceive black masculinity and black men as inherently threatening. At the same time, white rancher Cliven Bundy's standoff with federal authorities in Nevada and the armed occupation of a federal wildlife refuge on Northern Paiute lands in eastern Oregon by white militants (led by Bundy's sons) are the latest examples of a decades-long fight against what some rural men in the West see as federal encroachment onto grazing lands and their rights as individuals. Whiteness shapes white rural men's grievances as they assert their frustration over a loss of their perceived rightful privileges as white men and largely protects them from overtly violent responses from law enforcement, unlike black men. Their own often racist and anti-immigrant rhetoric belies the racial nature of these white men's political project. The increasing visibility of white supremacist and white nationalist organizing since the 2016 U.S. presidential election further affirms the bigoted nature of these movements.

Many have pointed out that race and masculinity are central to understanding both cases. Yet the notion that these particular black and white masculinities are so inherently connected to space is often left out of these analyses. Space is central to these racialized masculinities—one symbolizing the inner city and, therefore, ghettoized urban space, in stark contrast to the wide-open spaces of the "cowboy West." Societal forces are swiftly changing these spaces in the early twenty-first century, presenting threats to both groups. In urban space, rapid gentrification of many cities is squeezing racially and economically marginalized communities. And in rural space, continued economic woes in an age of global neoliberal economics threaten rural men's traditional livelihoods.

Trans men's narratives lay bare the spatially based ideals of masculinity that, like those urban and rural ideals, men negotiate in the contemporary United States. The masculine ideals that emerged from interviewees' discussions of masculinity incorporated not only an urban/rural dichotomy but also suburban ideals of normalcy. These ideals emerged primarily from questions about how interviewees define their own masculinity, what kinds of expectations men face in their particular geographic context, and what they reported experiencing in actual interactions, as well as what they anticipated when they moved through different spaces and places. The four most common spatially based ideals interviewees discussed, forming a continuum from the most masculine to the most feminized, were hypermasculine men, regular guys, progressive men, and faggy men.[1] In addition, trans men's masculine ideals linked to each region on another continuum, with the West being most open and flexible and connected to the progressive man, the South being most restrictive and associated with hypermasculine men, and the Midwest as being in the middle and coupled with regular guys. Faggy men were not tied to a particular region, but there were some spatial variations in this ideal. While these ideals lay on a masculine–feminine continuum, this is not meant to say that particular men are more masculine and others more feminine, though they may conceive of themselves or others in that way.

These spatially based masculinities are ideals not only in that they have some influence on and are important categories for social analysis but also in that it would be rare to find a perfect example of one walking around. As ideals or images, they are not necessarily what individuals strive to be but rather a type that holds some collective meaning and works as an illustrative example. Further, the thug, redneck, and faggy man work as controlling images, in the sense that Patricia Hill Collins uses the term, to describe stereotypical racialized, gendered, and sexualized images that mask historical and contemporary power relations. In regard to African American women, Collins writes, "These controlling images are designed to make racism, sexism, poverty, and other forms of social injustice appear to be natural, normal, and inevitable parts of everyday life."[2] Controlling images of marginalized groups become a foil against which to define the normalcy of dominant groups. Thus, the regular guy is constructed as normal against these hypermasculine and feminized controlling images. Building on Collins's concept, trans men's narratives illustrate not only how controlling images work to inscribe and reinforce inequality but also the ways that men attempt to resist broader cultural meanings by taking on and reclaiming aspects of these disparaged images.

Though men can see themselves reflected in one type or another, they also engage in practices associated with other types or actions that do not fit neatly on this spectrum. Rather, this spectrum is meant to reflect that racialized, classed, and sexualized masculinity and femininity are *constructed* in opposition to each other and is a simple illustration of the normative pressures on most men to fall somewhere in the middle. While interviewees often described these spatially based ideals as if they were clear characters, the ideals are not easily reducible to individual men or the characteristics they take on.

Trans men's narratives of the continuum of ideals show that they most valued the regular guy ideal in the middle of the spectrum, which relied on a "Goldilocks masculinity." This hybrid masculinity holds somewhere between a domineering violent masculinity and an overly emotional or weak masculinity—not too hard and not too soft—that is fundamentally shaped by race, sexuality, and gender. This regular guy ideal is constructed in opposition to controlling images of excessive raced and sexualized others—the faggy man, the thug, and the redneck. Overall, it is clear that control across contexts is central to normative masculinities and how contemporary relations of gender, sexuality, and race are reinscribed. The black men murdered on the street and the white occupiers of federal land are linked not only in their relation to space but also as symbolic representations of masculinities that are not under control. In one instance, lives that must be eliminated; in the other, evidence that hypermasculinity and attendant racism and sexism are located only in rural spaces and particular regions.

Indeed, these masculine ideals are racial projects, which Michael Omi and Howard Winant define as "simultaneously an interpretation, representation, or explanation of racial identities and meanings, and an effort to organize and distribute resources (economic, political, and cultural) along particular racial lines."[3] Projects are large and small, from the realm of law and major social institutions to everyday interaction and individual behavior. Through focusing on the realm of interactions, individual behaviors, and symbolic meanings attached to masculinities, it is clear that these spatially based masculine ideals are simultaneously raced, classed, sexualized, and gendered projects.[4]

Like Goldilocks trying out the beds of the three bears, some masculine ideals are too hard, some too soft, and others just right. Investigating the spatially based, in-between masculinity that is constructed against both the borders of femininity and hypermasculinity and the effeminate controlling images connected to men addresses key questions: What is the larger effect of these changing masculine standards? Do the changes in masculine ideals affect unequal relations between women and men and among men? How are they wrapped up in sexual, racial, classed, and other inequalities? Part of the answer is that the Goldilocks masculinity—a hybrid masculinity that incorporates aspects of femininity and enlightened masculinities—reflects more of a surface than a substantive change to social relations.

MASCULINITIES IN THREE REGIONS

The West, Midwest, and South contain spatial and cultural variation within each region but, at the same time, share historical, political, and cultural processes and histories that produce particular regional masculine ideals. This history of the regions illustrates how landscape, industry, and social conditions have created the ground for unique masculinities in each place. A broad historical overview might seem to gloss over the many differences contained in each region, but it is meant to give some background on their geographic imaginaries: the mental images we have of spaces and places that give them much of their meaning and that these places have produced in the popular imagination and among interviewees.

These historic ideals are closely aligned, though not exclusively defined, by regional economic production, especially in rural spaces. The rural character of these masculine ideals illustrates that rurality is centrally tied to larger constructions of masculinity and, in particular, to the rural economic production often associated with agriculture and natural resource extraction and management.[5] These rural representations of the western cowboy, midwestern farmer, and southern good old boy are inherently racialized as white, since they are constructed against not just women but also men of color, based on the specific historical and contemporary gender and racial relations of the region. In addition to being racialized as white, they are also heterosexual and able-bodied ideals.

The West is characterized in the U.S. imagination as the frontier and as a vast open space awaiting conquest. As eastern cities in the 1800s became more crowded, the West became a pressure release valve where urban men could imagine reclaiming a virility supposedly denied in the ever more constrained city.[6] Yet as the West was increasingly settled by whites at the expense of Native people, the fantasy of a wide-open West became far from reality. This fantasy is embodied in the cowboy, a figure who originated with the vaquero, a key agent of Spanish colonization who produced beef to feed colonists and miners. Thus, the cowboy is inherently tied to "colonial mastery over indigenous peoples, animals, and landscapes."[7] The popular image of the cowboy as a mythic figure embodying heroic masculinity arose in the late nineteenth century in the United States, just as the cowboy himself was disappearing from the rangelands.[8] This creation, popularized in literature and film, emphasized independence and rugged individualism but has never truly represented the cowboy's actual life, which involved more routinized grunt work and little autonomy from cattle owners. While the cowboy is a white racialized image, a large number of actual cowboys were in fact Native American, Mexican, and black.[9] Yet the whiteness of the cowboy is popularly constructed in opposition to the Native American, the Chinese railroad worker, and the Mexican bandit. In contrast to the southern good old boy and the midwestern farmer, the cowboy was in more direct contact with Native Americans. This heroic and conservative stylistic image has spread globally as a symbol of traditional masculinity, even in urban spaces through country music bars.[10] Donning the cowboy aesthetic and attending events like rodeos in the twentieth century became a way for men to reclaim traditional manhood at a time when their masculinity was threatened by changing work, as well as competition from women and racialized immigrants.[11] The cowboy is the predominant image of masculinity in the West, but there are other localized versions, such as the lumberjack in the Pacific Northwest.

The Midwest sits in the literal and figurative center of the United States; in the popular imagination it is seen as the Heartland and the mass of the country or, alternately, as fly-over territory by urban coastal elites.[12] The midwestern masculine ideal emerged from an early pioneer and settler mentality that rests on the control and settlement of a supposed wild landscape from Native Americans.[13] While the pioneer mentality still underlies this ideal, it has morphed into the upstanding farmer of places like Iowa and Minnesota, often from Scandinavian or German descent, who historically tamed and now control the expanses of fertile land that make up the Corn Belt of the Midwest region.[14] The masculine ideal in the Industrial Belt, or now more commonly referred to as the Rust Belt, is the urban industrial worker steeped in union culture that is central to the large cities of Ohio, Michigan, and Wisconsin.[15] The Corn Belt retains some of its settler agricultural flavor and shares some characteristics with the West, while the Industrial Belt shares characteristics with the urbanized and industrialized Northeast. In reality, the idealized characteristics of both regions have diminished with the shuttering of traditional manufacturing and the replacement of family farming with large-scale industrial agriculture in the late twentieth through twenty-first centuries.[16] The loss of these traditional livelihoods has led midwestern men to compensatory acts in other arenas, such as asserting control in the home, owning guns, or brawling in bars.[17] The Corn Belt has an increasing Latinx population, and Rust Belt cities have high proportions of African Americans, which has increased through outmigration of whites from these former hubs of white working-class stability.[18]

The South is often centrally characterized in the popular imagination by the horrors of explicit antiblack racism, including chattel slavery, lynching, and Jim Crow segregation, on one hand, and by a genteel, mannered white aristocracy, on the other. Southerners themselves see values of community mindedness and mutual aid, a slower pace of life, and southern hospitality at the center of regional identity.[19] Historically, the predominant images of white masculinity in the South were of the poor but independent farmer and the upper-class genteel plantation owner or businessman. Since World War II, one prominent representation of the southern men is the sinister white man bent on racial and patriarchal control, determined to protect white supremacy and white southern womanhood from any encroachment of blackness.[20] In contrast, the other most prominent representation is the somewhat more benign good old boy. The good old boy comes in two forms: in its comic and popular version, like Andy Griffith and Luke and Bo from the *Dukes of Hazzard*, and a more serious, patriotic and blue-collar form. The redneck, a prominent ideal in trans men's narratives, is a more extreme variant of the good old boy. The good old boy is inherently rural, like the cowboy and the midwestern farmer, and particular areas within the South have variations of the good old boy connected to local industry, like the Appalachian coal miner.[21] This figure combines a rebelliousness and independence with a defense of traditional southern values. The ideal is clearly defined as white because if a black man engaged in the hell-raising misbehavior of the young good old boy, the same southern whites would not explain it with a tolerant "boys will be boys" attitude but rather violently punish the black man for this behavior.[22] This southern masculinity is predicated on the removal, including genocide and dispossession, of Native Americans from the land, like the midwestern farmer and cowboy, but opposition to blackness is at the center of white southern masculinity.

These historic masculine ideals are based mostly on imaginaries of rural spaces, which do not necessarily reflect contemporary economic and social realities. Neoliberal policies and politics have had tremendous effects globally, and the rural United States is no exception. The onset of capitalism, with its twin processes of urbanization and industrialization, has made for large shifts in the agricultural work and resource extraction that is central to U.S. rural life. In addition, rural gentrification has made survival while doing traditional rural work even more difficult. Rural masculinity varies between region, such as the more macho, machinery-dependent farmer of the South and the more stoic, less overly macho agrarian ideal of the midwestern farmer.[23] Overall, farming masculinity, like that of many resource-based rural occupations, tends to center on control and mastery of a feminized earth and nature, but traditional agrarian ideals and ethics can also contest capitalist impulses that are in conflict with stewardship of the land.[24] In addition, shifting farming practices, such as a turn to sustainable agriculture, necessitate more flexible masculinities, though traditional gender ideals and masculine identities may remain relatively unchanged.[25] The rural is also a place of white men's anger, such as the invocation by right-wing militia members of virtuous rural men alienated by increasingly liberal cities.[26] These histories about masculinities in rural spaces and the three regions help form the backdrop through which men negotiate competing masculine ideals in the contemporary United States.

HYPERMASCULINITIES: TOO HARD

No one wants to be "that guy." The trans men I interviewed practiced a wide range of masculinities and held conflicting views about how men should be. Yet not one of the men said that he wanted to fully embody the stereotypical hypermasculinity of an ultra-tough action hero. In fact, while some of the men took on a few of the traits of this mythic hypermasculine man, they more often defined themselves against this image. Interviewees described the ideal of the hypermasculine man as aggressive, violent, rigidly heterosexual, and conservative (both politically and as generally old-fashioned). This ideal is a strictly controlled masculinity that does not allow any expression of femininity. Interviewees' descriptors of hypermasculinity were consistent across discussions of particular regions, and they painted a classic picture of loud, aggressive, and swaggering men who typically had short hair and beards. While Raewyn Connell's notion of hegemonic masculinity is frequently conflated with hypermasculinity, or what is popularly referred to as *toxic masculinity*, this rejection of hypermasculinity suggests that it does not necessarily serve as a legitimator of patriarchy, an essential part of the definition of hegemonic masculinity.[27] That said, a small portion of the men openly identified as hypermasculine and took up certain aspects of the type. Overall, the hypermasculine man served as an extreme example of what not to be and provided material to construct normative masculinities against.

While it was not common for men to identify as hypermasculine at the time of the interview, interviewees frequently described themselves or other trans men as being hypermasculine early in transition. Chris, a white man living in urban Northern California, explained how some trans men behaved early in transition:

> Swearing a lot or walking in a certain way and sort of swaggering—they're all sort of physical things that I think [they were] trying to emulate. There were some people that were over the top and starting to talk about women in a certain way. That sort of less-than-nice way. As if that makes you more male. Becoming sort of an asshole. Sort of like a truck driver or a stereotypical, what we like to think of some truck driver that's all rough, but I think pretty ugly. Like putting your feet on the coffee table. I saw guys doing that.

As Chris's description shows, interviewees saw the hypermasculine man as inauthentic for trans men and a form of overcompensation for all men. Further, hypermasculinity took on particularly raced, classed, and sexualized meanings in trans men's narratives that reflected larger social ideals and images.

Rural Redneck Men

The term *redneck* came up frequently among interviewees, and they described redneck men with ease. Regardless of where they lived, trans men marked the redneck as the predominant pattern of practice for men in rural places. Historically, *redneck* emerged in the nineteenth century as a largely negative descriptor for rural poor white southern men.[28] While at times it has been used in media and everyday talk interchangeably with terms like *hillbilly* and *white trash, redneck* has moved beyond its regional roots. In the popular imagination, the redneck has come to represent poor and working-class men across U.S. regions, from urban midwestern factory workers to loggers in the Pacific Northwest.[29]

The image of the redneck that emerged from interviewees' narratives was a politically conservative, backward, and uneducated rural man wearing camo who enjoyed hunting and fishing. This image aligns well with popular images of the redneck.[30] Alan, a white man living in urban Kentucky, shared that redneck masculinity was synonymous with expectations for men where he grew up in rural Appalachia:

> Where I grew up, being a man was very much being a cardboard stereotype. It was, you have to grab yourself and spit and be bad to women and [be] domineering and macho pretty much. If you weren't anything like that, then you were automatically a limp-wristed fag. You're gonna go mud bogging on the weekends, cow tipping, all that kind of stuff, chew 'bacca, you know.[31] That's the rural South for you. . . . Yeah, if you think redneck, that's pretty much what it means to be a man where I come from.

The characteristics, aesthetics, and activities of rednecks, that Alan described, matched interviewees consistent descriptions of rednecks as white, rural, heterosexual, and hypermasculine. Thus, the controlling image was raced, gendered, sexualized, and space-based. This white rural working-class masculinity was tied to the control of women and nature (cow tipping and mud bogging) along with a crude interactional style. It is clear that the "fag" worked as a subordinated masculinity to define and defend the redneck against. Thus, the redneck is characterized not just for his distance from but also for his hatred of effeminate gay men.

Racism, along with homophobia and sexism, was at the core of the redneck that trans men described. Whiteness is central to the redneck ideal. Mason, a white man who lived in urban Tennessee, described his redneck brother:

> He likes rebel flags and trucks and stuff.... There's been some incidences where he's called me out for a bunch of stuff. Just being really rude and disrespectful, and called me a dyke.... He's a redneck, basically kind of like Republican and just kind of closed-minded.

Mason associates the Confederate flag with racism and bigotry rather than the Heritage Not Hate motto attached to Confederate flag–emblazoned items sold in gas stations and souvenir shops throughout the Southeast. If the decision of a person to wear dreadlocks is an example of a racial project, as Omi and Winant argue, then certainly flying the Confederate flag is a white racial project.[32] With or without this particular symbol, interviewees' narratives entwined the redneck with racism, homophobia, sexism, and violence, and the redneck was placed in rural spaces. Indeed, this is why trans men viewed rural spaces as particularly unsafe for anyone who was not like the redneck. Not only are the individual behaviors or characteristics associated with redneck men potentially racial projects, but the invocation of this controlling image is itself a white racial project.

To understand the redneck man as a racial project, it is important to complicate the representation of the redneck by looking more closely at what this racialized hypermasculine figure does in the larger cultural context, not just how men experience others as rednecks. Primarily, the redneck is an explicitly marked white racial subject who is used among white people to mark in-group boundaries, along lines of class and notions of decency, between poor whites and the usually unmarked middle or upper-class white subject.[33] According to Lucy Jarosz and Victoria Lawson's analysis across rural sites, the image of the redneck as "obsolescent" and "unsophisticated" in the changing rural spaces of the twenty-first century has been used by elites as a tool to frame rural white poverty as a matter of individual moral failing rather than as a result of structural inequality linked to increasing capitalist accumulation through resource extraction and rural gentrification.[34] This characterization of poor rural whites as backward mirrors larger narratives of modernization and colonization that frame particular places as needing a civilizing force that its current occupants are incapable of achieving. Thus, we can see that one of the most important functions of the redneck is to symbolically contain and explain white racism, along with other forms of bigotry, such as misogyny and homophobia. This allows whites to distance themselves from racism and the negative characteristics of whiteness, instead assigning them to a marginalized "regional culture and class" and opening space for an ideal type of "whiteness that is normative and superior."[35] The in-group dynamic allows middle- and upper-class whites a general sense of superiority, access to rural land and resources, and a claim to innocence from racism.

The redneck acts as a controlling image of poor rural whites and as a racial project that explains racism as a matter of explicit individual racial hatred rather than the more subtle acts of discrimination and structural policy. This is not to say whether individual rural whites subscribe to racist values but rather to point out that poor whites are unlikely to be in a position to engage in housing and employment discrimination and are not usually the ones directly making the policy decisions that uphold the prison–industrial complex, though they may vote for politicians who do.[36] In fact, members of militia and overt white supremacist groups, such as the Ku Klux Klan, are not just poor rural men but come from across class and urban/rural lines.[37] Thus, the redneck image helps elites distance themselves from and explain racial inequality.

At the same time the image of the redneck acts as a foil against which proper and purportedly nonracist whites can be distinguished, it also provides a symbolic space for expressions of twenty-first-century white, patriotic Christian conservatism. Comedians, such as Jeff Foxworthy and Larry the Cable Guy, and reality television stars, like the cast of *Duck Dynasty*, have popularized the resurgence and reclamation of the redneck in popular culture. This new redneck stands as a recuperation of masculinity and rural pride, but with a less overtly racist face than the typical representation of the redneck. This shift is an attempt to make the image more palatable for mass consumption. Instead of overt antiblack racism, this redneck expresses patriotic anger at foreign others and pokes fun at "yuppie men" or "metrosexuals."[38] He is still staunchly heterosexual, as shown in songs such as Justin Moore's "Bait a Hook," where a man tries to win back an ex-girlfriend by showing he can fish and drive a truck, in contrast to her new sushi-eating, Prius-driving metrosexual boyfriend. The Christian, conservative, and traditional gender values served with a working-class aesthetic emblematic of this new redneck present an "authentic" masculinity that is taken up by men across class positions when they "play redneck."[39] This cooptation is evident in the manner and dress of the Bundy family and other occupiers of the Malheur National Wildlife Refuge. They often wear cowboy hats and work clothes and drive pickup trucks that do not necessarily mirror their social and economic status or everyday work but instead appropriate working-class aesthetics. In all of these senses, the redneck may operate as a local hegemonic masculinity in some rural spaces, but only when the image goes beyond the stereotypical redneck ideal.

The three interviewees who identified with aspects of the redneck image tried to hold the complexity of these different histories and meanings. They did not dispute the connection between bigotry and the redneck but also saw positive attributes. For example, to Bobby, a white man in suburban Kentucky who grew up in rural Mississippi, self-sufficiency was synonymous to his identity as a redneck:

> Redneck to me is, your truck breaks down, you fix it. If the electricity and everything, we just got wiped off the grid, you know, all these city folks would either starve to death or be eating rotten food or wouldn't know how to get anything, but we'll survive. You know, you go kill something, you bring it home, you skin it, you cook it, you eat it. It's simple. But they'd starve to death 'cause they wouldn't have running water or anything like that. We don't care. We'll make it. To me, that's redneck.

Again, Bobby did not disagree with negative characterizations of the redneck, but these additional qualities show why one might want to transform it and take it on as a point of pride and a symbol of rural independence and self-sufficiency. By distancing themselves from the racism of the redneck through active antiracist practice, Bobby and other men could reclaim the values associated with survival amid rural poverty. These values are evident in groups such as Redneck Revolt, which describes itself as "a pro-worker, anti-racist organization that focuses on working class liberation from the oppressive systems which dominate our lives."[40] The group, formed in 2016 with an emphasis on community defense and antifascism, illustrates how the redneck can be used in the service of racial and class solidarity. This reclamation shows promise, but it remains to be seen if the category is truly salvageable.

For most of the men in this study, the redneck was an extreme form of hypermasculinity to define themselves against. It exemplified understandings of more restrictive ideals of masculinity in rural places and the South. Yet images like the redneck have complex and multiple meanings. One central operation of this controlling image is to define proper whiteness, placing white racism solely onto poor rural whites while absolving urban and suburban whites from their own guilt and blame for racism. Thus, the redneck is spatially situated in the rural while the whites who most often use this image as a foil are largely placed outside rural spaces.

Urban Thug Men

The varieties of urban masculinities that emerged from trans men's accounts mostly reflected subcultural, racial, and sexual lines in major cities. For example, Ben, an Asian American man, talked about riding a bus across town in order to describe his major midwestern city. The bus moved through a downtown business district of mostly white middle-class professional men and then through a white gay men's neighborhood to a Chinatown populated by working-class Asian men and, as the bus continued, to a predominately black neighborhood. Ben explained that one should not travel beyond Chinatown at night because it was dangerous. Who, exactly, did Ben fear?

The racialized and classed image of the thug was likely at the center of Ben's fear of the black neighborhood and larger fears of black and, perhaps, Latinx men in the United States. The thug, representing poor black men, stood in for urban hypermasculinity, like the redneck for poor rural whites. The thug is a well-circulated depiction of black masculinity that has its roots in slavery and the contemporary prison–industrial complex. Patricia Hill Collins explains that the "brute," or the exceptionally strong, big, unintelligent, and violent black man, emerged as one of several controlling images that both masked and justified the "objectification, commodification, and exploitation" of black bodies under chattel slavery.[41] The violent brute has most often been represented in media and popular discourse as a threat to white womanhood. Media portrayals of the brute intensified after emancipation during the period of Reconstruction, as did the practice of lynching black men, white supremacist violence that was justified with false claims of sexual assault against white women.[42] Thus, as black freedom increased, so did popular portrayals of black men as vicious and violent threats to whiteness and white femininity.

With the increasing migration of black people from the rural South to cities after the Civil War and into the twentieth century, a discourse of black crime became prevalent in social science and popular accounts. According to Khalil Gibran Muhammad, the use of racial crime statistics cemented the association between blackness and urban criminality—and thus offered a justification for proponents of black inferiority—that was central to the making of the urban United States.[43] Constructing black people as inherently criminal through racial statistics then became the basis for blaming racial inequality on either biological or cultural causes, as opposed to seeing the main sources of black punishment in the agencies, police, and other institutions dominated by whites. As Michelle Alexander and Douglas Blackmon, among others, have shown, the enslavement and segregation of black people did not end after the Civil War but has continued to today in the criminal and prison systems.[44] The association between blackness and criminality that continues to justify racial inequality and state violence toward black people is perpetuated by news media accounts that disproportionately show black people as lawbreakers and white people as law defenders—such as attorneys, police, and judges.[45]

The thug is the contemporary version of the brute and represents a clear symbol of black criminality that excuses the expansion of the prison–industrial complex and disproportionate confinement and murder of black people. In an era of color-blind racism, explicitly racist language has fallen out of favor and has been replaced by coded language like *thug* and *ghetto*, as opposed to more explicit racial epithets.[46] Along with this coded language, we continue to see the controlling image of the thug used to explain contemporary crime, such as black and Latinx criminality and the media portrayal of "wilding" in the Central Park jogger case in 1989.[47] Images of the uncontrolled thug are central in contemporary killings of black men by police, such as in the cases of Michael Brown, Oscar Grant, and Tamir Rice.[48] These portrayals effectively shift blame for the deaths of black men onto their supposed violence and ferocity rather than onto the police officers who pull the trigger. It is important to note that black girls and women, like Sandra Bland and Kayla Moore, are also subjected to this racialized violence and death at the hands of the state.[49] These narratives of black threat are likely part of a logic that leads to increased urban policing and excuses gentrification of urban black neighborhoods.

The thug is not the only racialized hypermasculinity symbolically connected to people of color. The "macho" image portrays Latinx men as dangerous, savage, and thus less fully human—operating similarly but differently from the thug in various geographic and historical contexts. This image is certainly connected to the figure of the "bad hombre" that emerged in the 2016 U.S. presidential election, which portrays Mexican and other Latinx immigrants as inherently dangerous and criminal. The valorization of the thug and the macho have been thoroughly critiqued and complicated by black and Chicana and Latinx feminists to show not only how hypermasculinity can be damaging to black and Latinx communities but also how these images are used to criminalize black and Latinx men.[50] Among Connell's multiple masculinities, the thug and macho would be considered marginalized masculinities.[51]

The thug is the racialized hypermasculinity of urban spaces and a black racial project that infuses everyday interaction, just as the redneck is the racialized hypermasculinity of rural spaces. Each black trans man reported that others applied the hypermasculine and violent image of the thug to them regularly in everyday interaction. The expectations of the thug construed them as dangerous, which was highlighted when others saw them as newly threatening at work and in their interactions with police as men. This gives further evidence that the controlling image of the thug is difficult for black men to escape and generally puts them at a deficit in interactions because others assume they are untrustworthy and criminal from the start. Encountering racial stereotypes, profiling, and microaggressions, not to mention the threat of extreme violence, creates a heavy burden for black men in everyday interaction and may lead to preemptive strategies to fend off being subsumed in this image.[52] Though few of the black men interviewees identified as a thug, they did find that people treated them as if they were thugs, no matter how they presented themselves. All of this attests to the power of this particular racial project.

While descriptions of the redneck as a representation of rural spaces came easily, when I asked interviewees to describe typical or ideal men or masculinities in urban spaces, most had difficulty describing one or two and instead attempted to describe a multitude of masculine styles and groupings. When comparing typical urban and rural masculinities, men said things like "it's more broad," "the entire spectrum," or "at least five kinds" to describe urban masculinities. In trying to explain this, Sebastian, a white man living in a large city in the Great Lakes region, said:

> I think naturally in larger cities you get a greater diversity of expression, and you get a lot more subgroups in communities that develop in a larger city than you do in a small town where everything is pretty homogenous.

Yet when talking about hypermasculinity, many of the men, especially white men, used coded references to urban hypermasculinity. Thus, the image of the thug emerged in nonblack trans men's accounts in much less explicit terms than the redneck, which aligns with a colorblind racial discourse.[53] Instead, it was black men for the most part who named and grappled with the image of the thug most explicitly, as this controlling image was hard for them to escape.

In light of the ubiquitous thug image, black interviewees talked about efforts to push against this ideal. For example, Ethan, a black man living in a midsized Michigan city, described his brother, whose masculinity he admired:

> He's honest. He goes to work every day. He provides for his sons. He's not the typical black male that you would think. He doesn't drink. He doesn't smoke weed and all that kind of stuff. He goes to work every day. He's in the house with his children, because most black males, you know, they're not in the house with their children. He has one baby momma, and he's been with this same woman for like thirteen years.

Ethan holds up this portrait of his brother, very much a regular guy, against the hypermasculinity of the thug. Ethan himself seems to share a belief in the range of stereotypes that make up this controlling image.

Like most descriptions of the thug, Ethan's narrative suggests that the thug's poverty is a matter of personal failing rather than employing a more critical understanding that sees both the image of the thug and the material conditions of black men in the United States as the product of systematic processes and structural power relations.[54]

Distancing oneself from the stigmatized thug is understandable, but it also illustrates how the thug can function as an image against which to define middle-class black propriety and respectability. On one hand, this is part of a larger quest to challenge notions of black pathology and push against racialized and classed hierarchies of masculinity. On the other hand, it is also an embrace of white middle- and upper-class notions of respectability. As popularized in gangsta rap in the late twentieth century, which itself repackages white historical constructions of violent black masculinity, the thug also operates as a reclaimed symbol of resistance to these politics of respectability.[55] Leo, a black man living in San Francisco, takes the thug further by both embracing and transforming this controlling image when describing his masculinity. He said, "I'm an intelli-thug! Because I'm so nonviolent. I'm Rastafarian, so I'm nonviolent altogether, but at the same time I'm race conscious." Thus, Leo embraces the race conscious and liberationist potential of the thug but distances himself from violence. Michael Jeffries illustrates that figures such as Tupac Shakur represent a more nuanced vision of the thug, as a hard and violent figure that is also capable of vulnerability. In this reclaimed vein, the thug embraces the criminal label, along with overt and sometimes subtle critiques of morality, freedom, and justice, that is both embraced and reviled by the larger U.S. consuming public.[56] This "complex cool" of the thug, illustrated in some ways by Leo, shows both the constraint of the ubiquitous controlling image and its potential for subversion and resistance.

Middle-class men also took up the thug as an aesthetic in complex ways. Ben, from a major midwestern city, described a friend who took on this thug masculinity even though he came from a privileged background:

> He looks like he would be a thug, but he's a radio personality, and so like he just dresses according to the attire of the radio show of the people he interviews, 'cause he's interviewed Lupe, Eminem, and Wiz Khalifa, all these big rappers in the hip-hop scene. So the way he dresses is kind of in that genre, but he's never had a speeding ticket, never been to jail, you know what I mean? Has

always lived on the good side of town; his parents are still married. So it's kind of like looks can be deceiving when you're trying to, I guess, portray yourself in a certain, you know, a certain venue, or get certain street credibility.

In Ben's estimation, his friend adopts the aesthetics and practices of the thug for work even though his biography does not line up with the poverty and broken homes connected to the controlling image of the thug.[57] Perhaps it was not this version of the thug that Ben feared when he earlier described crossing his city on the late-night bus. In fact, the adoption of the thug persona by his friend likely appeals to the many hip-hop consumers who are actually white, suburban, middle-class teens. Thus, in particular contexts the thug as an aesthetic becomes an asset, but only when it stays on the surface.

While white interviewees' discussions of the thug were less overt, some said that there was a black urban masculinity but that they could not presume to even describe it. White interviewees had particular difficulty when asked about their experiences of race, though men of color in general saw race as central to their experiences as men. Many white men acknowledged that racialized ideals existed in urban spaces, but they seemed reluctant to describe them. On the other hand, the same men talked about rednecks with ease and, frequently, in a derisive manner. Though it is always difficult to define absences and interpret silence, the whiteness of the redneck allowed for more openness for all interviewees in talking about poor men, while white interviewees seemed hesitant to represent themselves as racist by presuming to talk about thugs. Stereotypes about rednecks are more socially acceptable, whereas "racetalk" necessitates impression management on the part of white speakers so that they avoid being viewed by others as racist.[58] This further illustrates how talking about whiteness, due to its invisibility in discourse, does not usually count as racetalk at all. It is also possible that some white men did not have ideas about urban racialized ideals or about men of color due to the separation of hypersegregated cities, though the discomfort evident when I tried to probe white interviewees on this belied an underlying tension.

In sum, no one wants to be "that guy." None of the men I interviewed fully embraced hypermasculinity as an ideal for themselves, but mostly as material to define themselves against. These narratives are examples of discursive distancing, where men distance themselves from hegemonic and hypermasculinities by framing their own masculinity as more enlightened.[59] Even the men who embraced thug and redneck identities felt the need to modify the image in an attempt to transform its meaning. It is heartening to find a group of men who reject many of the most toxic aspects of contemporary masculinity, yet something more complex is also happening. It turns out that "that guy" takes the blame for many social ills and becomes a way for other men to proclaim their own innocence.

FAGGY MEN: TOO SOFT

Just as the thug and the redneck controlling images allow some men to distance themselves from hypermasculinity, as well as culpability for sexism, racism, and homophobia, another controlling image allows them to distance themselves from its opposite, excessive effeminacy. Ken, a white man in urban California, explained the consequences he sees in being perceived as effeminate:

> I think it's really scary to be a male that's perceived as faggy. I mean you get that from the gay community, you get that from the straight community, you get that from women. Like, if you don't act like a real man, then you don't really matter.

It is well established that dominant contemporary masculinities in the United States often rest on a distancing from homosexuality through both overt and subtle forms of homophobia.[60] C. J. Pascoe compellingly argues that the ubiquitous fag discourse employed by high school boys is as much, if not more, about masculinity as it is about sexuality. Because of this, the repudiation of the fag and its use in shoring up normative masculinity can exist alongside acceptance of gay men themselves.

The fag discourse operates to police boys across racial groups, though the label *fag* operates differently for boys of color.[61] For example, in Marlon Riggs's analysis of the prevalence of faggy black men, or snap queens, in 1990s black popular culture representation, he illustrates that this figure is both desexualized as a hyperfeminized joke and posed as a sexual threat in the midst of the early AIDS crisis. Both dangerous and ridiculous, this figure worked as an other for black men to affirm their masculinity and sexuality against.[62] Similarly, the faggy man that emerged from trans men's narratives operated as an ideal for most men to define themselves against.

The ideal of the faggy man was most closely tied to femininity in interviewees' accounts of contemporary masculine ideals. Interviewees most frequently described this ideal as effeminate, flamboyant, and expressive. Since the patterns of practice associated with this ideal refer to men, particularly gay men, one might call it a masculinity rather than femininity. At the same time, this image is connected to some feminized and effeminate expressions. Further, the faggy man represents a subordinated masculinity among the types that Connell names.[63] Various interviewees saw the faggy man equally as positive and as the object of derision and humor, and they described both themselves and other men or their practices as "faggy." The image of the faggy man lines up with stereotypical ideas about how gay men do masculinity, and thus faggy practices mean the man will be read by others as gay. Again, most interviewees acknowledged that men could have sex with other men and not be extremely effeminate; thus, not all gay men were faggy men.

Few, if any, of the interviewees would use "fag" as an epithet like the high school boys C. J. Pascoe studied, but this controlling image was still used to construct a normative sexual and racialized masculinity. In most cases, trans men's histories in LGBT communities and antihomophobic attitudes stopped them short of hurling this loaded homophobic phrase in a negative way. Yet the extreme faggy man still operated as a specter through which normative ideals of masculinity were constructed against for the majority of interviewees, regardless of their sexual orientation. In addition to being overly expressive, the faggy man is silly and unserious like the snap queens analyzed by Marlon Riggs. Where the hypermasculine thug and redneck are violent and threatening, the faggy man is ridiculous.[64] Luke, a pansexual white man living in rural Indiana, described his friend who exemplified the faggy man:

> He couldn't keep his wrists straight if he was in splints. He was [*laughter*] dramatic. I mean dramatic. The hair in a bouffant. You just could tell immediately. Really, anyone could. And he really got very mistreated out in public. . . . Guys would say, "You fuckin' faggot," and cross the street.

Luke and other interviewees certainly would not harass another man for this effeminate display, but the key distinction here is that being a faggy man and being gay are not the same thing. In this instance, the faggy man is rejected as too silly and feminine by gay and straight men alike. Several interviewees noted the proliferation of terms like "no femmes," "masc 4 masc," or "straight acting for straight acting" on gay dating apps and websites. These preferences suggest that effeminacy is not only an object of mockery but also sexually and romantically unattractive. As Ken, a queer white man living in urban Northern California, observed, "Being a faggoty person still, even in the gay community, can be a bad thing." In the aptly titled "No Fats, Femmes, or Asians," C. Walter Han illustrates that these dating and sexual preferences reject fat bodies and, along with a general rejection of femininity, are often racist and work to reinforce stereotypes of feminized Asian men.[65] In these cases, gay or queer-identified men use the figure of the faggy man to construct a racialized and gendered normative gay masculinity. Thus, the faggy man is a sexual, gendered, and racial project.

Though trans men's narratives tended to associate the faggy man with urban spaces, interviewees described a particularly rigid faggy masculinity in rural places. In the same sense that interviewees saw hypermasculinity as excessive, some of the men described particular images of the faggy man in rural places as being equally exaggerated. Michael, a queer white man living in urban California, explained this when talking about gay men in rural Appalachia where he grew up:

> There is this limp-wristed expectation of what a gay man looks like in the South that I've never been fond of, and it's still there, which amazes me ... but it's still alive and well in bars throughout the South. Lisps, oh my god, even down to the lisp. It's crazy. I like a dandy, but, you know.

Michael had a touch of affection for effeminacy in the softer masculine aesthetic of the dandy, but the excess of the faggy man was just too much for him. This excessive faggy masculinity was one extreme, with the hypermasculine redneck at the other end. As Alan, a white man living in urban Kentucky, said when describing the ideals of his rural Appalachian hometown, "You have this dichotomy of übermasculinity versus flimsy fag boy thing." In these narratives, gay men exist in rural spaces but are locked into an inauthentic and exaggerated state in opposition to the redneck. In practice, rural men could express an array of masculinities; however, this was not how rural ideal types were constructed in trans men's discussions of masculinities. Overall, this depiction of faggy men means that effeminacy is still largely reviled across contexts in the United States.

While the prevalent image of the faggy man as something to define normative masculinity against provides evidence of the continuing relevance of homophobia to contemporary U.S. manhood, a few interviewees reclaimed this image by embracing it as a positive descriptor for themselves. Alec, a white queer man in urban Northern California, described his general demeanor as faggy because of his personal style and his tight girly clothes:

> I always thought that I was kind of like a faggy boy, and people used to think that when I was a girl. So it's always what's fit. Like I'm kind of male. I'm kind of masculine, but I'm definitely faggy, and I like to look pretty, and I like to get dressed.

Like Alec, Jeffrey, a white queer man living in a college town in California, also embraced being faggy as central to his identity. He found that this actually helped him to avoid the intellectual posturing in his graduate program by cisgender heterosexual men: "For the most part, men leave me alone at school because they perceive me to be a faggot. That's my impression." Jeffrey sought out spaces, such as radical faerie gatherings, that embraced effeminacy but also found that as a trans man he felt excluded at times in gay men's spaces. He reported not being comfortable around some gay men because of their degrading talk about women and body parts that many, but certainly not all, women and trans men have. He said:

> There's a certain kind of faggotry that is so antivagina. There's no other way to say that, and it's really gross. I have overheard so much vagina bashing that I'm like, "This is so misogynist. Like, how do you not get this?"

While faggy masculinity is certainly a subordinated masculinity, the outrageous camp humor associated with it can still perpetuate the subordination of women and enforce normative ideas about particular bodies. Thus, the gendered and sexual project of the faggy man is a constant negotiation for the men who embrace aspects of this controlling image. Further, while only a few of the men fully embraced an identity as a faggy man, more of the interviewees described engaging in faggy practices in particular spaces. Yet some of these same men still repudiated faggy practices as being out of place in most contexts and disciplined their own and others' behavior accordingly in those spaces.

The caricatures represented by each of these controlling images work to dehumanize particular men—the thug and redneck are so violent and hypermasculine and the faggy man is so fey and boisterous that they cannot be real. Each is marked by excess and an inability to constrain themselves properly. These racialized and sexualized ideals represent extremes that some men adopt and transform but most men use as poles to define themselves against.

REGULAR GUYS: JUST RIGHT

If hypermasculinity was too hard and extreme effeminacy was too soft, what was "just right"? In comparing the hypermasculine ideal of Israeli masculinity with what he saw in the United States, Levi, a white Jewish man living in the urban West, explained:[66]

> I think American men are more aware of the advances of feminism in the past fifty years and that they tone down their aggression. They tone down kind of possessiveness about women or men, depending on their attractiveness or attraction. . . . There are exceptions, like rednecks and assholes, but American men tend to be more neutral.

Levi's description exemplifies the most common ideal that interviewees both described and wanted to emulate. In contrast to both hypermasculinity and extreme effeminacy, a majority of the men I interviewed strove to be a regular guy. The ideal for regular guys was defined most by what they are not, hypermasculine or extremely feminine, rather than what they are. The regular guy represents a balance between being solidly and authentically masculine and being secure enough in one's masculinity to not need to defend oneself against any appearance of femininity. This predominant ideal embodied through a Goldilocks masculinity attempts the "just right" balance between extremes. Like in Kathryne Young's ethnography of men in a Hawaiian cockfighting community, a model of masculine balance means that men respond to the gender dynamics of particular spaces, such as incorporating subordinated masculinities in particular settings, even among men who are not particularly privileged in other places.[67] Similarly, the regular guy incorporates hybrid masculinities, a mix of dominant and subordinate practices and styles that ensures enduring inequitable social relations amid political and social challenges to that dominance.

Across the three regions, interviewees painted a picture of a regular guy that is heterosexual or homonormative, cares for and provides for his family, likes sports, knows how to fix things, and is fairly "laid back." Operating as a default normal, interviewees most closely connected regular guys to a supposedly neutral suburban middle-class white ideal, though regular guys existed across a range of spatial contexts, racial identities, and class positions. The regular guy is a middle-class ideal, built on notions of a traditional breadwinner. There was some variation between region in interviewees' narratives, with the South connected to more traditional masculinities and the West associated with a more open style. Overall, the regular guy was tied most closely to midwestern and suburban ideals of normalcy, though there were variations in each region and in urban and rural places.

Interviewees defined the regular guy primarily through his relations with women and other men. Seth, a mixed-race (black and white) man living in urban Minnesota, exemplified both the balance and relational qualities of the regular guy:

> I don't want to be a guy that people are afraid of. I want to be a good guy. I want to be a nice guy, but not too nice that you're always the friend, you know. I want to be respectful of women. If there's anything about being a man that's number one, it's being respectful of women, is treating women well. It's not being a douchebag. It's not treating other guys like shit because it's gonna make me feel better.

Seth resists the violent controlling image of the thug by demonstrating his respect toward women and other men. The regular guy does not want to provoke fear in others and treat other people badly, especially women. At the same time, he does not want to be so kind that he becomes unattractive to women because he's "too nice," a sort of feminized position that makes him a less attractive object of heterosexual desire. Jack, a white man living in rural Tennessee, illustrated the rural South version of this in-between ideal well when he said, "I just wanna be a regular old Joe. I'm not the worst of the barrel, and I'm not the cream."

Traditional elements of masculinity are incorporated into this regular guy style, but consent and partnership in the nuclear family are, at least symbolically, important in separating the regular guy from hypermasculinity. Taking traditionally gendered roles in the family, such as being a husband or father, was central, though not required, for the regular guy. Yet to maintain the more relaxed stance of this middle-of-the road image, regular guys strove to maintain at least a façade of consent rather than being the explicit head of household ruling with an iron fist. This mirrors Kathleen Gerson's "neotraditional" men who derive their self-respect from work and thus seek partnerships that prioritize their career even though they profess more egalitarian ideals about their relationships with women partners.[68] Interviewees' narratives show that the regular guy defines himself as a husband and father against a hypermasculine and domineering man, while maintaining a fairly traditional gender division of labor with his partner. Rather than forcing these roles in the family, the regular guy sees himself as being in a conventional relationship because his and his partner's preferences happen to line up that way. Tom, a white man living in suburban California, shared a vision of himself as a husband and father that exemplifies this balance:

> I know exactly what I don't wanna be. I've seen so many relationships that my female friends have gone through with really lousy guys. I wanna be supportive. I do wanna be the breadwinner in my family. I think it's important to me because it's important for my wife, 'cause she wants to stay home and she wants to be there with the kids, and I want her to, too. I don't want my kids to grow up where we're not home. I think that sucks. And if that's what she wants, I wanna give that to her. I'm not a stay-at-home-with-the-kids person at all. I have no maternal instincts. I share in taking care of him, but it's not for me to stay home and be a mom. Mostly, I think just being what my wife wants me to be as far as contributing to the family and feeling a sense of worth. I think for guys that's important to feel like you're taking care of your family, and that's what I want. That's what I've always wanted. And she

allows me to be in that role and pursue that role, and that's how I feel good. I don't wanna be supported. I don't like that feeling.

This example illustrates how men like Tom establish themselves as fathers and husbands against femininity and hypermasculinity. These narratives do not necessarily devalue traditional feminine tasks in the family, such as being a stay-at-home parent; instead, they characterize the tasks as a personal preference or matter of personality. The regular guy embodies the romanticized notion of suburban normality and family as a middle-class breadwinner for the contemporary era. This is a separate spheres ideology—that suggests men should be providers out in the world and women should be caregivers in the home—with a kinder, gentler face.[69]

Tom's description of his role in the family is representative of narratives of the regular guy in the West, but this varied across regions. The regular guy in the Midwest or Southeast is more likely to take on a stricter role as the decision maker and true head of the household. The southern or midwestern regular guy still distinguishes himself from hypermasculinity with his respect for his wife or partner and their opinions and needs, but he has the final say in most matters. This mirrors the relational nature of ascendant middle-class masculinities that are constructed in contrast to subordinated working-class masculinities in Karen Pyke's analysis of relationship dynamics of heterosexual marriages.[70] Men who portrayed themselves as regular guys were not afraid of femininity, and most mentioned a few feminine coded tasks that they liked to perform, such as cooking or sewing, but at the same time, like Seth, they were careful to not present as "too feminine," in contrast to faggy men.

Through Tom's description we see how the regular guy is infused with traditional gentlemanly manners, but not the rigidity and control associated with hypermasculinity. This parallels the distinction between machismo and caballerismo in Mexican and other Latinx cultural contexts.[71] The caballero is not the vaquero of the cowboy West but rather draws on the image of a chivalrous knight and scholar to symbolize patriarchal protection. The regular guy, like the caballero, reinforces patriarchal relations without the control and violence of the macho.[72] For example, Diego, a Latinx man living in suburban Atlanta, said that he wanted to maintain a traditionally gendered division of labor in the household with his partner, but this meant some negotiation:

She loves cooking for me; she loves cleaning for me.... But it's just the little comments that I make here and there. Or like, I'll tell her not to do something. I'll be like, "You're not supposed to do that." Like, she'll go outside just because I haven't gotten to something. She'll start doing that. I won't get mad, but I'll be like, "No, what are you doing?" And like, "That's my job; that's what I'm supposed to do."

While Diego pushes to maintain the traditional division of labor to maintain their suburban home and lifestyle, he distances himself from hypermasculinity by not being angry or violent as he negotiates this labor. He sees himself as the protector and provider rather than a controlling oppressor.

Though heterosexuality is central to the regular guy, homophobia is more closely tied to hypermasculinity. This is not to say that men who have sex with other men or identify as gay cannot be regular guys. For example, Ken described the kind of man gay men sought in their "masc4masc" dating ads: "They're looking for a man who is very straight acting and who they can maybe feel comfortable sitting in a fine restaurant with and not necessarily being read immediately as gay." This illustrates it is not exclusive heterosexuality that makes one a regular guy but primarily being read by others as heterosexual and distancing oneself from excessively faggy men. This normative masculine ideal clearly draws on notions of middle-class respectability that the outrageous behavior of a flamboyant man would disrupt. Thus, the homonormative dating and sexual preferences for "straight-acting" and masculine men among gay men stems from revering this ideal. At the same time, the regular guy stands in contrast to homophobia and the overt racial, gender, and other bigotry of hypermasculinity. Once again, upholding the regular guy means distancing oneself from both hypermasculinity and excessive effeminacy.

In the Goldilocks masculinity that characterizes the ideal of the regular guy, we see the complex balance of contemporary U.S. masculine ideals. This is a hybrid masculinity in that it represents incorporation of feminist and other challenges to the contemporary gender order in ways that are largely aesthetic or symbolic. The regular guy likely represents some improvements to the toxic nature of some masculinities, but within this ideal men retain control of the patriarchal home, reproduce the nuclear family, and continue to distance themselves from women and effeminacy, along with subtly reinforcing white middle-class suburban normativity. Where this ideal has perhaps moved away from the overtly patriarchal, homophobic, and racist masculine ideals of the past, it does not appear to actually offer a sustained challenge to the normative structures that hold these social inequities firmly in place.

PROGRESSIVE MEN

The progressive man emerged from interviewees' narratives as an ideal they could aspire to and an alternative to normative notions of masculinity. This ideal was best characterized by its active rejection of hypermasculinity and many aspects of the regular guy ideal. Like the regular guy, interviewees' narratives defined the progressive man by the kinds of interactions he wants to have with women and other men, but more than the regular guy, the progressive man takes on explicit projects of equity and justice, especially related to gender, race, and sexuality. The progressive man's expression of masculinity is primarily a project of self-improvement. In other words, he sees his masculinity as a constant quest to be better. Though individual enactments of being a progressive man varied quite a bit among interviewees, their commonality was an overall project to consciously work to undermine inequality.

Rather than judging the comfort of the three bears' beds, the progressive man might instead question whether entering another person's home and using their resources without permission resembles a problematic colonialist mentality. Interviewees used fairly consistent descriptors for progressive men across regions, such as being "open," "aware of privilege," "egalitarian," and "vulnerable." In contrast to the association of hypermasculinity with poor and working-class men, the progressive man is educated and worldly, though not necessarily wealthy. Thus, there is a classed dimension to the progressive man in terms of education and bearing.

The progressive man ideal resembles aspects of the "sensitive new-age guy," who was almost as ridiculous as the faggy man in some interviewees' accounts, yet progressive men worked to resist this stereotype. The "sensitive new-age guy" label emerged as something of a joke in response to the emergence of profeminist men in the late twentieth century.[73] Progressive men instead emphasized a sharp political edge and project of constant self-transformation in order to help distance themselves from an image that is sensitive to social ills but wholly ineffective. Thus, this ideal indicates a critical awareness of the trappings of earlier versions of profeminist or feminist men along with critiques of hypermasculine men and the regular guy.

Interviewees often admired qualities of the progressive man and held men who approximated this ideal as masculine models. Bert, a white man living in a college town in North Carolina, described two men who were his close friends that exemplified particular aspects of the progressive man:

> They both very beautifully modeled a kind of masculinity that I admired. There was a softness to it, an openness. They were both really opinionated and really strong flavors, but very sweet. I have a couple men that I still sort of look to as the kind of masculinity that I admire and I think pretty unilaterally. They're just really open to people, and they're sensitive. They're aware of their place in a world amongst others. And I think that's really beautiful.

In Bert's glowing description, it is clear he aspired to be a similar kind of man. James, a white man in urban California, said that sensitivity and empathy were central to his masculinity. As a young person in the punk scene of a city near the Great Lakes, figures such as Ian MacKaye of the band Fugazi provided a model for this sensitive and politically engaged masculinity in contrast to the violence and hypermasculinity that characterized his local scene.

The project of transformation is especially important for progressive men. Malcolm, a white man living in urban Georgia, described his friend, another young trans man, whom he admires:

> He's really conscious of how privilege works and how he gains it and what it means to him; also what it means for him to transition and being Latino and how that works for him. That that's really complicated, too. And I think he works through that in a really good way. He just thinks about everything. And in a lot of ways I look to him for like how I wanna construct my masculinity. You always have to be looking at what you're doing and aware of how you could be sexist. I think that's something really critical for me, too, like being a white man in the South. That has so many terrible connotations and so many things that I don't want to be.

Perhaps subtly referring to the redneck and good old boy, Malcolm wants to distance himself from both gendered and racial connotations of southern masculinity. Taking on the transformative project of the progressive man was especially important for a man like Malcolm, whose political commitments meant a consciousness of his place as a white man in the systems of racial and gender inequality in the U.S. South. This illustrates how interviewees evaluated progressive men by their engagements with racial justice, like the white man who understands his racial privilege and combats white supremacy. Thus, the progressive man ideal is still a racial project, but it is what Omi and Winant refer to as an "anti-racist project."[74]

Like the regular guy, his relations with others, especially his intimate partnerships, define the progressive man. The progressive man's relationships are demarcated by flexibility and openness. For example, Alec, a white man in urban Northern California, described some aspects of his relationship with his partner:

> She opens the doors for me sometimes. I'm not always the perfect gentleman because our relationship isn't built on that. I'm not the breadwinner. We both bring in the same amount of money. We both do the same amount of housework. Actually, I do all the cooking in our relationship. So there are a lot of things that just when you look at your standard heterosexual couple, where you think of the men as the breadwinners and the women as the housewives, taking care of the house and the man being really like [*manly voice*] strong and loving and caring and taking care of the woman and carrying her around, and opening doors and being kind of aggressive, and I'm just not any of those things. I want a piña colada with an umbrella in the pool with all the women [*laugh*]. I mean, that's the other thing: I like girly drinks. I like beer, but if I'm in Vegas in a pool, I want something like girly and ridiculous.

As Alec's narrative shows, the progressive man rejects aggression and hypermasculinity in addition to the gendered roles in relationships typical of the regular guy. Where the regular guy is masculine but is not afraid of femininity or effeminacy, the progressive man actively embraces aspects of femininity. Another notable way that the progressive man embraces femininity is in not being afraid to be seen as gay regardless of his sexual practices or identities. This shows that there is some overlap between the more feminine practices of the progressive man and the faggy man. Yet there are men who do a faggy masculinity without being a progressive man and vice versa.

Overall, the progressive man ideal appeared as an alternative way to be a man that allowed interviewees a way out of the constraints of normative masculinities and a path toward making change. It was clear that the progressive man attempted to go beyond the surface aesthetics and shallow discursive distancing of the regular guy. While promising as a project of change, this progressive ideal requires vigilance not only to work against being "that guy" but also to avoid solely glorifying the progressive man himself, which might once again recenter particular groups of men rather than shifting inequitable power relations. Thus, trans men admired this ideal, but it was difficult to consistently put into practice, especially considering the predominance of the regular guy. Trans men, from their experiences of being treated as women, may tip more toward the progressive guy than some other groups of men, but most interviewees wanted to be regular guys. Despite their own preferences, their narratives of contemporary masculinity tap into their experiences as men and with the larger cultural contexts of the contemporary United States.

CONCLUSION

The West, Midwest, and South each have a unique history of regional masculinities connected to their landscape, economic circumstances, and social conditions. The geographic imaginaries of each region draw mostly on traditional rural occupations and histories to prescribe regional masculine standards. In the twenty-first century, it is clear that some of the predominate characteristics of traditional masculinities are no longer valued as they once were. Racialized hypermasculinities, such as the controlling images of the thug and redneck, as well as excessive effeminacies like the faggy man, operate as gendered, racial, and sexual projects tied to particular spaces that pose some men as excessive and out of control. In contrast to these spatially inflected controlling images, most men strive toward being a regular guy and achieving a Goldilocks masculinity. This regular guy is not overtly macho, appears to be heterosexual but is not homophobic, and cares for and provides for his family. This is a middle-class suburban ideal of normalcy, even if this ideal exists across regions and urban and rural spaces. While regular guys tend to have normative gendered relations with their partners, these are based not on authoritarian control but on consent and personal preference between partners. The progressive man represents a less common but promising ideal. He is more overtly focused on living in ways that challenge social inequities in both his personal life and the broader political realm.

The regular guy seems like an improvement over the hypermasculine, emotionally cold, and domineering normative masculinities that have existed in varied times and places. It is certainly positive that this ideal offers more flexibility for men to enact a wider range of human characteristics and behaviors. Yet as C. J. Pascoe and Tristen Bridges remind us, it is not just a change in how masculinities look that leads to changes in the larger gender order, or for that matter the race, class, or sexual orders. Instead, we should look for evidence of how these masculinities actually create substantive change in the racially and sexually tinged inequality between women and men, as well as among groups of men.[75] In this sense, the Goldilocks masculinity at the center of the regular guy likely falls short. The regular guy is still constructed in opposition to femininity, whether it's women or faggy men, and is a white middle-class ideal constructed in contrast to particularly racialized and classed images of hypermasculinity. Rather than substantive change, Goldilocks masculinity represents an incorporation of more palatable standards in the economic and political context of neoliberalism and a response to challenges posed by feminist, racial justice, and LGBT movements. Yet through distancing themselves from controlling images of hypermasculinity and faggy masculinity, as well as femininity, the regular guy does not really challenge his suitability for power. Rather, he displaces culpability for ongoing racism, sexism, and heterosexism onto marginalized others. Further, those class, race, and sexually privileged men will come closest to embodying the normative regular guy, whereas men of color, poor men, or effeminate men may never be able to fully achieve this standard beyond selected contexts, at least partially due to the prevalence and effects of controlling images.

All of these dynamics suggest that flexibility rather than rigidity is crucial to contemporary masculinities. Even Donald Trump, who often embodies some of the most abhorrent traits of hypermasculinity, still shifts his masculine practices between contexts to retain dominance in light of the reduced legitimacy of hypermasculinity. Tristan Bridges and James Messerschmidt show how through these fluid masculinities Trump takes on the role of protector in one moment and bully in another.[76] Further, C. J. Pascoe emphasizes how both Trump's actions and much of the discourse opposing them rely on "dominance practices over women and other men as well as repudiation practices that position other men as unmasculine failures."[77] Amid the rise of other strongmen globally, including Vladimir Putin in Russia, Rodrigo Duterte in the Philippines, and Norendra Modi in India, the aura of a domineering and strong yet tender and protective in some moments leader is doing the global political work of legitimating forms of patriarchal, heteronormative, and economically exploitative control that are bringing social inequality to new levels.

The key to the regular guy is not just flexibility in terms of incorporating subordinated or marginalized masculine practices but rather adaptability to the demands of the spaces and places he moves through in everyday life. This may mean finding "masculine balance" in a hyperlocal context.[78] Indeed, striving for a Goldilocks masculinity means engaging in masculine practices that hit the just-right balance that makes them "in place" in a particular setting, while constructing other men and other masculinities as "out of place." From the streets of the gentrifying inner city to the ranches dotting the wide expanses of the West, this contest of masculine ideals represents key contemporary struggles over power and social inequality. In the following chapters, I will return often to these masculine controlling images as racialized, sexualized, gendered, and classed projects and the effects of a Goldilocks masculinity on the contemporary gender order. Some readers might wonder if the ideals that emerged from trans men's narratives reflect trends among men as a broader group. This raises the question: Who, exactly, is a man?

2
One Is Not Born a Man
SOCIAL RECOGNITION AND
SITUATED GENDERED KNOWLEDGES

Wesley was a forty-four-year-old white man who lived in a midsized city near the Appalachian region at the time I interviewed him. He had transitioned twenty years before we met. Early in his transition, Wesley lived in a large city on the West Coast, but he was uncomfortable there because he felt like people often read him as transgender or thought he was a butch woman. He had moved from that city to a southern state a number of years before the interview partly because he wanted to be seen by others solely as a man. Wesley shared with me a remarkable story about an interaction he had with a neighbor early in his time living in the Southeast.

Wesley had very large breasts before getting chest reconstruction surgery but was comfortable without a shirt on, especially in the yard of his home, which at that time was in a rural area.[1] Wesley's next-door neighbor in that rural community did not see his large breasts as being in conflict with recognizing Wesley as a man:

> Went out, he saw me, huge breasts, couple of times. I was out one day mowing the lawn, and he came over, and he was speaking to my chest. He'd look at my eyes, look at my chest, and he says, "You know, dude, I've gotta apologize." And I'm like, "For what?" ... He goes, "You know, man, that's some nasty glandular problem you have. You mean no one's helped you fix that?"

After Wesley had chest reconstruction surgery, the neighbor brought over beers to celebrate and continue their neighborly relationship.

The neighbor, whom Wesley described as a redneck, could have read Wesley's body in a number of different ways. He likely chose the option that made the most sense—that Wesley was a cisgender man with large breasts due to some kind of untreated medical problem. It is

|| 59

easy, and neatly fits stereotypes of poor white rural people, to think of this as some kind of ignorance or simplicity on the part of the neighbor. Yet if we take a moment to see Wesley through the neighbor's eyes, we can understand how his assessment of Wesley represents not a lack of knowledge but instead a particular knowledge that is rooted in the rural Southeast about who is a man, what masculinities are acceptable, and how men should interact with one another.

The interaction suggests that the knowledge the neighbor was operating with is based on a binary and essentialist understanding of gender, meaning that there are only men and women, that each person fits in one of those categories, and that there is no crossing over those groups. Even if he knew that transgender people existed, this gender knowledge might dictate that trans people would not be found in this place, but only in cities and outside the Southeast. That the neighbor saw Wesley performing white heterosexual working-class rural masculinities additionally set the ground for the neighbor to accept Wesley's nonnormative body as falling onto one side of a gender binary.[2] Thus, Wesley displaying the appropriate racialized, sexualized, and classed masculinities connected to that place, as well as normalizing his own body by unapologetically going shirtless, solidified the neighbor placing him in the category of man.

The recognition of Wesley as a man and the raced and sexualized assessment of his masculinity also shaped how the neighbor treated him. This recognition led to the neighbor engaging him in over-the-fence neighbor talk, showing concern for what the neighbor clearly perceived as an unusual body—one that was perhaps embarrassing due to its womanly implications—and then bringing him into the homosocial fold by offering him a beer once the problem was "fixed." This had the effect of conferring recognition of Wesley's identity not just as a man but also as a man who fit that place.

This encounter shows that Wesley got exactly what he wanted from moving to the rural Southeast—the recognition as a man that he was often denied by people operating with a more expansive gender knowledge that included transgender people. Though Wesley thought this incident was rather remarkable—that he was recognized as a man despite the presence of his large, uncovered breasts—it illustrates the ways he was included in homosocial interactions and spaces in the rural Southeast because others consistently recognized him as a man. It would be false to understand this recognition as an incident of some sort of deception on Wesley's part, because he was being recognized for exactly who he saw himself to be in terms of gender—a man. Thus, the local knowledge of gender helped the neighbor see Wesley in a way that felt authentic to Wesley himself.

The process of recognition as a man in interaction occurs in light of varying contextual gender, racial, and sexual knowledges. Inhabiting the social category of man is not based in biology, or even solely in one's identity or legal classification, but is rather a process tied to social assessment and interaction. In other words, trans men's accounts of recognition suggest that for all men one is not born a man but rather becomes one again and again as they encounter the gender, racial, and sexual knowledges and related expectations of different social contexts. The social experience of being a man is a becoming that happens through recognition rather than a static or fixed trait, or individual identity.

RECOGNITION AND GENDER KNOWLEDGES

Gender in interaction starts at the moment a person categorizes another as a man or a woman, or as something else entirely. This moment becomes the basis for the social action that follows. According to West and Zimmerman's foundational work, once one is categorized as a man or a woman, then one is accountable to the situated and historically specific normative gender expectations connected to that category.[3] The moment of categorization is potentially a moment of *recognition*. I follow Raewyn Connell's use of *recognition* rather than the controversial term *passing*, both to better represent trans men's view of themselves and to ground the process of categorization, or being seen by others, as inherently social.[4] Recognition not only is a more polite description of passing but also highlights that categorization is a social process for all people.[5] Indeed, gender recognition, based on norms that vary across contexts and are embedded in space, can be the basis for being considered fully human, and a lack of recognition can deny some individuals the possibility of livable lives.[6]

Authenticity is an essential part of being socially recognized as a man. I use *authenticity* to refer to the idea that what an individual is doing or saying or how they are presenting themselves are true representations of the self rather than mere sincerity, which is an alignment between what one is feeling and what one is expressing.[7] This means that trans men achieve authenticity when they express themselves as the gender they see themselves as and others recognize them as such. At the same time, my use of *authenticity* does not assume a conception of a unified and easily identifiable self that can be "truly" expressed; the definition reflects instead commonly held beliefs about the self and authenticity.[8] While it is a popular idea in this moment that individuals have a core internal being that can be discovered and then authentically expressed, I operate with the understanding that this internal sense is more likely formed by interaction and experiences and through the available language and ideas of our particular time and place. This does not make any particular identity or gender category any less real or valid than any other but refers instead to a generally more malleable idea of the self and identity for all people. Regardless, social recognition as a man can further legitimize the internal sense of being a man and, importantly, open up social action in line with being recognized in that category. For my interviewees, gaining social recognition was an active process that occurred at various points and in various forms of gender presentation, ranging from early in transition to later when people did or did not see them as men or transgender or both.

Trans men's narratives illustrate that contextually based gender knowledges that are simultaneously racialized and sexualized shape processes of recognition and authenticity. These gender knowledges represent norms that prescribe not only how gender should be done but also what gender categories even exist and who can inhabit them.[9] Gender knowledges are primary to, but not separable from, race and sexuality in the determination of who is a man and who is not. An intersectional analysis extends understandings of gender and recognition to demonstrate the centrality of racial and sexual recognition as well.

In my research with trans men, I found that some spatial and institutional contexts offered more expansive notions of who is a man, while others relied on more restrictive ideas. The more expansive notions often relied on a person's self-definition—if you see yourself as a man, then you are a man—and the knowledge that not all men were assigned male at birth, as well as acknowledging the existence of transgender people and genders that do not fit an either/or binary. More restrictive gender knowledges relied on a binary and essentialist understanding of who counts as a man—there are only men, and men are people who were assigned male at birth. Both these expansive and narrow gender knowledges allow for different forms of recognition—as a man, as properly masculine, and as transgender. It bears emphasizing that those individuals who had more restrictive or narrow gender knowledges were not necessarily less complex thinkers than those with more expansive knowledges. That is, expansive knowledges do not necessarily refer to knowing more, but to knowing differently.

While focusing here on interaction, gender knowledges play out at the individual level, as well as in legal classification and policy. Raewyn Connell writes about self-knowledge of gender for "transsexuals" as a key moment of recognition, despite embodiment or assignment to a particular sex.[10] Yet this self-recognition is not unique to transgender people, as all people operate with a gender self-knowledge and, to a lesser or greater extent, may have to grapple with contradictions between self-knowledge and their particular embodiments or social positions. Cisgender men and women, too, must reconcile the fact that they do not always achieve normative bodily ideals of manhood or womanhood, such as having chest protrusions that are too large or too small for their respective gender. Indeed, it seems that few people actually achieve these nearly impossible gender standards. Managing the consequences of categorization and potential accountability in interaction is based on this gendered subjectivity.[11] Legal classification and policy debates, often based on cisgender people's imagined interactions with transgender people, are also key arenas where gender recognition is based on varied and competing knowledges.[12] Both individual self-knowledge and the knowledges employed in policy based on imagined interactions rely on historical and culturally located discourses of gender, sexuality, and race, which rely on medical, psychiatric, and media accounts that both construct and naturalize various forms of difference.[13] These are taken up in uneven ways and have unexpected effects as they are deployed across spatial and institutional contexts.

The moments of recognition in trans men's stories illuminate how gender knowledge is operationalized as everyday common sense in the categorization of others in interaction. This common sense is related to other media and scientific discourses but is not reducible to them. Much work has been done to understand how gender operates in interaction, but fewer scholars have investigated the moment of categorization and how it can vary. Trans men's narratives of deployments of categorization and recognition illustrate that these moments are crucial for establishing social positionings of gender, race, and sexuality. At the same time, these stories show that the underlying beliefs and knowledges that lead to practical recognition are based in particular spaces and places.

CONTEXTS OF RECOGNITION

In discussing the social process of transition for transgender people, Raewyn Connell writes:

> It is a matter of creating everyday life on new terms. Transition is reentry into the historical dynamic of gender, an event in time that launches an interactive social process. A great deal, then, rests on the responses of others, in public arenas as well as private.... In the positive case, recognition as a woman need not involve passing. Recognition can equally be a matter of pragmatic acceptance by those with whom one lives and works.[14]

Though she focuses on trans women, Connell's words ring true in trans men's narratives. To transition means to reenter gender relations from a different position through an inherently social and interactive process. Transition is not just a personal change involving bodily transformations but is a social process that begins with recognition of a gender identity tied up with notions of authenticity. Recognition as a man is facilitated in particular spaces, and as Connell implies, it can happen with or without knowledge of a transgender past. When trans men moved through contexts where individuals knew of their transgender history, they could encounter both expansive and restrictive knowledges of who was a man and could be recognized as such or not based on those knowledges. These spatially specific gender knowledges exist on one hand as informal discourses, or everyday common sense, and on the other hand as matters of formal policy in a variety of spatial and institutional contexts.

Organizations

The trans men I interviewed had mixed experiences with recognition as men in the contexts they moved in and out of in their everyday lives when their transgender history was known to others. Some shared stories of surprising acceptance and affirmation in unexpected places, such as an easy and institutionally supported open transition at a conservative corporate workplace, while others recounted nearly insurmountable barriers and hostility—being continuously misgendered at school or fired from a job. These instances of misrecognition, harassment, and violence are important, but here I primarily focus on moments of recognition as men in particular institutional and interactional contexts to illustrate common experiences of recognition.[15]

Transgender support groups were one key place where trans men gained recognition as men, regardless of their outward appearance. Andrew, a white man living in suburban Tennessee, described this expansive knowledge in support groups, "If you tell me you're a guy, then you're a guy. 'What do you want to be called?' And that's it." While these same support groups could at times enforce norms of masculinity or hierarchies of trans legitimacy, they simultaneously affirmed an expansive gender knowledge that relied on self-definition.[16]

In some organizational contexts, expansive gender knowledges could lead to recognition as a man and actually help to reframe parts of bodies associated with female or male secondary sex characteristics. Ian, a white man who lived in urban Minnesota, was a member of a fraternity made up of mostly gay men. They accepted all self-identified men by policy and also deployed an expansive gender knowledge in practice. He described a trip with his fraternity brothers:

> I haven't had top surgery, but this summer we had a retreat at one of the guys' cabins up at this little lake in the middle of nowhere, really secluded, and I was really self-conscious. I love to swim. I love swimming. . . . And I hate, I just feel so uncomfortable. But the guys were like, "Dude, we don't care. No one's gonna judge you. No one's gonna stare at you." And so I spent the entire weekend in the lake [without a shirt on]. That was extremely validating.

The fraternity as an organization granted Ian recognition through their policy that allowed all self-identified men to join. In addition, his brothers further recognized him by accepting his body through normalizing his chest and promising not to give it undo attention through staring. Any man with larger than typical breasts might feel uncomfortable with his chest uncovered, but through knowing his transgender status and encouraging him to swim without a shirt on, Ian's brothers recognized his chest as a man's chest.[17] This kind of expansive gender knowledge put into practice allowed for recognition of trans men in these contexts, even when their bodies did not have typical male characteristics.

Family Matters

The family as an institution made for a complex site of recognition. It was a key space where interviewees sought recognition from those who had some sense of their transgender history. While the examples here illustrate moments of recognition as men, interviewees also experienced insistent misrecognition from some family members. This misrecognition, like all misrecognition, could be deeply painful and marginalizing for those who experienced it.[18] When parents, siblings, children, and other family members recognized interviewees as men, it was particularly meaningful because family often had difficulty using new names and pronouns. Tom, a white man living in suburban Northern California, was married to a woman and had a six-year-old stepson:

> My son's rad. I think he always thought I was a guy anyway 'cause kids are so black-and-white. When they see short hair and men's clothes, you are a male then. That's how our society is. I think explaining to him that I was a girl in the beginning was harder than telling him I was gonna be his dad now. . . . He jumped into that right away, 'cause he would already call me "Dad," by accident.

His son's response affirmed the authenticity of Tom's deeply held gender identity as a man, even before transition. Tom's masculinity was now in line with him being a man and a "dad," and thus he entered the realm of cultural intelligibility and was better aligned with the more restrictive knowledge held by his son.

Explaining to his son he was a man actually made Tom "in place" in the normative family structure, where masculine people are dads and men are married to moms. At the same time, this acceptance relies on an expansive gender knowledge that recognizes dads have not always been hes.[19] This example demonstrates not only the power of normative family formations and how they can be simultaneously challenged and reaffirmed but also that some gender knowledges might rely on a binary not based on biological essentialism. Thus, gender binaries in the family, as well as in other spaces, are reproduced at times even when the individuals are not cisgender or heterosexual.

Over time, a masculine presentation could seemingly erase more distant family members' knowledge of who the interviewees were prior to transition. This illustrates the strength of dominant knowledges and how routinized categorization becomes over time. Morgan, a white man who lived in rural North Carolina, had transitioned ten years before the interview. He and his partner had been together for fifteen years. Morgan had met most of her family when he lived as a woman, and his transition had been common knowledge in the family. He recently attended a funeral for a member of his partner's family:

> Her great-aunt down here in Jefferson County . . . she says to Sally [his partner], "Honey, I'm so glad you found a man" [*laughter*]. "It's just the right thing to do." But she had met me before. And I don't think she put two and two together.

Morgan had a thick mustache now but said that he otherwise looked about the same as when he lived as a woman. Plus, his gender-ambiguous name had also not changed. He explained that other family members similarly did not see him as the same person, and thus he got recognition in the family as a man. Even though the family knew him before, they seemed to assume he was a different person based on his more typically male presentation, his ostensibly heterosexual relationship, and the restrictive gender knowledges they relied on.

Interactional Spaces

Being recognized as a man by strangers and others who were unaware of their transgender biography was often a vital sign of authenticity for interviewees, but the reliability of this recognition varied across spatial contexts. Interviewees consistently reported they were more easily seen as men when they were not in major cities that had large LGBT populations. For example, Raphael, a Mexican American man living in Chicago, had these experiences when traveling from his neighborhood to Kansas for a wedding:

> I live in Robertstown, which is very openly gay and queer friendly. It's funny 'cause I still get called "ma'am" in certain situations, which I'm totally fine with. And sometimes, I'm called "sir." . . . Outside of my city, as an example, I went to a wedding in Kansas City, and no one questioned whether I was male or not; it was just automatically "sir" everywhere. I notice in different areas it's not even a question, but because this [area] is so openly gay friendly and queer friendly, I think people try to be, I don't know, politically correct, or they just don't assume.

According to Raphael, the expansive knowledge in his city, which included butch women and transgender people, gave people a broader set of gender categories with which to understand trans men's gender presentations. Trans men were likely to be categorized in more narrow ways in places with more restrictive gender knowledges, like where Raphael visited in Kansas. Other men noted a shift when moving from places like Pittsburgh or rural Ohio, where they were consistently recognized as men, to San Francisco, where they were more often read as transgender or as butch women. These moments of recognition also relied on regional and other locally based knowledges where certain cues, such as a haircut or a particular piece of clothing, might mean the difference between being recognized as men or not.

The particular knowledges present in different spatial contexts shaped racial recognition as well. With a complex racial identity, including African American, Indigenous, and Mexican backgrounds, Gabriel found he was read as biracial or black in the Deep South city where he grew up but not in the city a few hours away where he attended university.

> It was different for me that I was now no longer being read as biracial but by being read as specifically Hispanic and then people trying to figure out if I was Cuban, Puerto Rican, or what have you from the Latin areas. Which was weird for me because I'm Mexican. It's a very different setup, so it was weird for me. Like, I really don't know the difference between the Dominican Republic and Puerto Rico. I'm learning.

Gabriel's story parallels Chandra Mohanty's description of being read differently in terms of race as she lived and traveled through different regions of the United States.[20] Thus, Gabriel was categorized in different ways when he encountered new racial knowledges, and this meant he too had to learn the nuances of ethnic and national identities contained in this particular knowledge.[21] Both gender and racial categorization occur in everyday interactions along with their attendant meanings and treatment; in fact, other kinds of status can potentially shape racial and gender categorization.[22] Though gender is often most prominent in interviewees' accounts of their assessment as a man or not, race and sexuality are interwoven into these assessments.

Spatially based recognitions both affirmed and negated the complexity of trans men's identities. Some interviewees appreciated that others saw them as both transgender and a man, whereas others found it highly insulting. Levi had moved from a smaller city in Pennsylvania to urban Northern California and experienced a major shift in recognition due to spatially based gender knowledges:

> There I passed all the time! No question! Never a question! Even before I had surgery. No question. People just always treated me like a guy, and I got so comfortable and so easy with it, and my masculinity was reinforced by the fact that everyone just took for granted that I was a guy. There was no question. Coming here, and everyone's trying to be all politically correct. Like, "What's your pronoun preference?" And I'm like, "Fuck you! You can't tell?" And it pissed me off.

Levi's reaction illustrates that these narrow knowledges grant authenticity to people who most strongly identify as men because they become like any other guy. Levi's increased comfort with the consistent and unquestioned recognition as a man shows that this recognition can be a powerful affirmation of a gender self-knowledge. Checking for a person's correct pronouns is usually an attempt to honor an individual's self-knowledge and to recognize that an individual's gender might not be apparent from looking at them. Yet this example suggests the question can be discrediting and a moment of misrecognition, a sort of undoing, when individuals ask it only of people they read as transgender.[23]

These well-meaning moments of misrecognition and questioning illustrate how more expansive knowledges are not always preferable or more accurate at assessing gender, race, or sexuality. Like Wesley at the outset of the chapter, a number of men I interviewed had or planned to relocate to places with more restrictive gender knowledges so that they could live being recognized solely as men. These movements reflect spatially based notions of safety and are more available to white men who resemble raced, classed, and sexualized ideals of particular geographic contexts. Overall, the unexpected effects of different knowledges trouble notions of urban gender, racial, and sexual sophistication.

While recognition as a man could affirm self-knowledge for men like Levi, most interviewees reported that being recognized solely as a man actually presented a limited view of who they were. Aaron, a white man in Chicago, explained:

> Sometimes, I think the most problematic part of really passing as much as I do is that I start to feel like my whole history is invisible . . . and that's isolating. Because people make a lot of false assumptions about not just who you are but where you've been and your entire life.

Spatially based knowledges that lead to recognition as a man also leave less room for trans men who feel a strong connection to their past or identify as nonbinary. Thus, for some interviewees the cost of recognition as a man and the sometimes crucial social intelligibility that goes along with it conflicted with authenticity to complex gendered selves—not just as a man or not but including whether one is transgender or not, nonbinary or not—especially amid more restrictive gender knowledges.

Chest Reconstruction

Bodies are significant in interaction and in recognition. The imagined presence of particular genitals and their sexual implications are central in categorization through policy and interaction.[24] However, genitals are not the only area where gender and sexuality play out on the body. Indeed, Eric Plemons suggests that facial feminization surgery may be surpassing genital reconstruction surgery as the most significant aspect of a medical transition for trans women.[25] Other areas of the body, such as chests, are significant in the production of gender and sexuality in interaction and for recognition based on contextual gender knowledges.[26] The ways that chests are read, reread, and transformed in interaction present a particularly good example of the influence of gender knowledges on the relationship between gendered and sexual embodiment and recognition.

Men's and women's chests are treated quite differently across public and private spaces. Men typically have greater social permission to expose their chests than women, especially in public, largely because women's chests are viewed as sexual objects. A man's exposed chest can be shown on television with little fanfare, but women's exposed chests are far more controversial.[27] For example, in a documentary that included the chest reconstruction surgery of a trans man, his nipples were blurred during the beginning of the surgery. However, once a significant amount of tissue was removed and his now smaller nipples were reattached, they were no longer blurred.[28] According to the logic of the producers or censors, the reattachment was the crucial moment when his chest went from one that needed to be blurred out to one that could be shown.

However, the exposure of men's chests can become quite fraught when they do not conform to embodied gendered ideals. For example, when a boy or a man has gynecomastia, a medicalized condition where a large amount of breast tissue grows, their bodies can be considered a source of embarrassment that should be covered.[29] In fact, gynecomastia is quite common in people assigned male at birth. It affects over 50 percent of male-assigned people as infants in the first few weeks after birth, during puberty, and as they are aging.[30] The presence of breast tissue does not constitute a health problem in and of itself but becomes a problem due to social stigma. As Robyn Longhurst has found, these "man-breasts" are often considered abject, sources of simultaneous horror and fascination for others, and can be a threat to a masculine sense of self for men and other masculine people.[31] For instance, butch women might desire to have chests with smaller protrusions either for practical purposes or so that their bodies fit their masculine ideal.[32] Thus, chest protrusions in general are out of place when they cause conflict with embodying masculinity.

Wesley, Ian, and Jason's experiences illustrate that varying gender knowledges can reshape the fleshy material body in interaction, marking men's chest protrusions as abject or normalized depending on the space and a reconstructed chest as potentially sexy. This marking is crucial to the process of social recognition and of these people as socially embodied men. In the story of Wesley and his neighbor, Wesley normalized his own breasts, but they were clearly an object of fascination and disbelief to the neighbor. Wesley thought the neighbor was attracted to his large breasts but simultaneously revolted that he had an ostensibly heterosexual desire for large chest protrusions on a man's body. Within the neighbor's narrow gender knowledge, Wesley's chest protrusions could only be abject appendages on a man's body that necessitated medical intervention. Like Wesley's neighbor, Ian's fraternity brothers saw his chest as a man's chest when they encouraged him not to wear a shirt during their trip to the lakeside cabin, but his chest was normalized rather than abject. Not staring or giving his chest protrusions undue attention illustrates that his chest was not an object of heterosexual desire, which would have been incongruent with recognizing him as a man. As a fraternity made up of mostly gay men, Ian's chest and its potential heterosexual implications might have made him out of place with his fraternity brothers. Instead, the expansive gender knowledge that welcomed Ian into the group as a matter of policy was reinforced in social interaction to transform the meaning of his chest and to treat Ian as the man he is.[33]

Part of trans men's work to reclaim and normalize their bodies is also about transforming language, which is a powerful tool for gaining authenticity. Like other particularly gendered zones of the body, trans men often work to linguistically reframe their chests based on self-knowledge. For example, Henry, in talking about his decision to get chest reconstruction surgery, said with a laugh, "Can't help that I was born with chesticles instead of testicles." This individual work is important, but the reframing is particularly impactful when it is backed by others' behavior in interaction, such as not staring, that socially affirms men's embodied status.

Like Ian, Jason, a white man living in suburban Ohio, found recognition as a man in gay men's spaces, where his chest was not treated as a deficit. Bear communities that generally accepted a wide range of bodies were especially welcoming to Jason and other men.[34] In describing this recognition, Jason shared an early experience at a Bear event:

> There was this huge Bear dance party. Oh my God. I gotta tell you, it was amazing. I'm out there, I'm dancing, not wearing my shirt, and I scarred pretty bad after my surgery. And my friend that I was

there with, he was like, "Honey, you spent a lot of money for those scars. Show 'em the hell off."

The expansive gender knowledge employed by his friend to encourage Jason to go shirtless and show off his scars transformed the scars into a source of accomplishment, whereas they might have been seen as a discrediting visual reminder of past incoherencies in his gender embodiment. The space was welcoming due to the combination of an expansive gender knowledge, where a history of breasts did not discredit categorization as a man, and an acceptance of a range of bodies that are scarred, fat, hairy, and differently shaped.[35]

This recognition of Jason was not just as a man but as a sexually attractive man. He went on to describe how the other Bears treated him at the party:

> Just dancing and men just all around me, grinding on me, and making out with random guys, and it was just so open and welcoming and comfortable. In the Bear community, the biggest compliment you can get from another Bear is for him to look at you and say, "Woof." Okay? And there was this tall good-looking guy, and as I was walking by, and he looked at me, and he winked, and he was like, "Woof."

By dancing without his shirt and showing his chest scars, Jason opened up the possibility that strangers would recognize him as transgender. Due to the expansive gender knowledge employed in the queer space of the dance party, other men recognized him in the homoerotic context as a man through dancing with him, making out with him, and giving him that customary "woof." To some degree, like Wesley, it is possible that the absence of his former chest protrusions made him a man who was compatible with the dominant sexual meanings of the space.

Wesley, Ian, and Jason's experiences of embodiment across these interactional spaces illustrate the power of gender knowledges to reconstitute the material flesh of the body. These stories show that the material body does not hold a static meaning. Even the presence or absence of flesh, such as breast tissue, which holds central meaning in dominant ideas of femaleness and maleness, is interpreted by others in different ways depending on the space. These framings and reframings shaped how others treated the men in interaction, especially in regard to the status of breasts in heterosexual desire.

CONFLICTS OF RECOGNITION

While gender knowledges are spatially and institutionally based, they are not always consistent among the individuals interacting in a space, and this leads to conflicting assessments. Trans individuals themselves can, of course, intervene to assert their status, but the conflict is often settled by others doing what Jane Ward describes as "giving gender."[36] This is a form of gender labor where a person affirms the potentially contested gender of another. For example, Alec, a white man living in urban Northern California, worked in a men's sex club that employed an expansive gender knowledge by welcoming all self-identified men as customers and workers. Yet he said there were times when some customers' assessments did not align with the policy:

> He [a coworker] had just started taking T a few months before. I don't really like to use the word *passing*, but this person didn't pass enough for the men who were coming in the club to go, "Oh yes, this person is a man." One day it was me, this person, and then another trans guy who was the manager working. So it was all three trans guys staff, and this customer came up to me and the manager and said, "What is that dyke doing sitting at the front counter?" [*laugh*]. And we both just looked at each other because we're both trans guys, and we're like, "This is so fucked up," and we were just like, "We don't see any dyke here. There is no dyke in the building. This is a men's space. There's only men in here."

The policy of the club to accept all self-identified men as workers and customers gave the coworker one form of recognition, and Alec and the manager provided another form by "giving gender" through affirming to the customer that their coworker was a man. In effect, both policy and practice enforced an expansive knowledge.

When family members persistently misrecognized trans men, strangers often provided recognition far more easily. Oscar, an Asian and white man living in suburban Northern California, was early in his transition. He reported that his family and friends would not use the correct pronouns and name. He said:

> It still bothers me when people still call me "Octavia" because I feel like they're disrespecting me.... When they want to call me "he" and "Oscar," I feel really respected. It's nice of them to do that. That's why I'm actually more comfortable talking to strangers who just met me, because they treat me how I want to be treated, which is as a guy. They don't think of me as Octavia still, and they don't slip into Octavia mode.

Oscar's ability to be read as a man provided recognition his family would not. Thus, it was usually in public spaces with strangers rather than the space of the home with family where Oscar found recognition.

In public contexts, family members who did not use correct pronouns or other terms of address for the interviewee created conflict when strangers recognized them as men. For example, if a server in a restaurant correctly called Oscar "he" but his family did not, it caused confusion for the server. Thus, the same gender knowledge, in this case likely restrictive for both his family and the server, can have differing and unexpected effects. His family's restrictive gender knowledge, along with knowledge of his history, led to misgendering, whereas the server's led to recognition as a man. Rather than discrediting the trans man, this recognition usually created embarrassment for the family member because they seemed to be the one who was getting it wrong. Family members then often started giving recognition, at least in public. Whether this caused a total shift or just a shift in public, this recognition from strangers was instrumental in shifting family members' attitudes. This process illustrates one of the many social aspects of gender, that recognition from strangers made trans men's gender identities more legitimate to family members. At the very least, in public it forced the family member to make a choice between either disrupting the interaction and marking themselves as an incompetent actor or going along with it.

BE A MAN

Gender knowledges operate not just in terms of being categorized as a man or not; rather, trans men's narratives show that particular ways of performing or doing gender help individuals stake their claim in that category. Thus, gender knowledges also contain ideas about contextually appropriate masculinities. Trans men are not passive in the process of recognition but engage particular masculinities in order to be seen as men, especially at times when they have more trouble achieving recognition.

Early in transition, most interviewees reported pressure from others to conform to some form of normative masculinities in an effort to be recognized as a man. This meant distancing themselves from anything considered womanly, not only from femininity but also from female masculinity. Levi, a white man living in urban Northern California, described a common experience of this:

> When I was first coming out, people were like, "Oh, well you can't walk that way. You have to walk like a guy. You can't make your words go up at the end of the sentence. You have to keep it like this, a flat intonation." These are the things I got. "When you look at your nails, you have to do this, not this." . . . This is how you have to be if you're going to be a man.

Restrictive suggestions on how to present as acceptably masculine came from other trans men, transgender advice websites, family members, and medical and psychiatric professionals. This instruction reminded trans men that normative masculinities were central to expectations for men and could be a way of avoiding having to explain themselves or defend their incumbency in this category.

Incorporating these normative masculine practices was a strategy for some trans men to ensure their recognition as men. However, many of these practices became more flexible as time went on. Dominic, a white man living in a town on the Great Lakes, spoke about this early transition time:

> I wouldn't say I was overcompensating during the beginning of my transition, but I definitely think I tried harder to be more masculine. . . . I was more concerned about it before, watching kind of how I acted and stuff, 'cause I didn't really wanna be perceived as a gay guy or whatever, but now I just don't care.

Safety was part of Dominic's motivation for not wanting to be perceived as gay, but recognition and authenticity were at stake, too. Heterosexuality is so central to normative masculinity that Dominic felt he had to distance himself from seeming gay in order to be recognized as a man—just like the teen boys C. J. Pascoe studied who constantly defended their masculinity through engaging in the fag discourse.[37] Overall, interviewees were more likely to conform to the expectations of normative masculinities when they worried most that their gender identity would be misrecognized.[38]

Consistent recognition by others as a man was the most common reason interviewees gave for this increasing flexibility in their gender expression over time. This reliable recognition allowed them to move away from normative masculinities and to be men in a way that felt more authentic. In some cases, it even allowed them to embrace aspects of femininity. Finn, a white man in urban Minnesota, who described himself as effeminate, said:

> Actually, one of the things that was enabled by transitioning is my ability to be more feminine without being perceived as something that I wasn't. It's odd because when I was a bull dyke it was very important for some reason to still be perceived in a very masculine way, maybe for reasons of gaining respect or something. So I couldn't be feminine. And now my masculinity is not questioned, and so I can be effeminate if I want to be. I can wear pink if I want to. You know, I can dance if I want to. I can shake my hips, and I don't have to just do the straight white boy shuffle.

This comfort with femininity allows Finn not just more freedom in dress but an embodied connection to his hips, a typically feminized and fraught part of the body that is also malleable when used in different ways.[39] Further, this loosening of the hips and new dance possibilities appear to distance him from a white, straight, normative masculinity.[40] Not all of the interviewees embraced femininity or even rejected all traces of normative masculinities, but nearly all reported some level of increasing flexibility over time.

Trans men's narratives of increasing flexibility focused on the process of coming into authenticity. These stories show that a man must be recognized not just as a man but also as the kind of man he wants to be, which adds another layer to the process of recognition. Turning back to Wesley's interaction with his neighbor, we see that beyond just recognizing him as a man, the neighbor recognized Wesley as the kind of man he wanted to share a beer with and have neighborly conversations with over the fence. Being that kind of man is about race, sexuality, and also the particularities of gender expression—not just for trans men but for all men.

INTERACTIONAL EFFECTS OF RECOGNITION

Recognition as a man not only was an affirmation of gender identity but also led to major shifts for trans men in a range of social interactions in everyday life. As Douglas Schrock and Michael Schwalbe write, "For an individual male to enjoy the benefits that derive from membership in the dominant gender group, he must present himself to others as a particular kind of social being: a man."[41] While Schrock and Schwalbe suggest that a body assigned male at birth is necessary to become a man, their larger point is that the social arena is where the meanings of social difference and inequality are worked out. An individual gaining recognition as a man means they will be treated by others as such and receive the social benefits and disadvantages of that social position.

Every man I interviewed spoke to marked differences in the general treatment of men and women. This difference centered on being included in men's backstage talk and behavior, being given respect, being treated as competent, and receiving shifting sexual attention. Treatment is a consequence of categorization and recognition, so when one is recognized, they are treated accordingly. It is in this treatment where key forms of gender inequality are produced.[42] Chris, a white man in urban Northern California, shared the changes in interaction he noticed when others started consistently recognizing him as a man:

> There's these very subtle little things daily. Like, just walking down the street, or when the bagger bags the groceries, they're going to expect you to pick 'em up. [In restaurants] they sort of give the check to you at the table and push it towards the man. They talk to the man not the woman, and that is sort of not nice, but I realize that that is done a lot. Yeah, restaurants, and I'm like, "Talk to her," because she's the wine expert and all that stuff. Like, giving me the wine to taste, and I'm like [*shrugs and holds hands up in the air*].

This assumption by others, that by virtue of being a man one has the ability to pick up a bag of groceries or do other tasks that require physical strength, highlights the relationship between masculinity and assumed physical ability. Chris's own past experience of a debilitating illness that left him with little physical strength illustrates that loss or lack of strength can diminish a sense of masculine independence.[43] This same independence and assumed competence came into play in restaurants where he was expected to order the food, know what his partner wanted to eat, and pay the bill at the end of the meal. Like Chris, all but a few men reported marked differences in how they were treated by others in interaction, especially by strangers, when they were recognized as men. The few who did not report a difference believed this was because they had always been seen as men by others.

Several interviewees said that this different treatment set them apart from trans men who were not frequently read as men. Mario, a white man in urban California, explained, "You can't even begin to know or prepare yourself for how things change once everyone views you as male, especially strangers, . . . and the way that your outlook on life changes because of that, and your behavior has to change." These new expectations and others' behaviors toward them due to recognition as men affected how trans men acted. This different treatment affects how trans men interact and is key to the social experience of being a man; therefore, recognition sparks a whole range of gendered, racialized, and sexualized interactional effects. At the level of interaction, this is where these categories are worked out as a matter of our everyday social worlds and, most important, as a site of the creation and re-creation of social inequality.

Backstage

Being included in men's backstage talk and behavior, meaning men's talk and actions when women are not present, was the most commonly reported difference when others recognized interviewees as men; indeed, over one-third of them mentioned this.[44] Some talk focused on men's bodies and discussions about sports and heavy machinery, while other talk focused on sexuality. They explained that this backstage talk and behavior allowed a release from the more constrained behavior that some men feel compelled to perform around women.

Backstage talk most frequently consisted of open discussions of sex and what some men named as misogynist talk about women. Heteronormativity was enforced in much of this sexual talk about women; it was a sort of homosocial heterosexual bonding. Dominic described his new experience with this talk:

> They'll just say a lot of things about women, . . . nasty things about women, in a very sexual way that I would never hear if I was a female, because they would never say that in front of me. So them presuming me as male, I think they feel more comfortable saying these things to me.

Inclusion in this talk was often surprising for interviewees at first, and whether they were comfortable with the content of the talk, it gave them a sense of recognition as men and an indication they were now part of a world not available to them when they had been recognized as women.

Being included in backstage talk by other men also had a transformative effect on trans men over time. Men like Mario reported a new understanding of backstage talk:

> It's not surprising the way that guys will talk about sex without a girl there . . . because when you're a girl and hear that kind of talk it seems like a guy's being an asshole, but you're a guy and you hear that kind of talk, it's like your perspective is different. Girls don't talk that way, because they see it as disrespectful, when it's not that they're always being disrespectful. It's just that they're talking in the way that guys do, and so it's not.

Mario affirms his authenticity by distinguishing himself from women through his inclusion and understanding of backstage talk. This moment also illustrates the transformative effects of different treatment and assessment as men noticed their shifting behavior in light of this recognition.[45] For example, as they were recognized more frequently as men, interviewees reported censoring themselves around women. At the same time, these explanations naturalize the heteronormativity and misogyny of this kind of talk, making it just a matter of gender difference—something men understand and women do not. Progressive men intervened in this talk at times but were more likely to do so in contexts where they felt safer.[46]

Respect

Getting increased respect from others was the next most common experience reported by interviewees and was mentioned almost as often as backstage talk. This respect came in the form of being listened to, being given space by others, and being treated as respectable. Saul, a white man in urban California, explained the change in how people treated him:

> You get more physical space. People are less inclined to step into my space as a guy. I also feel that people attend to my voice. It's deeper, and so people pay attention more readily. Those are the big things, . . . being seen, being heard. Getting space.

More than one-quarter of interviewees mentioned people listened to them more and gave them more physical space when they were recognized as men. Only a few reported they did not. Both being listened to and the freedom of movement they experienced made them feel more empowered in a range of spaces.

Increased respect often meant being seen as respectable and receiving better treatment as a customer, but this varied based on race and class. For example, Casey, an Asian and white man in urban California, reported he was treated better in stores when recognized as a man. Workers were more polite to him and gave him a higher level of service. On the other hand, Holden, a white man in suburban Wisconsin who worked in a retail clothing store, believed the better treatment he received in stores was due to being seen not only as a man but as a white man. He said:

> Being looked at as, like, a white male, . . . getting some of the privileges that go along with [that]. Being helped in a grocery store or even at work there's been some loss prevention, so people are being looked at more closely. I feel like some people are prejudiced, racist, the people that I work with. So, being treated differently by them.

Holden believed his white male privilege caused the better treatment he received as a customer in stores, whereas he saw his coworkers treat men of color as automatically suspicious. Further, this privilege meant his supervisors and coworkers treated him as automatically innocent in a recent theft investigation at work. Comparing Casey's and Holden's accounts suggests that gender, race, and class are all implicated in this different treatment. Holden talked about black and Latinx men being targets of scrutiny as potential thieves because they were simultaneously viewed as poor and, consequently, likely to steal. Thus, being recognized as white, or perhaps Asian like Casey, might make them seem less threatening. This better treatment meant one not only got more respect but also was seen as respectable while shopping.

Competence

Trans men frequently reported that others began to see them as competent and knowledgeable when they were recognized as men. This experience was especially prevalent in spaces marked as masculine—like hardware stores and auto repair shops. Luke, a white man in rural Indiana, explained:

> I've had really bad experiences at automotive places. If you don't know what you're talking about and you're a woman, they will screw you over in a second.... And I walk in there, and they're like, "Hello, sir," and they're totally different. I can be standing next to a woman, and they're treating her differently than they're treating me. They're really serious with me, and they're getting down to the nitty-gritty, and they're getting real detailed with me, and then, "Oh, I can knock this off," and, "I can take that off" [the bill]. But they're not doing the same for her.

Luke got more respect as a man in these contexts, and the presumption of competency and knowledge meant better service and lower prices. Again, this different treatment was triggered by the gender knowledge of the space that assumes men's competency and expertise in mechanical tasks. Interviewees were astonished that as the same person they would get treated very differently.

Mirroring Kristen Schilt's findings, this assumption of competence followed men into the workplace but was mediated by race.[47] Brandon, a white man in the suburbs of a midsized Michigan city, somewhat sarcastically described his experience at his internship at a nonprofit organization: "I'm apparently good at setting up internet, which I had to do twice now, and setting up phones because I'm a dude, and apparently, I'm technologically literate." This assumption of competency varied for men based on race and other aspects of social location. The experience of Ethan, a black man in the suburbs of another midsized

Michigan city, shows that gendered knowledges that assume black men are violent affected his interactions with the patients and their families in the care facility where he worked. He said he experienced quite a shift at nursing jobs when he went from being seen as a woman to being read as a man:

> [Before,] it was easier for me to get a job, interact with my residents, interact with family members, but since I am transitioning, it's difficult, a little harder. The patients are standoffish, and so are the family members. I'm trying to explain to 'em that, you know, "I have your family's best interests in mind. Because what you see does not necessarily mean I'm gonna hurt your family."

As a black man, he is no longer seen as competent doing the same work; indeed, the stereotypical image of a dangerous black man is in direct conflict with the type of care work he does on the job.[48]

Returning to Gabriel's earlier example of encountering different racial knowledges as he moved to different parts of the Southeast, clearly the ethnic and racial knowledges of these places also shaped assumptions of competence. For example, while growing up, Gabriel often received preferential treatment from teachers in his grade school in a predominately black neighborhood because of his lighter complexion. When describing his experience with teachers, he said, "Even some of the black ones who had kinda internalized a lot of racism themselves would favor me just because I was the brown kid who wasn't that brown." This preferential treatment likely saved Gabriel from the fate of many black and Latinx boys, who are often treated more as criminals than as achievers in the U.S. educational system.[49] Thus, colorism as well as different racial categorizations affected how interviewees were recognized and seen as competent across varied contexts.

Sexual Attentions

Trans men became new objects of heterosexual attraction when straight women recognized them as men in everyday interaction. Sexualized situations are especially important for recognition, since they raise particular limits to recognition where bodies come into play as part of the prospect of sexual intimacy.[50] A majority of the interviewees had sexual interest and relationships with women prior to transition, but transition shifted these interactions, especially with women who did not know their transgender history. Bert, a white man living in a college town in North Carolina, described a surprising new experience:

> One of the things that was really shocking to me when I began transitioning was how women would hit on me. Particularly older women. Who never would talk to me before, really. I was working in a store down the street, and these older women would be incredibly flirtatious. It was a shock to me. . . . I didn't know that women were like that. I'd never had like quite that attention.

Though he had primarily had relationships with women throughout his life, this new heterosexual attention from older women was striking. A general presumption of heterosexuality meant that Bert and other men were seen as worthy objects of flirting by more women. By the same token, others found it was more difficult to have friendships with women because the pressures and presumptions of heterosexuality gave new meaning to interactions. Actions in the past that would have been unremarkable became fraught with possible significance and could even be seen as newly sexually threatening. Black men in particular reported that others, especially white women, saw them more often as sexually threatening than as an object of sexual interest.

Being recognized, or misrecognized, by others as heterosexual grants trans men a certain normative approval, but depending on the man and his partner, not all heterosexualities are created equal.[51] Leo, a black man in San Francisco, experienced disdain rather than acceptance in what others viewed as an ostensibly heterosexual interracial relationship:

> I definitely get looks when I'm with my wife, who is white. Especially older people who, like, you just see physically, can see them trip out. Little old white ladies scrunching their faces in disgust. Old black women kind of looking my wife up and down and just kind of giving her a look.

While they were recognized as a heterosexual couple, Leo and his wife's experience illustrates Cathy Cohen's point that not all heterosexualities receive heteronormative approval.[52] The treatment Leo and his wife received from older black and white women shows their disapproval of them as an interracial couple. Bert's experiences of being the object of attraction were also likely shaped by his whiteness, but he did not explicitly mention race in his narrative.

Queer spaces where there were more expansive gender knowledges could provide nuanced recognitions and sexual attentions, such as Jason's experience among Bears, but at the same time were still shaped by assumptions of heterosexuality. For example, when interviewees were recognized as men, they were often less noticeable to queer women in queer spaces as potential sexual partners than they had been before transition. Queer women were desirable sexual partners for many interviewees because of shared culture and values, as well as often having knowledge of trans men's bodies and an ability to openly communicate, which made for satisfying sexual experiences. Recognition as a man invited potential attention from heterosexual women and gay men, yet this same presumption of heterosexuality made it difficult to approach queer women as potential sexual partners. In contrast, some men saw the ability to maintain a sexual relationship with ostensibly heterosexual women as a confirmation of their authenticity as men, whereas sexual interest from queer- or lesbian-identified women made them feel less authentic. For the most part, though, as Carla Pfeffer and Jane Ward also found, the gender labors of queer and lesbian women in these relationships meant they generally affirmed trans men's gender identities.[53]

CONCLUSION

Interviewees responded in a number of ways to the different treatment they encountered when others recognized them as men. Some men embraced this as a form of recognition and authenticity, while others rejected aspects of the masculine expectations placed on them. Overall, these accounts were filled with ambivalence: moments of pride and self-worth as their authenticity as men was confirmed by others and instances of discomfort when they felt as if their whole self was not recognized, as well as discomfort when this treatment did not line up with their social and political ideals. The differing treatment itself indicates the continuing salience of gender, race, and sexuality and how difference and inequality are perpetuated in everyday interactions. The ambivalence in their reactions evidences an awareness that moving from being socially recognized as a woman to a man confers a great deal of privilege, though that privilege is mutually constituted by other social identities and not all changes are positive. Recognition leads not just to different treatment from others but to being implicated in social relations of misogyny, racism, and heterosexism in new ways.[54]

Trans men encounter different spatially based situated knowledges that shape recognition as men in social interaction. The dispersion of knowledge of transgender possibilities made for shifts in recognition based on place in that they were more likely to be recognized solely as men where there was little knowledge of transgender people. Prior knowledge of an individual man's transgender biography could shape this recognition, but it could also be forgotten over time or just accepted. Conversely, strangers could assume a trans history in ways that discredited interviewees' identities as men. The meanings of bodies themselves could be reconfigured and transformed through recognition based on spatially based knowledges. Recognition as a man provided a sense of authenticity but also meant being treated differently by other social actors. This differing treatment had a transformative effect as men sought to balance an authenticity to themselves and the consequences of interaction. This recognition and treatment as men created an ambiguous empowerment that sometimes denied their complex gendered, racial, and sexual identities and also implicated them in relations of social inequality through interaction.[55] Regardless of their desires or political intent, the men often found they were brought into new experiences of social privilege and domination. Thus, gaining recognition that was firmly tied to authenticity had effects beyond simply being seen as a man or not.

Recognition through self-knowledge, policy, and social interaction are all paths to becoming a man. In an ideal world, recognition through policy and social interaction would always follow from self-knowledge, but this is not always the case.[56] Each path has particular barriers to recognition, whether it is fear of coming to a self-knowledge that conflicts with societal expectations or policies that restrict changes to birth certificates or access to bathrooms. One of the key differences among these paths is the effect or consequence of each kind of recognition. Legal recognition might lead to access to formal rights but would not guarantee recognition in social interaction or vice versa.

It is possible this notion of authenticity and recognition is unique to trans men, perhaps because they have had to make what seems like a special effort to achieve recognition for themselves as men. Yet manhood and masculinity are highly contested for all men. There are many examples of how ostensibly cisgender men are compelled to constantly prove their authenticity as men, starting with the frequent refrain to "man up" or "be a man." Some men, misguidedly, even use the trope of the "real man" to support women's or feminist causes, seen in the refrain "Real men protect women's rights" displayed in recent protest signs.[57] The protest signs held by black men that read "I am a Man" from the 1968 Memphis sanitation strike show that full membership in this category is also always a racialized proposition. Finally, the notion of becoming is evident not just in trans men's narratives but in those of cisgender men. This becoming is clear in the following words attributed to U.S. president James A. Garfield: "I mean to make myself a man, and if I succeed in that, I shall succeed in everything else."[58] While every group of men confronts unique challenges in being recognized and achieving authenticity, it is precisely that process of becoming that creates some cohesion across this social category and shows that what it means to become a man is a shifting target based on spatially and contextually specific knowledges.

Going back to the opening story of Wesley and his neighbor, although both Wesley and I focused on the remarkable transformative moment when the redneck neighbor recognized Wesley and transformed the expected meaning of his chest, we must remember that the neighbor also had to be recognized as a man through the gender knowledges of that particular place. He too has been shaped and will continue to be shaped by negotiating the situated gender knowledges and attendant expectations for who is a man and how a man ought to be. While we know the neighbor, unlike Wesley, was assigned male at birth, it is clear that he too was not born a man. Instead, he had to become one.

3

"Strong When I Need to Be, Soft When I Need to Be"

SITUATED EMOTIONAL CONTROL AND MASCULINITIES

Henry, a white man living in suburban Indiana, had a desire for a wider emotional life than men were typically allowed. Rather than hiding emotional expressions, such as crying, behind a façade of toughness, Henry believed that men should express their feelings more publicly.

> I told my mom, "If I turn out to be half the man that dad was, I'm gonna be twice the man that lots of people are." 'Cause I think men get too much of the "Boys don't cry" and "You have to be tough" and "You have to do this. You can't do that." And I really think the world would be a better place if people would just be themselves.... If something's sad and you feel like crying, cry. It doesn't matter if you're a man. Men get sad. You know? It's okay to cry.

Yet since starting testosterone seven years before, it had become more difficult for him to do just that. He felt more distant from his emotions in general, and his ability to cry had diminished greatly:

> I have found that since the testosterone it's very hard for me to do so. It takes a lot. Used to be [*snapping fingers*] just like that. Oh, yeah. But, I just wanna be the kind of man that accepts people for who they are. You know? Be strong when I need to be, soft when I need to be.

Henry's description of an idealized emotional life for men that combines control and emotion exemplifies the most common pattern that emerged in regard to emotion across the stories of the men I interviewed; rather than being unable to express emotions or, conversely, being overly emotive, the ideal man should be soft when he needs to be and strong when he needs to be.

While Henry thought it was okay for men to cry, other men I interviewed saw this kind of emotional expression as weak and excessive. Yet even men who saw themselves as particularly tough and who ridiculed excessive emotions identified places where a softer approach was more desirable. For example, Aidan, a white man in urban Tennessee, explained:

> I'm not really into sissy things [*laughs*]. [What are sissy things?] Whining. I call everyone I know a titty baby. At some point or time in their life, they would get called a titty baby by me. You know, "Suck it up. Quit cryin.'" I like to fish and wakeboard and go out on the boat. You know, different things like that compared to other sissy guys who don't wanna get wet or sweat. I'm not really worried about bugs or animals. I'm not gonna go pick up a snake. If there is one, I'll figure out how to get it away from me. I'm not gonna like run and scream. So, things like that. But as far as like my partner goes, . . . I'm kind of a ladies' man. Pretty sweet and sensitive and all. I think about her a lot and different ways to do surprises and stuff like that. Kind of a typical like traditional guy, you know?

Out in the world, Aidan saw himself as rough and tumble but able to handle dangerous situations with a calm rationality that "sissy guys" lack. Yet the tenderness and consideration that would make others an object of his ridicule were perfectly acceptable in the context of his relationship with his partner. It was his ability to be tough in the world and soft at home that made him a proper man.

Aidan and Henry differ in tone, but both challenge the notion that men are, or at least should be, emotionless. Instead, they share the sentiment that men should express particular emotions in the right spaces. Whether Aidan is comparing himself to "sissy guys" or Henry to men who cannot cry when they are sad, they both mark other men as unable to do emotion appropriately. Stephanie Shields argues that rather than being emotionless, a particular set of masculine emotions, when displayed appropriately, are more representative of the masculine ideal in the contemporary United States. Manly emotions, in Shields's telling, are characterized by being strongly felt but under control.[1] In the same vein, Michael Messner draws from contemporary presidential politics to argue that this wider emotional expression for powerful men may not signal a substantive change in the gender order but rather an incorporation of critiques of masculinity.[2] The display of situationally appropriate but controlled emotion further legitimizes some men's suitability for leadership. Accordingly, contextually appropriate emotional displays do not necessarily stop men from wielding or benefiting from institutional power.[3]

Socially desirable masculine emotional displays are relational in that they form in contrast to women's emotions, which are constructed in broader social narratives as excessive and illegitimate in their scope, and to other men, who are either overly rational (e.g., Al Gore in the 2000 presidential contest) or who show excessive anger or violence. Sarah Ahmed, in her work on the cultural politics of emotion, illustrates that there is a long-standing dichotomy constructed in Western thought that defines reason and rationality as superior to emotion, where man and whiteness are valued as modern and "others" are closer to nature and more savage.[4] Stereotypes often depict women, Latinx people, and black people as excessively emotional or as not having appropriate emotions, such as the image of the aggressive and controlling black matriarch or the angry black man.[5] It is clear that gender, race, sexuality, and class together shape the appropriateness of certain emotions and emotional displays.

The social understanding of emotion I use here to consider men's emotional lives draws on sociological and social psychological approaches to emotion. These perspectives focus on the social influences and norms that shape emotional displays and how people think about and label their feelings.[6] A geographic understanding of emotion offers further insight into how emotion is named and mediated through places and environments. Social and geographic understandings of emotion offer tools to move beyond just thinking about emotions as something that happens within individuals to considering how they are socially, culturally, and spatially constituted.[7] Emotion became a particularly important topic of analysis in other disciplines as part of the "affective turn" in the humanities, an effort to bring together theorizing of the interplay between the body and the mind. Following Deborah Gould, affect is the "nonconscious and unnamed, but nevertheless registered, experiences of bodily energy and intensity that arise in response to stimuli impinging on the body," and emotion is "one's personal expression of what one is feeling in a given moment, an expression that is structured by social convention, by culture."[8] Emotion, then, is the expression of affect. It is that which is named or expressed. In this formulation, affect cannot be fully captured by emotion, and as such, there is always something left out or lost between affect and emotion. This distinction allows for an examination of both the bodily effects of stimuli and emotions as they are expressed, in addition to the analytic space to examine what is lost as affect is expressed as emotion.[9] Including attention to affect in understanding trans men's narratives of emotion draws out a wider understanding of the role of self-discipline in contemporary masculinities.

Rather than a topic I intended to focus on in the interviews, emotion and affect emerged as a strong current in interviewees' discussions of transition, their own masculinity, and broader contemporary ideals of masculinity in the United States. In fact, I had not planned to spend much time on discussing the physical aspects of transition, partly since earlier work had covered these topics and especially because these details often speak more to the prurient interests of cisgender people than the needs of trans men. Yet it became clear that managing their new positions in the emotional economies and feeling rules of a range of settings are particularly salient parts of trans men's narratives of manhood and masculinity. Indeed, these stories of bodily change actually reflect how larger narratives of masculinity, testosterone, and a masculine ideal of emotional control affect this particular group of men. Their descriptions of affective changes with transition illustrated that managing and controlling affective states are central to achieving appropriate emotion. Calm, crying, anger, and sexual urges were the most common areas of affective changes that interviewees reported, and these changes featured prominently in their narratives of emotional control. These narratives are examples of Goldilocks masculinity.

The Goldilocks ideal for everyday men that emerged from trans men's narratives calls on men to be emotionally expressive when the space or situation calls for it and to be calm and rational when appropriate. A social understanding of emotion and affect shows how discourses of emotional control are a key way of creating and maintaining gender, racial, and sexual inequality. On the spectrum of masculine ideals that emerged from interviewees' accounts of contemporary U.S. masculinity, from the faggy and the progressive man on the softer end to the hypermasculine classed and racialized thug and redneck on the harder end, this contextually appropriate emotion is central to finding the sweet spot in the middle. Thus, expressing the right emotions in the right spaces is crucial to meeting the most valued masculine ideal of being a regular guy and achieving a Goldilocks masculinity in contrast to classed, racial, and sexual others. These understandings of emotion incorporate naturalized discourses of difference and reinforce the ideal of the self-disciplining emotional subject. The experience of transition is particular to trans men, but this ideal is tied to larger shifts in the relationship between normative masculinities and emotion in the contemporary United States. By understanding how emotional control across contexts represents a surface change to contemporary masculine ideals but does not necessarily shift the domination of some men over women and other men, we can further see how a hybrid masculinity represents a shallow rather than a substantive change to gender relations.

AFFECTIVE TRANSITIONS

The sixty men, out of sixty-six interviewees, who had undergone hormone therapy reported that using testosterone was the most significant marker of affective change related to transition that they had experienced. The physical and emotional changes associated with testosterone were a significant marker for those men who did take it as part of their transition, though a few of the interviewees who had not taken testosterone lived their daily lives being recognized as men. Almost all of those who did use it reported the hormone created significant differences between themselves and people who had not hormonally transitioned, whether other trans men or nonbinary trans people. As Mario, a white man in urban California, said:

> Hormones do so much in your body. I mean, they really do. They do so much to your brain. They do so much to you emotionally; they do so much to you sexually and physically. There is such a huge difference between like a genderqueer person and a person who has transitioned.

Like in broader discourses of testosterone's effects on cisgender men, trans men attributed their difference from women and nonbinary people to testosterone's varied changes to their physical bodies (hair growth, muscle and fat redistribution, deepening of the voice, and other physical changes were common) and, perhaps more important, a range of emotional and other affective changes.

It should not be surprising that hormones are so central to these discourses of difference among trans men. They line up with commonsense understandings that purport gender differences are the direct effect of neurological, hormonal, and evolutionary differences between male and female bodies. However, the prevailing findings of contemporary scientific research in these areas show that plasticity in things like brain function and complex relationships between bodies and their historical, cultural, and social contexts are more accurate explanations for human behavior than gender or sexual difference.[10]

The common idea that testosterone is at the heart of gender differences, such as men being more aggressive and violent than women, is likely, as biologist Robert Sapolsky argues, oversimplified if not altogether incorrect.[11] A naturally occurring hormone in both male and female bodies, testosterone was first synthesized in the United States in 1935. According to John Hoberman's history of testosterone, since that time there have been attempts to use it to increase energy, sexual stimulation, and athletic performance, although synthetic testosterone has never gained widespread use, except for a black market life as an athletic performance enhancer.[12] Research examining the relationship between higher levels of testosterone in individuals—whether occurring prenatally, through natural production after birth, or via the administration of synthetic hormones—and differences in aggression, language, toughness, and status within groups shows little correlation between the two.[13]

Testosterone therapy is widely used by trans men as part of a medical transition, though there have been few, if any, widespread studies of the effects of testosterone in terms of emotion and other psychological effects. Trans men's reports of changes due to testosterone are likely to be influenced by measurable changes to the body, in addition to being influenced by the strong cultural ideas about testosterone that influence all people. These influences are difficult or impossible to untangle from one another, but it is clear that among the men I interviewed the effects and their interpretation of those effects varied from one individual to the next.

The few men I interviewed who had not taken testosterone—most planned to start eventually—reported that one of their main delays was their fear of the emotional changes that testosterone would bring. During a discussion of his decision to wait to start testosterone, though he already had a doctor's prescription, Mason, a white man living in urban Tennessee, said what he feared most:

> The emotional changes, like the negative ones. I don't wanna become unemotional. I've heard people, like, they can't cry or they just don't know how to process stuff and their frustration turns to anger or violence or whatever. That's just not who I am. So, that's just what scares me.

Mason was worried he would become the stereotypical inexpressive or even angry man upon taking testosterone. Interviewees shared similar fears of emotional changes throughout their stories; however, the results reported by men who did use testosterone were in fact more complex.

Feeling Calm and Feeling Right

While interviewees broadly feared increased anger due to testosterone, and there were some instances of this, more than half of the men actually reported feeling calmer. More calm made for increased clarity and control in managing their inner states. This sudden or eventual calm was one of the most consistent reports from using testosterone. For most men calm meant that they had fewer feelings and that those feelings were less intense overall. These feelings of calm were part of an overall pattern of reported distance or dulling of emotion with transition.

A number of men actually went from having extreme problems with aggression and violence to feeling generally more composed and reporting significantly less anger after starting testosterone. This often signaled a departure from hypermasculine violence toward the calm self-control of the regular guy and moving closer to Goldilocks masculinity. It is notable that the surprise many men reported as they became calmer upon starting testosterone reflected the strength of the popularly constructed connection between testosterone and aggression. Aidan described his mental state before testosterone as "really aggressive. I wasn't happy with myself, my life, with anything." Before taking testosterone, he hit his girlfriend on several occasions and even made her bleed. He expressed remorse as he recounted these incidents, even though he said she brought it upon herself and used other, similar language as an excuse for his violence. Regardless, he did not want to continue to be aggressive and violent:

> I don't wanna hurt anyone. It killed me to see her bleed. It was a terrible experience. I felt so bad about it, but I just snapped. You just don't make decisions at that time—it just fucking happens. So, since I've been on the T and transitioning, I'm a lot more calm. I don't get mad about things. I don't get frustrated. You know, a lot of people will say it's like compared to 'roid rage or whatever. You get really aggressive—and I don't. Like, I've had one time that I got mad. I just like flipped my shit, and it was at my GPS, so my GPS can handle my wrath. That was the only time. Everything else, I actually think I handle things a lot more calmly than ever before.

Aidan went from being a more dominating, hypermasculine man in the space of the home to being a man who could control his violence and who was more able to engage with his girlfriend in the less rigid partnership characteristic of the regular guy and the idealized white middle-class family norm. Being calm gave him a sense of control over his formerly unruly emotions. This control was particularly evident when he could direct his anger in an appropriate direction, toward an object rather than a person.

This newfound sense of calm was often difficult for the men to name, other than saying they finally "felt right" in their bodies. The effort to put these feelings into words, the translation of the bodily sensations of affect into named feelings, in any stage of life is an inherently social undertaking regardless of the chemical source of that affect. For example, the ability to name one's emotions is gendered in the sense that being "in touch" with one's emotions is a feminized characteristic. Aaron, a white man living in Chicago, recalled a similar feeling:

> I went on testosterone, and emotionally . . . I felt so much better. I started feeling really comfortable in my body in a way I hadn't expected or looked for or been aware that I wasn't feeling. I was aware that I wasn't super comfortable, but it was like this huge weight that I didn't know I was carrying.

This general bodily sense of "feeling right" was an overall positive feeling that confirmed taking testosterone was the right decision. In addition to showing how these men associated testosterone with feeling more comfortable in their bodies, this also illustrates an overall pattern where they had more difficulty naming and clearly defining some affective experiences after starting testosterone.

Some trans men who experienced this sense of calm or control attributed it to the higher level of testosterone in their bodies, while others attributed it more to satisfaction with the physical changes of transition and the benefits of being recognized by others as men. It is likely that a mix of the bodily effects of testosterone, the social changes of transition—a long-anticipated goal for many of the men—and having their gender identities reliably recognized by others shaped these changing feelings. These stories mirrored common age-based discourses of going from an impetuous hormonally driven youth to a calmer and more controlled man. Moving into the social status of man, as well as some men becoming more visibly gender conforming, contributed to feelings of confidence and calm as well. When trans men are recognized by others as men, they are generally afforded more respect and given space. This change increases feelings of confidence and calm, but better treatment varies depending on race and class. Thus, race- and class-privileged men are more likely to receive these emotional benefits. Overall, the ability to obtain an aura of calm and confidence aligns with the in-between balance of the regular guy and Goldilocks masculinity.

Boys Don't Cry

While he shared his story, I asked Simon, a white man living in a mid-sized city near Appalachia, what it meant to be a man in the South:

> To me, a southern man is strong. Well, I hope I'm strong, but I also know that I have a tender side. . . . And most southern men do have tender hearts; they just don't let 'em show very often. 'Cause, you know, you get told, "Boys don't cry. Man up. Grow a set." Whatever. I mean, I love sports, and almost every southern man does. See, to me, a man is not just tied up in manual labor or beatin' on the chest or the macho stuff. A man is crying when they put your daughter in your arms, or your son in your arms, because

you realize your whole life has just changed and something great's come into it.

Across trans men's narratives, they framed crying as the emotional expression most closely tied to women and femininity. Sobbing or uncontrollable tears were the antithesis of emotional control and rationality. This did not mean most of the men embraced the idea that boys do not or should not cry. Like Simon's southern man, it was understood as appropriate for a man to cry in particular situations, like meeting his newborn child. Thus, by crying in the appropriate spaces and moments, men could achieve a Goldilocks masculinity that was between controlling images of hypermasculine men who cannot cry and feminized faggy men and women who cannot help but express their overflowing emotions.

Formerly difficult-to-control feelings became controllable and appeared only in particular spaces and situations, making for a more predictable emotional life. Interviewees said that they could not cry as easily overall, not just that they should not cry in particular settings. Nearly every interviewee that mentioned crying reported they cried less often, and only a few mentioned they missed the ability to cry. In fact, nearly all of the men experienced the lack of excessive emotion, exemplified by fewer incidents of crying, as an overall positive change. They often linked these previous uncontrollable emotions and bodily feelings to the menstrual cycles most had experienced in the past. These former hormonal swings were chaotic in contrast to the control that went along with their new emotional states as men. As Phillip, a white man living in a midsized North Carolina city, explained:

> Emotionally, it's been different. Because I was so up and down before and I would cry all the time. You know, I was so depressed. . . . I would just have so much emotion as a woman, and now, I mean, yeah, do I still occasionally cry at some things? Like when my sister passed? Or if I just am frustrated with life a certain day? Is it a lot? No, not at all, but it's better. Because I was just, I felt so overwhelmed with emotion. . . . I mean, it was just terrible, and then the mood swings and everything was just ridiculous. More than normal [women], and without that, the quality of life's so much better.

Phillip's description of the affective turmoil he remembered before and the relative control over his emotions now mirrors the narratives most of the interviewees shared about their experiences. This contrast is especially clear between his life before, when he "would cry all the time," and his life now, in which he identifies particular spaces or events that prompt tears—his sister's death, for example. Phillip recounted later that these infrequent incidences of crying were unlikely to occur in public spaces. Thus, his formerly public expressions of emotion were relegated to more appropriate private spaces as well.

Trans men framed this new emotional control, especially between public and private spaces, as increased rationality in opposition to excessive emotional display. Rationality is an inherently raced, classed, and gendered concept, as it is closely associated with whiteness, discourses of Western modernity, and middle-class propriety.[14] This links the spatially based emotional control to the regular guy ideal and Goldilocks masculinity. Josh, a white man living in rural Northern California, had formerly experienced most emotions as just under the surface and ready to bubble out of him. This shifted with testosterone:

> I'm in more control of what it is I tell people and what I can tell people. 'Cause it just felt like [before], "God, I can't keep this in." And the whole crying when I was angry, because nobody gets that. They just think that you're all hurt or whatever. They don't get that you're so infuriated that that's the response that comes. I know a lot of women that that happens to. More than it doesn't. So, I don't get angry very often now, but when I do, it's more, it's not as visceral, it's not as visceral at all. It's more in my head, and I cannot just blurt out stuff. I can think about it and be more rational about it. . . . I have emotions and I feel them, but I'm not so emotional that I can't keep it under wraps. I really appreciate that. I mean, I still get touched by movies, but I don't cry so often at movies, but I still can.

In this narrative, Josh contrasted his newer rationality with women's excessive emotional display of crying, especially from anger and frustration as opposed to sadness. He could handle his emotions rationally, with his feelings being more linguistically nameable and less connected to his body. According to him, it was still okay to cry in a darkened movie theater, a public space that offers a measure of privacy, or other suitable contexts, but overall his feelings of anger and frustration were less visceral and more easily managed in a logical fashion.

Importantly, this ideal of increasing rationality and emotional control was not a total lack of emotion. Instead, the ideal reflected a desirable ability to self-regulate one's emotions so that they were expressed only in appropriately measured ways and in the right spaces. Even when transition narratives described an opening of emotional expression, it was still a narrative of spatially based emotional control. Paul, a white man also in rural Northern California, stringently avoided crying, especially in public, before transition. He felt like he had "something to prove" and that crying, even in a semipublic setting like his father's funeral, would be a sign of weakness, "and I didn't want to show weakness." After transition he felt more open and had even recently shed a few tears at a friend's wedding. When trying to explain his former state, he said:

> I think it had a lot to do with my brain being male and not realizing it. And always knowing that when you're younger, even though you're not male, if you're around other little boys, and they like skin their knees and they're like crying to their mom or their dad or whatever, especially their dad, and dads are all like, "Boys don't cry." You pick up on that. I think it had a little bit to do with that. But mainly the whole weakness thing, because that's another male thing. If you cry in front of people, you're showing weakness. Well, I'm not a weak person. I don't want to show anybody that I'm weak. So I'm going to do my damnedest to not show emotions, even if that is a detriment. That's just the way I felt when I was younger. Now, I don't really care, although I'm still not really a crier.

Thus, what Paul describes as an innate gender identity as a man made him more susceptible to the messages about emotional control boys around him received as children. Overall, it was the need to distance himself from vulnerability that was the primary driver for extreme emotional control that characterized his life before transition. Paul actually sees his increased emotional expression as a sign of strength as a man, with the insinuation being that men who cannot express emotions are doing so to cover for insecurity. At the same time, Paul continues to distance himself from being "a crier" and still notes it is appropriate only in particular spaces. His expressions have become more contextually appropriate and, thus, more rational than they were in the past.

Overall, trans men reported they did not cry as often after starting to take testosterone. The social expectations for men's emotionality likely had an effect on trans men's ability to cry, especially as they worried most about misrecognition of their gender when early in transition. While most of the men attributed their change in crying behavior directly to the effects of testosterone, they also had to contend with the strong cultural message that "boys don't cry." Some men missed the emotional release of crying, but most appreciated their increased emotional control and ability to rationally respond to stimulus. This rationality was a relative relief in contrast to the excessive and out-of-control feeling of crying. These narratives evidence a shift in bodily intensities and respondents' experience and articulation of these feelings in relation to emotional expression and emotional control. In the end the ideal relation to crying for most of these men was to be able to cry in particularly sad or sentimental spaces—such as funerals or weddings—whereas they wanted to maintain a controlled emotional display otherwise.

This spatially based control of their bodies was central to embodying Goldilocks masculinity and illustrates how bodies and affect figure into hybrid masculinities. In the face of the apparent myth of men's total inability to cry, many men will now cry in public. However, this does not necessarily mean men are showing a vulnerability that threatens the maintenance of patriarchal relations. As Pierrette Hondagneu-Sotelo and Michael Messner argue, "A situationally appropriate display of sensitivity such as crying, rather than signaling weakness, has instead become a legitimating sign."[15] Thus, crying in appropriate situations in the face of the myth that "boys don't cry" is a sign not necessarily of substantive change in social relations but that hybridity in emotional expression is the ascendant norm in everyday life.

Anger and Aggression

Stories of increased anger and aggression, sometimes referred to as "T-Rage" or "'roid [steroid] rage," appeared consistently in men's discussions of the effects they anticipated before taking testosterone, and some men did experience these feelings. For example, Dominic, a white man living in a town on the Great Lakes, explained his fear of increased anger and aggression:

> My therapist said, "You know, when you start T[estosterone], you might become more aggressive," or whatever, and I didn't wanna become more aggressive, but I definitely can feel that I am more aggressive now.

Despite his wishes, Dominic did experience increased aggression. However, although many of the men I interviewed expressed worries about increased anger and aggression, less than one-third reported actual increases in anger or aggression. As Robert Sapolsky explains, rather than a direct effect between testosterone and aggression, testosterone has a permissive effect, which means it does not cause aggression but exaggerates preexisting behavior and patterns of aggression. Thus, testosterone may encourage already existing aggression toward those with less power or status but will likely not produce increased aggression directed at higher-status individuals. In fact, socially learned patterns of aggression will often persist even when testosterone is removed from the body.[16] Cultural scripts about testosterone also have a permissive effect for men to enact particular expressions. For example, lab experiments have shown that people who believe testosterone causes certain aggressive and antisocial behaviors are more likely to enact those behaviors when they think they have been injected with it, even if they were actually injected with a neutral saline solution.[17]

Interestingly, during the interviews the men did not usually label anger as an emotion, though I name it as such for this analysis because anger is a cross-culturally common human emotion. The naming of affective feelings as emotions or not is a common way to distinguish gendered and racialized emotions.[18] This follows a general trend in which expressions associated with women are regarded as emotions and most of men's expressions are seen as something other than emotion.[19] Trans men's accounts mirrored this gender division. They labeled feminine-coded emotional expression as emotion and did not label affect more tied to masculinity as emotion.[20] Further, what is considered anger, especially appropriate anger, is classed and raced. In all, these narratives of anger and spatially based emotional control reinforced the Goldilocks ideal of masculinity.

The increase in emotions related to anger and aggression from those trans men who did report this experience ranged from mild irritation to intense feelings of rage. Much of the anger associated with testosterone therapy appeared early on in taking the hormone, as well as right between doses. Trans men's narratives often linked increases in anger to having too much testosterone or having a period of adjustment to new levels of this hormone in their body. Interviewees also connected heightened levels of anger and aggression to the timing of their testosterone doses. Casey, an Asian and white man living in urban California, described it as follows:

> I am more of a jerk sometimes. Especially if it's Wednesday, because I take my shot on Monday. So like, Wednesday is peak testosterone day, and if somebody gets on my nerves, I can feel like this little like grrr, this like anger bubble where I get like mouthy with them. Whereas normally I would never have raised my voice. Like, I don't think I ever raised my voice to my mom before T, and I would like stand up and like yell at her. That, and sometimes a weird thing that probably happens more on Wednesdays, but sometimes if a woman says something that makes me mad, I get this extra rage feeling, and I want to hurt her, and I'm like, "Whoa, what is this?" And it's like, "Wow!"

He went on to explain why he thought he had these new violent feelings toward some women:

> In my head I just label it as this monkey thing. It just feels like this real animal thing. Like, an immediate, it's like the dog pack or something, and you want to like pummel the dog back down into its place or something. It can be on the phone. A certain kind of woman voice where, where sometimes she won't even say anything bad, but she'll be like, "Can I put you on hold?" And if it's the wrong voice, then I'll be like, "Grrr, I just want to punch that woman!" [*laugh*]. Or just at the bank last week, some woman was like, "We might need to put a hold on this check." And I was like, "Grrr, I've been banking here for ten years!" And it didn't mean anything, but it was just like this rage, and I felt like, "Man, if this glass wasn't here, then I'd kick your ass!"

Notably, Casey reported experiencing these heightened moments of rage in connection with his dose cycle and saw them as biologically based. At the same time, these strong feelings of anger and aggression were not random, because they were directed solely at women, who were the most common targets for heightened levels of anger and aggression in trans men's narratives. Casey's expression of anger toward his mother in the private space of the family, rather than holding in his anger in the public space of the bank also likely reflected his understanding of spatially appropriate emotional display.

While Casey and other men reported increased verbal aggression and the desire to be physically aggressive, they often acknowledged they should restrain themselves from actually committing physical violence against women. In fact, it was this restraint and ability to control the expression of their anger that set them apart from other, raced and classed, men. He continued:

> Of course, I wouldn't [be physically violent toward women], but I could see how, depending on how people are socialized, *if that kind of thing is considered okay in your culture*, I could see how it could happen really easily and if you didn't have a million safety locks in place where you know it's bad that you don't hit women [*laugh*]. I could see how it could happen and how people could get conditioned to think that it's normal because it's in there. In the programming.

Here, Casey mixes biological and social explanations for more extreme types of aggression. In this way of thinking, testosterone in general makes one angrier, and fluctuations in the level of testosterone cause more extreme feelings of rage that produce violent aggression. If one is taught that this kind of violence is acceptable, then one might engage in it, though men who are taught not to can control these aggressive feelings. The key question becomes, who are these men who do not learn control?

Out of Control

When trans men described the hypermasculine men who could not control themselves, they talked about other trans men early in transition, but when talking about hypermasculine men more broadly, they evoked raced, classed, and sexualized ideas about masculinity and emotional control. Interviewees often critiqued other trans men and questioned the authenticity of their masculine practices for newly aggressive behavior that appeared along with transition. As Mario noted previously, there were substantial differences between people who had and had not undergone testosterone therapy. At the same time, he thought other trans men went too far in explaining all behavior changes through that narrative:

> I think for a lot of people things come out when they transition that were there before. You know, when people say you get 'roid rage kind of feelings? Like, you get really angry and violent? That is total bullshit unless you happen to have those things naturally. Testosterone does heighten things like that. I mean, if you're the kind of person that would let your anger get carried away, then you can get carried away if you have more testosterone in your body. That's always been very interesting to me, like the guys that transition and get to be like these really macho jerk-offs, and I wonder sometimes if part of it is like that is like their, the epitome of being a guy to them, of like being very macho and being like a very like, it's almost like they're continually having to prove their masculinity by being like that. I mean, maybe they're just kind of a jerk anyway. They're just kind of a jerk as a girl, and now they're more of a jerk as a guy, but I think the element of being like this macho asshole that's almost misogynist. That seems so inexfuckingscusable coming from where they come from, but it's almost like they take these liberties that they think they can get away with it because they're trans. Because they used to be female, it's impossible for them to be misogynistic, so they can say and do a lot of things.

Mario saw this hypermasculinity through expressions of anger, sexual dominance, and misogyny as a possible overcompensation for a threatened masculine self. At the same time, he questioned whether trans men take on this unquestioned hypermasculinity because they feel like they can "get away with it." Mario's explanations of changing behavior focused on the culturally permissive effects of testosterone, as well as a feminist critique of misogyny, but he still emphasized an ideal of individual control that aligns with Goldilocks masculinity.

The interviewees continued the theme of masculine compensation when speaking about anger and control for men more broadly but also evoked hypermasculine controlling images to explain differences in anger and violence. This worked as a rhetorical move to distance themselves from violent masculinities by shifting the blame for cultural violence to men in particular spaces.[21] In these images it is the thug and redneck—poor men, white rural men, and men of color in urban spaces—that supposedly are unable to control their rage and aggression. This lack of control and propensity for violence are central to what marks the masculinities of the redneck and thug as unacceptable. These narratives reify difference between men and women through the effects of testosterone—men are just biologically more aggressive—and difference between groups of men—those who can control their aggression and those who cannot. In this framing, violence against women is naturalized, marking it as an expression of individual men's aggression and their lack of ability to control it rather than an expression of power. Regular guys, on the other hand, can achieve that Goldilocks masculinity by expressing spatially appropriate emotion. While it is possible that testosterone therapy enables more aggressive behavior, it is telling that this aggression still follows lines of already existing social categories. Additionally, these narratives locate the cause of violence against women in the individual characteristics of men who are gendered, classed, and racialized as hypermasculine and distances other men, also gendered, raced, and classed, from culpability in a culture that promotes this violence.

Hypermasculinity as an individual trait was once again the source of violence and inequality and a foil for other men to construct their own acceptable Goldilocks masculinity against. These narratives that framed some men as especially uncontrolled and violent were especially prominent in contexts, such as therapeutic settings, that were supposed to offer a place for hypermasculine men to shed the tough demeanor they carried elsewhere. Wesley, living in a midsized city near the Appalachian region, organized a support group for cisgender men:

> I've actually facilitated men's groups for my job. Natal [cisgender] males sit there who are crying to each other about shit, problems they're having with their women, and they will get up, and when they walk out the door, they're right back to the "I'm a super redneck. I'm in control. And that bitch better have dinner waiting

for me when I get home and a cold beer on the table" kind of thing. But twenty minutes ago, they were crying about the fact that they can't get their woman to blow 'em when they want to. You know? So there's always another side to what you see outside. And if all you ever see is the outside, you might think you're not that. But the culture out here tells these guys you can't be weak in public. It's hard as hell to get men to show up to a friggin' support group. Which is why there's so much domestic abuse. There's a lot of domestic violence out here, a lot more per capita than other parts of the country.

Wesley's account draws on the ideal of the redneck to show that even these men could open up about their softer feelings and cry in the setting of the support group. These redneck men represented a hyper-controlled emotional life that Wesley tied to a propensity for domestic violence. For most of the interviewees, family was a space where they valued emotional openness; therefore, redneck men were marked as deficient because they supposedly could not control their anger at home.

These narratives of emotion framed uncontrollable men as improper self-disciplining emotional subjects and unsuitable citizens of the society. In a similar vein to Wesley, Saul, a white man living in urban California, talked about his work as a therapist at a treatment facility for mostly poor men of color:

> It's just not that comfortable for me to relate to really masculine guys. I had clients who were, either because they were overcompensating or whatever. I had this guy who was a little bit taller than me and really kind of buff, and every single session was a chess match. We were in there, and it was like fighting with him. I finally said, "Dude, what's up with this?" And he said, "Well, you're not the kind of person I would normally associate with" [*laugh*]. I'm like, "Really? Tell me more about that." Well, he basically meant that I'm too soft and that's kind of weird for him, and so we had to work through some of that. I think it was really valuable, but it wasn't easy [*laugh*]. You know, trying to get him to look at it was like, "What about you and the softer parts of you that you're not comfortable expressing?" These were guys with substance abuse problems, so you would get the front was very hard and defended, and inside they would be eleven-year-old

boys, and it was like, "Aww." And there would be sweetness there, and they couldn't show it to anybody because they would just be targets.

Even if Saul showed quite a bit of sympathy for his client's inability to express emotion, his narrative still marked his own ability to be soft in those settings as more desirable than his patient's comparatively deficient emotional expression. His somewhat paternalistic response when the men did show softer emotions framed them as immature adolescent boys on the inside. The therapeutic setting is a particularly important space for modern self-disciplining subjects to lay out their emotional sins, and an inability to do so is evidence that they are less evolved. This is not to say most men would not benefit from therapy and learning to be more emotionally expressive but rather to highlight how hypermasculinity frames racialized and classed groups of men as more savage and how this narrative turns the problem of violence into a problem of individual emotional control across spaces. This has the symbolic effect of marking these classed and raced men as less rational and modern, unable to achieve the control of Goldilocks masculinity.

Properly Angry

Most of the men I interviewed did not embrace excessive displays of anger but did identify particular spaces and ways of expressing anger that were acceptable. According to these narratives, anger was something to be used judiciously, often in more extreme situations, and was most appropriate when used in the service of others. Again, control was the key component of the proper relationship to anger for men. The control of anger, as an aspect of rationality, evoked the white, middle-class, subdued heterosexual propriety of the regular guy. In a nod to neoliberal ideals of individualism, anger in these narratives was a matter of individual control and exertion.

Interviewees' discussions of anger were most often coupled with their efforts to engage in emotion management and shift expressions of aggression. As conceptualized in the work of Arlie Hochshild, emotion management or emotion work is the process of bringing one's emotions in line or in response to the feeling rules of that setting.[22] Some men could control their anger through recognizing that anger and talking themselves down. Physical exercise was another common tactic to control anger and aggression. For example, Bobby, a white man living in suburban Kentucky, relayed this advice to trans men first starting testosterone:

> You're gonna have a attitude change. You're gonna be an asshole until you get your level right. Expect it. Okay? Make sure the people around you expect it. And if you can't control it, learn how [*pause*] quickly. Work out, punching bag, whatever you gotta do.... Because if you don't have a way to take the aggression out, you'll take it out on the people around—not physically, but you'll just gripe at the people around you. You don't mean to, but you don't have an opening beside the people around you if you don't learn to deal with it. Like me, I learned, you know, push-ups. If you get mad, you do push-ups. Just do it.

In Bobby's advice we can see the gym is the appropriate space not just to sculpt muscles but to express the affective impulses of anger. Clearly, many of the men experienced anger and rage, yet they managed those emotions in order to not be the violent men they disparaged.

Learning how to control emotions was the primary aim of emotion work in contexts such as work and family. Sean, a white man living in the rural upper Midwest, found that his anger hurt his work life and that he no longer wanted to be angry toward his wife:

> I would lose my temper a lot more early on in our relationship, and somewhere along the line, I just—I don't know what I thought, if I thought that I was being tougher somehow or if I was being stronger that way or showing strength. But I realized at some point that I was weaker to do that. I wasn't controlling myself; ... that's always what I thought about being a grown-up. Then I'd go, "Man, I have to do this self-control." That seems to be the theme of most of the lectures I give to my son.

Sean realized that to be truly strong he must control his anger and stop directing it at his wife. In a way, coming into being a "grown-up" reflects the age transition that's often mapped onto trans men's gender transitions. Yet it also signaled that maturity meant moving away from hypermasculinity toward a Goldilocks masculinity, with its spatially appropriate control. In this sense, control was another manifestation of the same underlying quality of masculine strength. The family space was an opportunity to help his son learn to appropriately control anger in order to manage emotions across contexts like his father.

To achieve this emotional control, the interviewees would often have to find a new target for their anger. Violent incidents among interviewees, whether before or after transition, were directed primarily toward women in the space of the family, and the ability to control these expressions of anger made them stronger men. Eric, a white man in a midsized Michigan city, had been particularly afraid of increased anger when using testosterone due to previous incidents of rage and physical violence:

> My anger got me in trouble once just a bit—probation for nine months and anger management. Basically, I assaulted someone. Anger. . . . It was my mom. As I've told you, my mom is close to me. We're much tighter these days. [Do you think that's something that could happen again?] Like me? I don't think so. I actually don't. I mean, sure, I get angry, but I tend to take it out on myself, sometimes physically, but you know, I have more internalized things, I guess. Which isn't always a good thing, but I don't see myself taking it out on other people.

In actuality, he found he was somewhat calmer with testosterone, like many of the men. He directed angry feelings toward himself instead of externalizing them through physical violence against others, which while still problematic showed he was working on establishing the spatially based control of Goldilocks masculinity.

Relabeling Aggression

While men attempt to manage their emotions, the labeling of those emotions is a social process in interaction that is racialized and classed. For example, expressions of anger are often legitimate only in particular contexts and when done by white middle-class men. In these cases, this appropriate anger is relabeled as assertiveness or as justified aggression. For men to achieve the emotional ideal of a self-disciplining subject, not only must they control their own expression based on the situated expectations of a context, but that expression must also be named by others as appropriate to the situation. Thus, when we move from the realm of affect to the realm of emotion, not only do we lose something about that feeling that is not captured in language, but race and other aspects of social location shape the way feelings are labeled and relabeled and judged as appropriate for the situation or not.

The moments when emotions are labeled become sites of contestation over meaning and the feeling rules of a particular context.[23] Gabriel, a multiracial (black, Mexican, and Indigenous) man living in a Deep South suburb, belonged to a fraternity that had a strong social justice mission. He described an incident with his fraternity brothers:

> Someone had posted a picture in a Facebook group that was trying to sell stuff. They were trying to sell their bedding, and behind the bed was a giant confederate flag. Somebody commented, "Hey, how much for the flag so I can burn it?" "Ha, ha, ha. Clever" [*laughter*]. And they were like, "Look, it's not racist." And I was like, "No, no, no, it is really." I basically got into this Facebook argument with this person. I'm like, "No, that's actually a really racist flag. Don't be offended that someone was offended at your flag." I remember I was rushing, I was a pledge at this point, and I remember asking some of my pledge brothers, "Hey, can you help me with this person?" Like, "You're white. Please tell your other white people to stop." And they didn't—they refused. Basically, for them it's like, "Well, this is bullying." And I'm like, "No, no, no, you don't understand. That flag is like bullying extreme." I was like just so distraught over the fact that they couldn't understand why this is such an issue.

Gabriel felt as though his fraternity brothers had minimized his reaction to the racist imagery, and they suggested he was overly aggressive toward, even bullying, the other man on Facebook. As Amy Wilkins and others have shown, black men's anger at racism is frequently characterized as excessive.[24]

It is illustrative to compare Gabriel's experience with another incident, in which Paul, a white man living in rural Northern California, challenged the behavior of others and had his action affirmed by other men. Paul described a recent incident when he was riding the bus:

These guys at the back of the bus, I'm at the front, and they're like using the F word every other word. In between me and them, so I knew anybody between me and them could hear, because if I could hear, they could hear—there was a mom with her kid there, between the guys in the back and me. So, when they finally took a breath, I said something like, "Do you honestly have to use the F word every other word? Because there is a child right here." And they're like, "What?" You know, so I repeated myself, and they were getting all agitated about what I was telling them. Then the bus driver backed me up. He goes, "If you don't knock it off, you can get off on the next stop." The bus driver kicked them off, and they wanted me to get off the bus so they could get in a fight with me. I'm like, "No." But blood pressure was going through the roof, so I thought it was an anger issue. I wrote it to the [online] group, and they were like, "No, you were just being assertive." And I'm like, "Oh." So, I think most of the people, when people assume that it's 'roid rage or whatever, it's most likely they're being more assertive.

In this scenario Paul used his newfound comfort and confidence that went along with transition, which he described earlier in the interview, to intervene in the men's behavior in the back of the bus on behalf of the woman and child. His narrative suggests the woman and child needed his protection against the crude behavior of the other men. In contrast to Gabriel's experience with the man with the Confederate flag, the driver affirmed the appropriateness of Paul's behavior when he ejected the offending men from the bus. In addition, through the online group, Paul relabeled what he initially named anger as assertiveness. As a white man, Paul's intervention was appropriate and controlled, whereas Gabriel's, usually read as a black man, was out of line and bullying.

The ideal of the self-disciplining emotional subject may be difficult to achieve if nearly any action could be relabeled as excessive anger. President Obama's careful avoidance of being seen as angry in order to soothe white racial fears, an experience very familiar to other professional black men, as Adia Harvey Wingfield shows, is a clear example of this dynamic.[25] As Ta-Nehisi Coates describes:

Part of Obama's genius is a remarkable ability to soothe race consciousness among whites. Any black person who's worked in the professional world is well acquainted with this trick. But never has it been practiced at such a high level, and never have its limits been so obviously exposed. This need to talk in dulcet tones, to never be angry regardless of the offense, bespeaks a strange and compromised integration indeed, revealing a country so infantile that it can countenance white acceptance of blacks only when they meet an Al Roker standard.[26]

The image of the angry black man, at the center of the thug controlling image, is present too in the realm of politics.[27] Thus, the power of whiteness allows Donald Trump to frequently lash out in anger during rallies or through social media but compels President Obama to control his emotions as a black man. The expectation of Goldilocks masculinity is still there, but it is racialized as well as gendered. The desirability of this hybrid for everyday men both supports this formation in the political realm and reflects how everyday men maintain their own legitimacy in local contexts. In other words, a man might aim to be a regular guy, but if others label every action he takes as aggression, he will always be a thug.

Altogether, the men I interviewed valued masculine control over anger. In their narratives anger can be appropriately expressed in order to help or protect people who are weaker or more marginalized than themselves, like women and children. Emotional displays were affirmed by others and themselves in interaction or upon reflecting on an interaction through relabeling them as assertiveness rather than aggression. This process frames the behavior as a rational response rather than an emotional one—again reinforcing classed, raced, and sexualized notions of spatially appropriate emotion. Throughout these narratives of anger, trans men used their bodily experience of anger to distinguish men from women. Crucially, these narratives also differentiated between the ideal of the self-disciplining emotional subject and the unacceptable men who were prone to uncontrolled violence. As with crying, this emotional control was about disciplining excessive emotionality at its core.

Affective Sexual Changes

Nearly half of the interviewees mentioned an increase in sexual desire as one of the most prominent affective changes with testosterone therapy.[28] These interviewees still valued an element of control over what they often described as nearly uncontrollable and difficult-to-describe bodily sexual urges during transition. Like anger, this tended to be stronger early on in transition and taper over time. Overall though, trans men reported experiencing lasting changes in their libido, sexual object choice, and other elements of sexuality.[29] Yet the most striking change for most men was the relationship between romantic emotions and sexuality, which was intertwined with the twin pressures of compulsory heterosexuality and gender conformity. These narratives of sexual desire and shifting emotional attachments mirrored larger discourses of masculinity and sexuality and, again, reaffirmed the value of Goldilocks masculinity. In this instance, it was more about detaching emotion from what had previously been a markedly emotional realm.

Barely Controlled Urges

The men who reported increases in sexual desire early on in testosterone therapy typically likened these feelings to those of a teen boy going through puberty: thinking about sex constantly, wanting to engage in sexual acts more frequently, and feeling sexual desire more intensely than before. As James, a white man living in urban California, explained, "A lot of guys find out when they start testosterone that sex changes a lot, as in how much more horny you are. The libido's bananas. It's out of control." Some men reported they initiated sex much more often with their partners. As part of this increased libido, men also described the urge to masturbate much more frequently and in places where they would not have before, such as several men mentioning masturbating in the bathroom at work in the first few months of taking testosterone. This trope of uncontrolled sexual urges at puberty is pervasive in U.S. popular culture and usually framed as humorous, such as the protagonist in the *American Pie* franchise who ultimately directs his urges to a freshly baked pie in the family kitchen. Like at work or on the kitchen counter of the suburban middle-class family home, these desires were often considered out of place in the spaces they occurred, even by the people themselves.

A majority of the interviewees that reported increased sexual desire mentioned a new and intense arousal from visual stimuli, but these desires, too, were often described as out of place. The men shared strikingly similar stories of barely controlled sexual urges in which they experienced intense arousal from looking at a woman in a nonsexual space, where trying to enact their desires would have been inappropriate or even threatening. These incidents involved interviewees staring at parts of women's bodies, which they thought was probably inappropriate but difficult to stop. For example, Phillip, a white man living in a midsized North Carolina city, shared this story about a former boss:

> I couldn't stand her, but I remember having a meeting with her one time, and I couldn't stop staring at her breasts. And I'm like, "Are you freakin' serious? Stop looking at 'em." I'm telling myself, literally, in my mind, "Stop looking at her tits," and, "What is my problem?" But I mean really, there's not much control, especially in that pubescent boy or, you know, adolescent boy thing. It's like this drive. I mean, it was, it was rough at first [*laugh*]. . . . I was not realizing it was gonna be that high, and I'm like, "She was in a lot of cleavage, I mean probably more than she should have been, you know." But, I'm like lookin' at 'em, and I'm like, "God, it's so obvious I'm doing it, too," and I couldn't stop. I'm like, "What the hell's gone wrong?" [*laughter*]. That's toned down of course.

The struggle evident in Phillip's internal discussion was a common feature of these stories, as was a narrative of empathy for adolescent boys experiencing the onset of puberty. These urges were not always heterosexual, as a few of the men reported a new intense interest in pornography made for gay men and interest in sex with men. Across these similar stories, the men emphasized the bodily and barely articulable sexual urges that attended their early days on testosterone, but as their physical transition progressed these urges became more easily controlled and less urgent.

Oft-repeated stories of these urges were so striking to each man because they felt like they were on the edge of losing control, a feeling that was especially disturbing in spaces where sexual feelings were out of place. These narratives show that sexuality is disciplined through notions of what spaces are appropriate for sexual urges. Thus, barely controlled sexual urges are another example of Goldilocks masculinity playing out in affect. Command of these desires signals a spatially appropriate masculine control. At times, the notion of appropriate emotional contexts mirrors distinctions between private and public space but also reaffirms how those spaces intersect with sexuality.[30] None of the men said that they had actually sexually assaulted a woman or that anyone had noticed their inappropriate looking, but they still felt ambivalent about these incidents. On one hand, they found these barely controlled sexual urges uncomfortable. On the other hand, the desires were a marker of coming into being a man, just like boys in puberty. This conferred a sense of authenticity as they recognized their own bodily impulses that lined up with the experiences of other men. In fact, their narratives did align with larger cultural discourses of men's sexuality, especially in the comparison to adolescent boys.

The more troubling issue is that these narratives of barely controlled urges subtly feed into the rape culture narrative of sexual assault being a result of men's natural irrepressible lust, as opposed to a feminist interpretation of sexual assault as a form of social domination. In other words, if these "good" men can hardly control their impulses, it becomes more understandable to some trans men that some other men cannot control themselves. There was a suggestion present across interviews that a total lack of control of their sexuality was a sign of hypermasculinity. It is clear here that the line is not necessarily just between having strong sexual urges or not but rather is a thinner line of being able to (barely) control those desires and express them in the proper spaces. Learning to control these excessive bodily urges, feelings that women and other people without as much testosterone coursing through their bodies could never understand, was part of the larger project of emotional control in different contexts. This control was at the heart of interviewees' ideals of themselves as men, since the majority of them strove to be regular guys and achieve a Goldilocks masculinity.

This raging-hormone vision of adolescent sexuality is not actually universal across contemporary cultures, which suggests that broader cultural narratives also shape trans men's accounts of testosterone and sex, as they do for cisgender boys and men.[31] It is important to note again that there was not only a wide range of narratives on the effects of hormones on each individual but also critiques of these narratives among interviewees. Jeffrey, a white man living in a college town in California, had misgivings about the connections other trans men made to new behaviors after starting testosterone:[32]

> When I was nineteen or twenty and getting ready to start taking T, I'd moved to the city to get T in a clinic. This culture, this big

bubble of young trans men that was coming up and we were all pretty new to it, and so was the medical industry, so there was not much dialogue checking the behaviors of transmasculine people. I was experiencing a lot of people in my immediate and extended community just totally using it as a free card. You know, like, "I'm more aggressive because of this," or, "I'm more horny because of this, and so I push boundaries, and I'm working it." Stuff like that. Okay, whatever, maybe your hormones are making you act in these more jerky ways, but now it's your responsibility to learn how to deal with it. And also as a person being on hormones, and, granted, I have been on low dose, however, I've been on it for a long time and a pretty wide range, and never anywhere in that range did I experience any of that sort of behavior that I felt like I could excuse. So, being somebody that didn't personally experience it, whenever I hear transmasculine people talking about that, it gets incredibly hard for me to believe, and I feel like it's an excuse.

This critique from trans men like Jeffrey exemplifies the possibilities of the progressive man to rethink dominant narratives of masculinity and biology. His counternarrative affirms the idea that the permissive effects of testosterone are likely related to different affective potentialities of the individual body and personality but also reflects a sense of cultural and social permission to experience and, in some cases, enact the "raging hormones" of the boy in puberty. The connection to adolescent boys further reifies the naturalized discourse of testosterone and puberty.

Sex among Men (Without Feeling)

One of the most significant and consistent changes that trans men reported with taking testosterone was that they felt less of a need for a romantic emotional component to their sexual activity than before. Jason, a white man living in suburban Ohio, shared:

I've tried to explain it to women and just be like [*smack*] that just need. It goes beyond want; it goes beyond . . . I don't need the touchy-feely. I don't need any of that. I just need to get off and go on about my day.

In going from sexual desire and emotion as intertwined to sexuality as an urge, narratives like Jason's evidence an exit from a particular emotional economy of gender and sexuality.[33] In a sense, this operates as a disavowal of emotion in some sexual spaces. This new orientation to emotion mirrors gendered notions of sexuality where women are more interested in emotional connection and men's sexual urges reflect affect. The affective sexual urges were often difficult to name for interviewees, in a prelinguistic sense. In general, as the men felt that their sexuality was less connected to romance or emotional expressiveness, sex with other men became more appealing.

A substantial portion of the interviewees divided and gendered their sexual relationships by engaging in sexual relationships devoid of romantic emotions with men, while reserving emotionally intimate sexual and romantic relations for women. A majority of the men I interviewed that talked about their sexuality said they no longer wanted or needed a romantic emotional component to sex. Instead, they wanted to satisfy their affective bodily desires without the "touchy-feely stuff" that Jason mentioned. For a number of the men, sex with men offered just that. Ian, a white man living in urban Minnesota, went from having relationships with mostly women to mostly men after his transition six years before the interview:

> Obviously, when you're taking hormones, it increases your sex drive, and I think my approach to sex is different. It shifted. Rather than being more of just an enjoyable and deep bonding relationship to being like this is just part of just a simple physical need. Like, there was a shift in mentality in that sense, but it was also how just like sexuality goes. Being comfortable with myself as a guy has really helped because now I feel like I can actually have relationships. You know, if I want to go out and meet somebody for sex, I can do that, and I don't have to feel weird about it being like, you know, because it's like, yeah, now if you don't like this that's fine. I was able to come to terms that I've always been attracted to guys. That's something I've known, but I've repressed it.

Thus, for Ian both the shift in his sexuality from an emotional base to an affective need, as well as his comfort in being seen as a man, allowed him to engage in sex with other men, whether through long-term relationships or shorter-term encounters.

In an interesting juxtaposition of the virilizing effects of testosterone usually associated with heterosexual men, more than one-third of the interviewees reported an increased sexual interest in men after taking testosterone, though some never acted on it.[34] Still more of the men mentioned this was a common experience for trans men. Felix, a white man living in urban Minnesota, talked about this potential as he pondered his decision to start taking testosterone:

> I think that's one of those things that I'm a little bit nervous about starting T. A friend of mine, who actually lives in another midwestern state, took me aside one day, and he was like, "You know that you will be taking gay juice, right?"

Using the phrase "gay juice," Felix's friend referenced the common idea that trans men develop a sexual interest in men as a direct effect of testosterone. Some trans men partially attributed this sexual exploration with other men to a fascination with other men's bodies. Sex with men provided a way to learn about embodied aspects of being a man through the exploration of others' manhood. In other words, this offered a way for men who had little experience with men's bodies to get an understanding of how parts, such as penises, feel and work.

Sex with men was also a less complicated outlet for increased sexual drives because it involved sexual engagement without emotional entanglement. Luke, a white man living in rural Indiana, also experienced a surprising change to his sexuality when he transitioned:

> When I started to transition, all hell broke loose. I found myself looking at guys all the time. I found myself wanting to have sex without protection [*pause*] in like cemeteries . . . anywhere I could find. It really tore me up. It turned my world upside down because I identified as a lesbian my entire freakin' life, even as a kid, and now this. And I'm like, "What?"

Eventually, he found a measure of relief in his new sexuality. Luke said casual encounters with men he met through a personals website were satisfying because they fit his new matter-of-fact sexual desires:

> In fifteen months, I've probably met about fourteen people. So, just for a one-night stand kind of thing. Yeah, I just want it

quick and easy, don't wanna cuddle, whatever. "Do it, please. Thank you."

Each of the fourteen people he found through the website were men, and these encounters satisfied his new higher sex drive. Sexual exchanges like these provided relief both from barely controlled sexual urges and from the demands of the emotional economies tied to their past or current sexual relationships with women.

Interestingly, in this new or heightened interest in sex with men, ten of the men I interviewed had sexual relationships with other men but stated they were interested in longer-term emotional relationships only with women.[35] Woody, a white man living in urban California, had considered himself bisexual when he first became sexually active in high school and had sexual relationships with both men and women for some time. When he became less comfortable living as a woman, he stopped having sexual relationships with men. Woody said he could not bear for them to see him as a woman, but once he transitioned, he was comfortable having sex with men again. He felt occasionally frustrated, however, with the fact that because he was a trans man, other men would assume he was more emotional:

> I'm supposed to be more sensitive and talk about my feelings and wanna cuddle. I'm like, "Actually, I just wanna suck your dick. I want you to fuck me. I want you to suck my dick, and then I want you to go home." You know, "I don't wanna talk about my feelings, and I don't wanna cuddle with you because that's weird and that's not what I'm into." And they're like, "Ah!" I've had these conversations with gay guys that know that I'm trans where they're just like, "It's like you're a straight guy," and I'm like, "Well, I kind of am a straight guy." I date exclusively women, but I sleep with men. I never date men; I just sleep with them, you know. And I have like friends that are guys that I sleep with, but it never turns into a romantic situation, and I'm okay with that. You know, I just don't have those feelings for men.

He went on to explain that he does have close emotional friendships with other men but that he does not mix sexual and romantic relationships with men. Like Jane Ward's str8-identified men, part of the way Woody maintains an identity as a straight guy is through the way he has sex with other men. In Ward's analysis, this means men associate themselves with "straight culture" while taking part in homosexual and homoerotic acts.[36] Woody went on to explain why he had not been able to have sex with men in the years leading up to transition and what had changed:

> It just never really happened again until I transitioned, and then it was like I kind of felt more comfortable being with a guy because I felt like I was finally getting to relate to them the way that I'd always wanted to, which is like, "I am your bro-dude-friend," you know, like, "and we're gonna have sex" and then like continue to be like broing down together.

This distinction between romantic and sexual relationships was another form of emotional control. For these men, romantic emotions were suitable only with women, whereas with men they could enjoy purely sexual pleasure without romantic entanglements because they labeled them as sexual and not emotional spaces. There were, however, men who had long-term romantic and emotional relationships with other men, whether these relationships were monogamous or not, and gained immense satisfaction from them, though they were a small minority among the trans men I interviewed.

Overall, the connection between heterosexuality and emotional relationships reified a form of heteronormativity in the institution of the family. This allowed those men to have sex with other men but avoid being tainted by feminine ideas of romance or the controlling image of the faggy man, who is overly emotional. In this hybrid masculine formation, which is another example of Goldilocks masculinity, sex with other men might be acceptable as long as it does not interfere with the emotional space of the heterosexual family. One could interpret this as a queer effort to delink the connection between sexuality and family, but these sexual practices still reproduce the normativity of emotion in the heterosexual family and thus potentially the superiority of heterosexuality.

CONCLUSION

Emotional control, related to calm, crying, anger, and sexuality, was central to trans men's narratives of the shifting affective states they experienced when taking testosterone. This journey frequently mapped onto the age-related narrative of boys becoming men through puberty and adolescence. Indeed, both transformation narratives draw on the same essentialist popular discourse of bodies, hormones, and sexuality. Most men feared increased anger and aggression before they started transition, but the majority actually felt more calm and rational after transition. Some men did experience increased anger, and that anger was directed mostly at women. While generally they reported a new distance from emotion, some strongly held feelings, such as sexual urges, grew in intensity. Increased sexual interest and practices with men would seem to contradict the traditional connection between idealized masculinity and heterosexuality; however, the connection between heterosexuality and intimacy was maintained through narrating sex with other men as unemotional. Again, these narratives of emotion, hormones, sexuality, and masculinity were quite similar, if not nearly the same, as those of cisgender men.

What is clear throughout these narratives is that trans men's idealized notions of emotion and masculinities were, for the most part, not the traditional ideal of the emotionless man, or the man who can express only anger. Rather, interviewees thought those men were problematic and regressive. Instead, the ideal emotional man of the contemporary period is one who is able to control his emotions, in that he uses his distance from emotions to be rational when the space calls for it and to be more emotionally expressive when appropriate. This is Goldilocks masculinity as played out through emotion and the body.

In this formulation, hypermasculine men, through racialized and classed depictions that invoke the thug and the redneck, could not control anger, aggression, and their sexuality. By claiming that the lack of appropriate emotion by some men is the primary cause for violence against women and others, men lay blame for these social problems solely on an individual's ability or inability to control themselves, rather than focusing on structural explanations for violence and inequality. In other words, good men can control their sexual urges and expressions of anger. They can even cry when the situation calls for it. Bad men, on the other hand, cannot control themselves and are the sole perpetrators of violence. Proper men can discipline their bodies, especially their affective experiences and expressions, whereas the bodies of women, feminine men, black men, and poor men are ungovernable. The process of labeling and relabeling emotional display is another means of creating gendered, raced, classed, and sexual difference when the meaning of a particular expression is contested.

Much of this narrative of masculinity and emotion relies on testosterone as a driver of emotional difference. Testosterone has material effects, but individual men experienced and interpreted these effects in a range of ways. It appears to be permissive in the sense of both exacerbating feelings already there and giving permission for particular behaviors and expressions. This permissive effect is both biologically and socially sourced. Thus, cultural narratives of testosterone and the related ideas about men's affect and emotion likely give just as much permission to name, express, and control particular feelings. Testosterone narratives, whether about adolescent boys or adult trans men, ignore the constellation of changes and events that occur simultaneously with chemical changes and both produce new or different affect. For example, trans men had to reckon with their decision to start taking testosterone itself. They also experienced the often-permanent physical changes, such as hair growth and fat redistribution, that went beyond shifts in their internal emotional state. In addition, these physical changes often simultaneously marked the achievement of a long-term goal and relief at satisfying a deep need for bodily change, not to mention the different forms of social recognition that a beard or other testosterone-induced changes make in social interaction. Some men found these changes exhilarating, while others were more ambivalent. In all, the centrality of biologically centered narratives of before and after testosterone say something both about the differing effects of this chemical on men's bodies and about the cultural story of testosterone as a powerful trope to draw on and explain moments of socially significant life changes.

This analysis of the contemporary emotional ideal offers further evidence of a hybrid masculine formation, the Goldilocks masculinity, that incorporates the challenges to existing gender and racial relations from feminists and other critics. Thus, while the normative ideal shifts from a lack of emotion to appropriate emotion, the basic premise that some, racialized, classed, and sexualized, people are in control and some are not remains the same. Those who can achieve the ideal of the self-disciplining emotional subject, who can be soft when they need to be and hard when they need to be, are suitable for power in the political realm and as proper citizens in everyday life.

Fear is also a powerful emotion that is gendered, classed, and racialized, and violence has many emotional components and consequences. The next two chapters continue to explore elements of affect and place through examining men's narratives of fear, vulnerability, and violence. Both spatially based fear and violence have the potential to discipline men's bodies according to normative ideas of sexuality, race, and gender.

4
Geography of Violence
SPATIAL FEARS AND THE REPRODUCTION OF INEQUALITY

The image of a woman walking down a deserted city street at night is a familiar one. On her way home from work or a party, she hears footsteps behind her. A furtive glance over her shoulder reveals a man a half block behind. Depending on who she sees, her body may tense, and her pace may quicken, but not so much that she draws attention to her fear. As her eyes search the shadowed block ahead, she wonders, "If he attacks, where will I run, what will I use to fight back, and would anyone hear my shouts for help?" At its core, this common image is about the vulnerability of women and how fear of violence is tied to space.

This vulnerability and attendant fear are encapsulated in the fear of violence Ethan, a black man, felt when he grew up living as a woman in his midsized Michigan city.[1] As he explained, this fear was pervasive and affected his access to public space:

> Growing up, that's always been a fear of mine, to be sexually assaulted. It was always on my mind, especially when I was younger and looked more like a female. That bothered me a lot, so I stayed in the house a lot of the time because that was a very big fear of mine. But as I got older and I started to change [transition], the fear level of that happening started coming down.

Though his fear of sexual assault went down with transition, he realized that, as a black man, others now saw him as dangerous in the same public places:

> I mean, you just notice certain things. Like, if you get in an elevator and it's a Caucasian woman in there, she'll hold her purse a little closer, or she'll move over to the corner, but since I've noticed stuff like that, when I get in an elevator, I will move to the other side. You know, 'cause I know I make them feel uncomfortable.

With Ethan's calm and sweet demeanor, it was hard for me to imagine anyone being afraid of him, but like the woman on the dark street, white women in elevators shifted their bodies and clutched their purses because Ethan apparently provoked their sense of vulnerability. Even though he was not afraid of violence against himself in these situations, Ethan too altered his behavior in response to other's fears so that he was perceived as less dangerous.

As a black man, Ethan also experienced increased scrutiny from the police:

> I get harassed a lot more by the police. And I really don't care for that. I don't have a criminal record. I've never been to jail. I've never been in handcuffs, but I've been spread-eagled plenty of times. And I'm not that type of person. So, for you just to [*siren sound*] pull up on me, just up out of the blue . . . and be like, "Okay, assume the position," I'm like, "Again?" You know, "You fit the description." "Of what? A typical black man?"

Ethan's experiences of harassment from the police also pushed him to avoid going out in public, though not as much as his fears of sexual assault did before he transitioned. The image of the thug followed Ethan through public spaces, even if it did not line up with how he saw himself. Ethan's fears and experiences of violence (of sexual violence when he lived as a woman and of being seen as dangerous while living as a man), as well as other's fears of him, shaped his behavior and the ways he was able to access different spaces.

Clearly, both fears and experiences of violence are connected to the context in which they happen and are shaped by race and gender. Both Ethan's map of fear and experiences of harassment altered his behavior when navigating the spaces of his city. As men and as transgender people, trans men have a complicated relationship to fear and violence. Like Ethan, most of the interviewees reported that they had feared sexual assault as women but that the fear diminished once they transitioned. In fact, they reported the jarring experience of women now being afraid of them when they walked down a dark street at night. Men of color, such as Ethan, were especially seen by others as dangerous in a number of settings. While many of the interviewees discussed a broad feeling of vulnerability as transgender people, men of color tended to be more concerned with the violence that might come from being recognized as black men.

Ethan's story demonstrates that broad narratives of vulnerability to violence and images of potential perpetrators shape men's everyday behavior and their experiences of violence. Trans men simultaneously negotiate pervasive images of transgender vulnerability and normative masculine ideals that suggest men should be neither excessively violent nor the victims of violence. Thus, managing fears and violence is another example of the Goldilocks masculinity at the center of the regular guy. In this case, Goldilocks masculinity is the sweet spot between being a hypermasculine perpetrator of violence—as in the controlling images of the thug, a black poor man in urban spaces, or the redneck, a white poor man in rural spaces—and not being a victim, like the image of the faggy man. By examining how trans men negotiate larger narratives of vulnerability and map out their fears based on region and other spaces, it becomes clear how this hybrid masculinity represents a shift away from promoting violence as a masculine ideal but simultaneously reproduces racial, sexual, class, and gender inequality.

NARRATING VULNERABILITY AND INNOCENCE

In the United States, the predominant image of vulnerability is that of a woman, usually white and middle class, walking alone at night. However, sexual assault by strangers, the fear at the core of this image of vulnerability, is actually an unlikely scenario. Women are much more likely to be assaulted by an acquaintance or someone they know rather than a stranger.[2] Feminist scholars in sociology and geography have long studied the effects of gendered vulnerability and fear. Sociologists such as Jocelyn Hollander and Esther Madríz and geographers such as Gill Valentine and Rachel Pain have shown the image of a vulnerable woman walking alone at night is a key component of a culture that shapes women's behavior and limits their access to public space.[3] Like Ethan, many people living as women avoid public space altogether because they fear they will be sexually assaulted. This leads them to spend more time at home and among family and friends, where they actually experience most gendered and sexual violence.

Fears and experiences of violence shape men's actions and how they practice masculinities as well, whether in being seen as violent or avoiding being a victim of violence. An imagined lack of vulnerability to violence is central to contemporary normative masculinities across most settings. This image of invulnerability increases most men's access to public space, since they are generally less afraid to do things like walk alone at night.[4] At the same time, men are more likely to experience physical assault by those strangers that women fear. Race, class, sexuality, and transgender status, among other categories of difference, also simultaneously shape these gendered patterns of fear and violence.[5] For example, the controlling image of the thug constitutes the most common image of perpetrators of violence.[6] Ethan's experience of being seen by others as newly dangerous, as well as a likely criminal by police, illustrates the effect of this common image. Once again, Ethan cannot escape the controlling image of the thug, which translates into increased harassment from police, as well as those subtle shifts in interaction that caused him to change his movements and behaviors in order to appear less threatening. Hypermasculine racialized controlling images like the thug construct certain men of color not only as threats to women and children generally but also as transphobic and homophobic threats to largely white lesbian, gay, and transgender people.[7]

While Ethan as a man was newly seen by others as dangerous, sociologist Laurel Westbrook has shown media and activist discourses also work to construct transgender people as inherently vulnerable. This is because the most common cultural images of trans people are as tragic victims of violence.[8] Recent surveys indicate that transgender people experience unacceptably high levels of violence and discrimination overall but that trans people of color, especially black trans people, tend to experience far higher rates of violence.[9] Yet these larger vulnerability discourses reinforce the vulnerability of all transgender people to incidents of spectacular violence, meaning murder or brutal assaults. These incidents of spectacular violence are much less frequent and tend to most often affect trans people who live at the intersections of class, race, and sexual marginalization. This vulnerability discourse also has a spatial dimension. In analyzing reactions to the murder of Brandon Teena, a trans man in small-town Nebraska, Jack Halberstam demonstrates that rural and midwestern transgender people are viewed as especially vulnerable, particularly by queer and transgender people in cities on the East and West Coasts.[10] Trans men face a contradiction: as men they are not supposed to be vulnerable, even though men are actually more likely to experience physical violence than women, but as trans people they are supposed to be inherently vulnerable.[11]

Events meant to empower transgender communities and address transphobic violence, such as Transgender Day of Remembrance (TDOR), can actually produce or reinforce trans vulnerability. A typical TDOR event involves a candlelight vigil and public reading of the names of murdered trans people from the prior year to bring awareness to their lives and the violence they have suffered.[12] TDOR serves the crucial purpose of giving activists and community members the space to reflect and mourn and a chance to build movement commitment and energy. At the same time, events like TDOR act as what I term *vulnerability rituals,* moments that performatively reinforce the notion of vulnerability of a group of people to violence. These moments often mark all transgender people as inherently vulnerable to heinous acts of violence but gloss over the fact that some trans people are much more vulnerable than others.[13]

The vulnerability produced at events like TDOR is all the more striking given that those who most often do the memorializing are white middle-class people on college campuses, while those being memorialized are nearly all poor trans women of color, who are simultaneously centered and erased in these narratives of violence. This dynamic related to TDOR is increasingly the subject of critique by scholars and activists alike, but media and community discourses still frequently reproduce notions of a broad vulnerability to extreme violence for all transgender people. In the course of his interview, Tim, a white and Latinx man who lived in suburban Georgia, talked about the omnipresence of the fear of transgender violence and whom he thought vulnerability rituals such as TDOR served. He said these fears when expressed by white trans people were overinflated:

> I feel it comes more from people who are less directly affected by the threat [of transphobic violence], and maybe that's not true in all spaces, but I don't know. I feel like Atlanta in particular has a fairly strong presence of older black trans women who are the people most at risk for assault for being trans. Who actually tend to use that discourse somewhat less than people with more power because I feel like when it comes from like this middle-class white person appealing to like terror and violence, it can mean

something.... [More] than coming from black people.... I really, really don't want to minimize the extent to which, especially when like black trans women talk about the threat of violence, how real that is, but I also feel like to some extent they don't talk about it as much as people who get more out of displaying their fear do.

What might more privileged people get out of displaying their fear in general and in vulnerability rituals such as TDOR? Showing this fear, regardless of whether it is actually felt, marks individuals as vulnerable and potentially absolves them of their culpability in other forms of inequality and violence. In this line of thinking, if they are vulnerable, then their actions or inactions that reinforce inequality become excusable because they are done as an act of understandable self-preservation. Indeed, trans people who are more privileged but also express vulnerability may draw resources away from the trans people who are more likely to actually experience violence. The racially, economically, and otherwise multiply marginalized trans people who actually experience this violence are often discredited as disrespectable, and the violence they experience is blamed on personal moral failings and other individual characteristics. Thus, there is a tension between whose voice is heard and whose claim to protection is seen as legitimate.

In an analysis of TDOR events and websites, Sarah Lamble refers to this dynamic, where white trans people invoke fears of transphobia through citing the violence overwhelmingly committed against trans women of color, as remaking white innocence.[14] Framing the violence as purely transphobic allows white people to distance themselves from culpability in white supremacy and antiblack violence. Lamble builds on Mary Louise Fellows and Sherene Razack's understanding of the "race to innocence," wherein marginalized people respond to their own complicity in the marginality of others by reinforcing or centering their own subordinated statuses and, thus, their innocence in producing or benefiting from the oppression of others.[15] "Moves to innocence" happen not just through claiming one's own oppression but also through asserting a lack of experience of the oppressions other groups face.[16] For example, when a white person in an organization is confronted with charges of institutional racism, they might not race to innocence by emphasizing their own marginalized statuses but instead might claim they cannot understand racism because they have no experience of it as a white person. Although they might have the best of intentions in making these claims, this person is still moving toward innocence because these claims make further invisible the privilege white supremacy systematically rewards to white people, even if mediated by class, sexuality, or other aspects of difference. The stories of fear produced by many of the trans men I interviewed followed this pattern: when they narrated their fears of extreme violence, they also narrated themselves into innocence. This is not to say interviewees or TDOR organizers have consciously intended to emphasize their marginality at the cost of others. Rather, their narratives of vulnerability that center only one social status, being transgender, erase the race, gender, sexual, and class inequalities that contribute to specific vulnerabilities and patterns of victimization.[17]

Furthering this discourse of vulnerability, Brandon Teena's story hung like a specter over trans men's discussions of fear and violence, which reinforced the controlling image of the violent, white, rural, poor redneck man. Without being prompted, nearly half of the interviewees mentioned Brandon Teena or the film *Boys Don't Cry*, which dramatized Teena's murder, in their discussion of violence. Ken, a white man living in urban California, shared a typical story of learning about Brandon Teena and how the story stayed with him:

> The Brandon Teena story, which they talked about and hyped, I'm really glad that that story is out there, but at the same time I remember before I ever even thought of transitioning I went to the youth group, and I was maybe nineteen. They showed the Brandon Teena documentary, and I had to get up and leave. Because I remember looking at pictures and thinking that that's me, that that could be me. It wasn't even so much that I was tied to the gender, at that point. Or the fact that he identified as male. It was that he looked like me, short hair, very sort of presenting as masculine. So, I think it was this built-in fear. From stuff like that.... But no, I've been very, very lucky, and sometimes I feel like I'm paranoid about this kind of stuff. I couldn't believe how much safer and how much better it felt once I moved here. It's not as if things don't happen here, because they do, but if something happened here, I feel like it's so much less than in a little redneck town. I definitely watch myself more [in a small town]. How I talk, and how people are perceiving me. I pay a lot more attention to that.

As Ken acknowledged, violence happens in major cities, but spectacular violence against trans men is associated with rural spaces. These fears reinforce the image of the bigoted single perpetrator, the violent redneck in rural spaces, as the source of transphobic and homophobic violence, rather than a consideration of the structural effects of racism or poverty that make some trans people more vulnerable. Teena's story worked as a vulnerability ritual that not just shadowed descriptions of rural violence but also fostered imaginings of the possibility of spectacular violence in all kinds of settings marked as unsafe.

In addition to creating a narrow focus on the source of violence, the kinds of fear both produced and recognized in vulnerability rituals act as powerful forms of social control that reproduce systems of social domination in spatially specific ways. For most of the men I interviewed, Teena's murder was the one incident they could actually name of the type of violence they feared most. In discussions of violence across the interviews, all participants combined could name only a small number of instances of spectacular violence committed against trans men they knew.[18] Thus, the fear provoked by Teena's story rather than direct experiences of violence shaped a sense of spatially based vulnerability. The effect of this spatial vulnerability is evident in Ken's heightened fear of violence for not being appropriately masculine in rural spaces and the relative safety he felt in his city. In the "redneck town," Ken watched his behavior so that others would not think he was gay, but in the city he felt less threatened. These fears tended to lead to more conforming behaviors for trans men—following the everyday rules of social interaction that re-create inequalities and not intervening when they observed racism, sexism, and homophobia in others, even if they said they wanted to. Thus, narratives of violence highlighted trans men's own vulnerability and encouraged more conforming behaviors. In the move to innocence, vulnerability became an excuse for conformity in their own behavior and complicity in the oppression of others.

Brandon Teena's story evoked the vulnerability of trans men, especially tied to rural spaces, but that same rurality and other aspects of his story became a way for interviewees to differentiate themselves from him. The obviousness of the threat to transgender people in rural places was a common explanation of this violence. Several interviewees wondered why Teena would stay in the town and why any transgender person would. Other men further differentiated themselves from Teena by positing he might be partially responsible for his own violent fate. For example, Colton, a white man living in suburban Wisconsin, explained:

> If you look at the situation with Brandon Teena, he was hanging out with drug dealers. He was hanging out in situations that would have been dangerous even if he wasn't trans. And he was also living in a very small-minded town at a time when these things were not as well known, and I think that probably made a difference. I would be wary of moving to certain parts of the country, and maybe without reason, you know. One thing that I think is nice about the Midwest is that it tends to be a very live-and-let-live kind of area, where it's as long as you're not messing with my personal freedom, then you can do what you want. Whereas I think there are some areas that are more fundamentalist, for example, where a person would be in more danger than they are here.

Colton lays out assumptions about where others will be tolerant of trans men and also about the activities that make one more likely to become a victim of violence. Like most other men I interviewed, Colton did not explicitly blame Brandon Teena for his own murder. Yet this process of differentiating themselves from the characteristics that lead to victimization does have this effect: it becomes a cautionary tale of how to avoid violence. In these explanations, conformity to a range of social mores becomes the way to prevent violence, rather than addressing the structural factors that might make some individuals more likely to experience victimization than others. The move to innocence here is about gaining a "toehold of respectability," where marginalized people can construct themselves to be aligned with normative social ideals in opposition to "degenerate" others.[19]

Balancing threats of victimization, spatially based fears, and claims to innocence also invoke the racial, gender, sexual, and class projects wrapped up in the ideals of the thug, redneck, faggy man, and regular guy. The thug and redneck often stand as the hypermasculine sources of violence in urban or suburban and rural spaces, respectively. Victimization, on the other hand, is a sign of weakness and therefore can potentially delegitimize men's hold on normative masculinity, taking a man closer to the femininity of women and the effeminacy of faggy men. Thus, being either a violent perpetrator or a victim of violence can make a man illegitimate in regard to proper masculine ideals. This dynamic provides further evidence of the predominance of the regular guy ideal, where one should be neither overly violent nor a victim. In this Goldilocks masculinity, some fear is acceptable, since extreme violence is the property of those classed and racialized men who cannot control themselves, but being a victim is a sign that a man is "too soft" or too deviant. Overall, this means men must carefully navigate their spatially based fears based on region and other spaces in order to avoid victimization. These narratives of the causes of victimization, along with discussions of violence that evidence a disjuncture between spatially mapped fears and actual experiences of spectacular violence, may displace attention from the larger systems that actually make some people more vulnerable to violence.

SPATIAL CONTEXTS OF VIOLENCE

Trans men's ideas about violence and place shape their fears of violence, which are both very real concerns for safety and also moves toward innocence. Interviewees mapped their perceptions of safety spatially, and this varied based on race, sexuality, ability, and class. A sense of trans vulnerability heightened the fears of homophobic, racist, and other violence they likely shared with cisgender men. Overall, interviewees mapped the specter of spectacular violence, including severe physical assaults, murder, and sexual assault, onto particular places, and this encouraged a space-based conformity to gender, sexual, and racial standards. As geographers Gill Valentine and Alec Brownlow have argued, while women report higher levels of fear in general, both men and women map out their fears spatially as "geographies of fear" and what I also refer to as geographies of safety.[20] At a basic level, this means both men and women tend to think some places and spaces are more dangerous than others, and they attempt to avoid or manage their interactions within these spaces accordingly. Men's geographies of fear have been mapped in specific urban contexts, noting how men engage in constant work both to avoid victimization and to perform fearlessness, yet there has been less investigation into how these fears are based on the region where they live and their geographic imaginaries of other spaces. Further, there is a lack of knowledge of how these geographic imaginaries shape the intersection of fears of transphobic and homophobic violence.

Regions figured prominently in the interviewees' geographies of safety. Both the region they lived in and their imaginaries or prior experiences of other regions shaped their fears. These fears based on region were broad and mostly focused on concerns about general social conservatism, along with the idea that the people found in those places were prone to violence. This assessment of the potential for violence often drew on the redneck controlling image and, thus, was a racialized, gendered, and classed judgment. Men who currently lived or had lived in each region tended to articulate a more nuanced geography of safety in each place—of which an urban and rural distinction was one of the primary organizers. Overall, interviewees tended to describe the West as the most tolerant of the U.S. regions due to a perception that, on the West Coast at least, a wide range of masculinities were acceptable and there was greater acceptance of LGBT people. The Southeast was characterized by both trans men who had never lived there and those who had as the least tolerant of the three regions. The Midwest was generally viewed as somewhere in the middle, as both more open and tolerant than the South but less so than the West, though really only slightly better than the South according to men from the West. The reality of legal protections for transgender people at the state level actually mirrors the interviewees' mapping. The twenty states that ban discrimination based on gender identity or expression, as of 2018, are clustered on the West Coast and in the Northeast, with three states in the Midwest and none in the Southeast offering such protections.[21] Crucially, whether these ideas about space and safety were accurate assessments of the potential for violence, they still affected trans men's interactions as they inhabited or traveled through these places.

West

Overall, interviewees living in the West characterized everywhere outside major cities on the coasts as unsafe and undesirable, though they described more subtle understandings of safety in the places they lived. For example, there was consensus among men living in the San Francisco Bay Area about which places were safer than others. They mapped their geography of safety as follows: the Castro, the gay neighborhood, was safer than other neighborhoods; San Francisco was a safer city than others; the San Francisco Bay Area was safer than nearly everywhere else outside it. Men from the West characterized the South and the Midwest and rural places in general as far less safe for trans men than the West Coast.

Generally, the men I interviewed who had spent their lives as trans men in a place like the San Francisco Bay Area described a sense of freedom to express a range of masculinities and, perhaps, to live more openly as transgender because they felt little threat of transgender-related violence. For these men, living elsewhere not only seemed difficult but was almost unimaginable based on their spatial understanding of the possibility of violence. Woody, a white man, described how his lack of fear living in this area allowed him more freedom in interacting with a broad range of people:

> I might be spoiled because I live in the Bay Area, so there's not really the same threat of violence that there is in other parts of the country or the rest of the world. I might feel different in places like that.

He imagined a different life for himself in other places where his interactions would be more restricted. Leo, a black man, also thought his life would have been significantly different if he did not live within the safety of the Bay Area. He explained:

> In the Bay Area guys are just spread out. There's a lot of us, but we blend in really well and are just scattered to the four winds as far as the greater Bay Area. I've often thought of what my life would be like if my parents never moved us out of Texas. It's really hard to comprehend.

Like most interviewees, Leo felt more comfortable in a place where there were more trans men and easy access to resources. He felt particularly safe with the knowledge that there would be trans men wherever he went in the local area. The inability to imagine trans men living in more dangerous places created a sense of social distance from those inconceivable lives.

In direct conversation about safety, nearly all of the men in the Bay Area and urban parts of the West said most other places were unsafe for trans men. At the same time, more than half of this subset mentioned elsewhere in their interviews that those more dangerous places actually provided a form of safety because they allowed trans men to remain unrecognized as transgender. Alec, a white man living in urban Northern California, shared an experience moving from the Midwest to California that exemplifies this pattern:

> I started passing in Ohio probably sooner than I would have passed out here, if that makes any kind of sense. I think here there would have been more support for, "I'm trans—please use male pronouns," than there would be in Ohio, but I think there was that automatic sort of switch. Whether or not they recognized that I was a trans guy or not, they just recognized that I was a guy [in the Midwest].

The same openness to transgender identities and understanding of politics that made places like the Bay Area feel safe also made it more difficult to be recognized as a man. Encountering the different gender knowledges of these spaces had unexpected effects on both their recognition as men and their sense of safety. According to this experience across interviews, when people do not have an understanding of a third category of gender, transgender in this case, then they are likely to choose man or woman when they are categorizing another person.

In fact, moving to a place where they could blend in held an appeal for some trans men, especially if they could fit with the raced, gendered, and classed expectations of that place. In contrast to the overall depiction of trans men's lives outside cities as unlivable, about a third of interviewees talked about men they knew who had moved from cities like San Francisco to small towns in supposedly dangerous parts of the country. In these accounts, the same lack of knowledge of transgender identities that allowed Alec to be read as a man in the Midwest gave trans men the opportunity to move to a town and blend in and just be a man.[22] Drew, a white man, explained this pattern when talking about men he knew who had transitioned before him when he lived in San Francisco:

> I was pretty good friends with this guy that transitioned like five years before. Then randomly he, well, most of them moved. A lot of the guys I knew back then moved to like seriously to like

small towns. Just really stealth-like in a trailer and just not be part of the queer community at all. I remember that happening and being like, "Whoa." It was a trip. I understand the concept a lot more now, but at the time I was like, really? You're just going to leave San Francisco and go live in like Arizona in a trailer? Okay. I understand what their journey was. They just didn't feel gay at all or part of the queer community. I still super feel part of the queer community because I've been part of it for so long. I can't imagine leaving it. It's part of the security blanket with all my friends. I can't imagine just going off and then not being a part of it.

Drew found a crucial sense of safety and belonging as a queer person in queer communities, which he thought would be unavailable in a small town. Yet he found that the further he went along in his transition, the more the notion of living in a small town appealed to him. When he talked about retirement, he said:

I wonder if I would just be one of those guys that would get a little cabin in fucking Wyoming or Montana and go fly fishing and retire and just live there and just be like a dude in town. I can see myself doing something like that. Even now, I think about moving to the suburbs, like if I want to get a house or something. I don't think I would be out to my neighbors at all. I would just be like this straight guy with my girlfriend living in like a freaking suburb.

Thus, while these "other" places were where many men mapped their fears, a number of those same men identified aspects of those places that made them safer as trans men. Suburban spaces perhaps offered not only an in-between place free of the threat of the violent rural redneck but also the opportunity to blend in as a regular guy. For men like Drew, there was an appeal to the idea of living out a more conventional life now that they appeared no different from cisgender men to their suburban neighbors. Ultimately, this movement enacts a fantasy of white normative masculinities, whether as a working-class rural man or a suburban middle-class man, at the same time that it might shore up their identity as men and a particular aspect of safety. For some trans men, the desire to blend in could also be an escape from identity itself. Certainly, these same fantasies operate for many transgender and cisgender men alike in urban centers when they seek to escape constraints of contemporary masculinities to the supposed relief of rural and even suburban idylls.[23]

Trans men's narratives of a lack of awareness of transgender possibilities construct suburban and nonmetropolitan spaces as less modern than the cities where there is both broad knowledge and some legal protection for transgender people. Yet these supposedly less modern spaces allow trans men to find safety in a place where they imagine they will solely be recognized as a man.[24] This life may only be available to men who can enact particular gender, racial, and sexual subjectivities. In any case, the safety of the city offers a bind for trans men who wish to leave transgender and queer identities and histories behind.

Midwest

Trans men living in the Midwest mapped out a more varied and detailed geography of safety than those in the West, though it was also racialized and classed. Felix, a white man, was happy living in urban Minnesota after stints living in a more conservative city. He had a possible move for work in his future, and I asked him if there were any places he would not want to live. He responded:

> I would avoid the South. I mean, basically we're looking at an electoral map, pretty much the red states. It's almost that cut-and-dried. Also, the sort of the Middle West. Yeah, the South and sort of the big square states I would probably avoid. I mean, maybe Colorado, but still I would feel much more comfortable on the coasts. That would be the only conceivable place I would look for jobs.

Like other people living in major cities, he believed large cities on the East and West Coasts to be most safe, yet his feeling of safety, like those of other midwestern trans men, showed a finer distinction. When I asked if there was anywhere he felt unsafe traveling, he laid out a more nuanced geography of safety:

> I would say the Iron Range. So west, closer to the Dakotas. Basically, the whole stretch of the side of the state I would avoid. Whereas starting with the Twin Cities and up to Duluth and then even farther, like, along the North Shore of Lake Superior, that is just a lovely little corridor of kind of, yeah, there's some kind of

aspects of rural life; you know, if it snows ten feet, you're not going anywhere for a couple of months. And you'll see the occasional incendiary yard sign. But for the most part because it's touristy, it's really open-minded, and I feel perfectly safe. I vacation there every year, feel perfectly safe. And then, even I traveled down south for work to a couple of the smaller towns in Rochester; even that's okay. I think it's like, when you get into sort of a little farther out and then like, in Michele Bachmann country, in St. Cloud. I would not go to St. Cloud. I'm just like, "Nah, I'm not going there."

The rural areas he actually traveled to, those geared toward tourism and educational and medical industries, felt safer than the area that had elected one of the most radically conservative politicians of the era. Thus, unlike most men in the West, Felix saw more nuance in rural places, even if he did not necessarily want to live in them. To some extent, rural gentrification based on tourism and particular industries, like the Mayo Clinic located in the Rochester area, made some rural areas friendlier, whereas the western side of the state was still not. Electoral politics stood proxy for the kinds of conservative and potentially violent people trans men expected to find in these places. Like Felix, the majority of men in the Midwest painted their broad map of safety using the language of "red states" and "blue states." These labels were particularly salient, as Barack Obama's reelection in 2012 occurred during the month-long trip when I conducted most of the Midwest interviews. This specific language was not necessary for trans men in the West, who depicted most places outside the West Coast as dangerous. At the same time, the language was too broad for men in the Southeast, who all lived in "red states."

Again, there were few clear incidents of spectacular violence against trans men that Midwest interviewees could name, beyond the story of Brandon Teena. When I inquired if they knew any trans people who had experienced physical violence or heightened harassment, the men turned to stories of violence against trans women of color, like the ones featured in TDOR. In fact, the one incident of spectacular violence against a trans person that Felix mentioned happened in the place where he felt most safe—his own neighborhood:

> Have you been up on the CeCe McDonald murder? That would be the biggest one that comes to recent memory. I think that some

of my friends have had one, of incidents of like vocal harassment, and that especially goes for the kind of genderqueer kids who are passing by a different bar on their way to a show or something. But nothing. As far as I can tell, aside from the CeCe McDonald thing, nothing violent. But that was a big deal. And I actually live like a few blocks from there. It's been interesting because we live in a very liberal neighborhood, and then this crazy thing happens in front of the grocery store that I go shop at. That was weird. I don't know if you know the story, but basically the guy [Dean Schmitz] and his friends started, basically initiated an attack on CeCe, and she stabbed him with a sewing scissors. And it turns out he had a giant swastika tattooed on his chest and stuff like that, which they admitted her history in court of having written bad checks, but they would not admit the evidence that he had a giant swastika tattooed on his chest.

From reports of the incident, the violence against McDonald was likely motivated by a combination of racism, transphobia, and homophobia. Felix said the incident made him feel "more wary" in his neighborhood for a time, but this diminished because the area he lived in was known to be safe for LGBT people. While Felix believed the attack was at least partially motivated by racism, his expression of fear also acted as a move to innocence, away from the privileges he gains as a white man, who also presents as straight and middle class, and the measure of safety it allows him.

Though there is a pervasive idea that individuals who will commit acts of spectacular violence are disproportionately found in rural places, home of the racist redneck, cases like CeCe McDonald's show those individuals are also in the major cities viewed as most safe for transgender people. John Howard, in his queer history of the South, argues that queer people in rural places use their local knowledge to avoid particularly violent or homophobic people.[25] Similarly, trans people living in rural places are more likely to know and avoid those people they perceive as dangerous, whereas urban trans people, like Felix or CeCe McDonald, may not know which of the strangers around them is likely to be violent. The politics reflected by the swastika hidden under Dean Schmitz's shirt might not be known in an urban space but would likely be common knowledge in a small rural community. There were no more reports of this kind of violence in rural places than in urban places across the interviews; rather, trans men's stories were similar across spaces in their lack of experience of physical violence overall.

The specter of violence limited where Felix felt safe to travel and live, which restricted his job prospects; however, as he would agree, through being recognized as a white middle-class man, he was not subject to scrutiny by the same people who attacked CeCe McDonald. The lack of surveillance allowed him to feel safe in a large city and maintain the belief that potential violence was somewhere outside it. The larger institution of the criminal justice system reaches across these spatial contexts. At the same time, the system is very much tied to the control of urban communities of color.[26] In fact, that system may be the ultimate perpetrator of violence against CeCe McDonald, who served nineteen months in a men's prison for defending herself against violence, and against many trans women of color who face particular and disproportionate brutalities in this system.[27] Felix, as a white middle-class man, is more likely to avoid both the scrutiny of the white supremacist who attacked McDonald and the apparatuses of the prison–industrial complex that punished McDonald for defending herself from attack. Again, though he truly felt this fear and an attendant lack of safety, the narrative also allowed him a claim to innocence in the interlocking structural inequalities at work in the situation.

Those living in rural places in the Midwest also plotted a more finely graded geography of safety, where particular rural spaces were safer than others. For example, Dominic, a white man, had recently moved nearby the large conservative rural town in the Midwest where he grew up. Other interviewees from Dominic's state characterized this section of the state as particularly unsafe for LGBT people. His experiences of homophobia growing up and attending a local college in the town gave weight to the assumptions of those living outside the area. He explained:

> When I was in high school—back in '03 is when I graduated—if people were gay, they didn't come out for sure, definitely in my high school. 'Cause I remember this one couple, this one girl who was kind of out, because she'd walk around with her, holding her girlfriend's hand, and that was the only one lesbian couple I knew of in my whole high school. It wasn't till years later where I found out through a couple friends of mine that people actually ended

up—or not ended up—but just came out. So, you don't really
hear too much about it, but it does exist. Does that make sense?
The large town is a kind of the more hush-hush type of place.
When I was a lesbian—and I'm with my girlfriend, I'd get looks,
for sure.

This climate made him fear reprisal if his current work were to find out he was transgender.

While this entire part of the state was seen as unsafe by trans men living in large cities elsewhere, Dominic now lived fifteen minutes away from his hometown in a smaller town that was a vacation destination for gays and lesbians from around the region.[28] This part of the state both confirmed and was contrary to the characterizations of safety and danger by trans men living elsewhere. Dominic's local knowledge allowed him to make more subtle distinctions in marking the places that were safe and the places that were not. He was afraid of people in the larger town knowing he was transgender, but he was able to cultivate a community of gay and lesbian people with whom he could be open in the smaller town.

Though rural midwestern trans men, like Dominic, saw more variation in the rural Midwest, they too characterized the South as particularly intolerant; only a small minority even allowed that some of the large cities, or more tolerant areas, such as the Raleigh/Durham/Chapel Hill area of North Carolina, might be safer. A few of the men went so far as to suggest the more intolerant midwestern places were actually somehow polluted with cultural values from the South. Brandon, a white man who lived in the suburbs of a midsized Michigan city, had a geography of safety that exemplified this pattern. When discussing what places he considered dangerous or where he would be less comfortable traveling, he named parts of particular midwestern states, rural areas, and the South. Prior to the interview, he had spent time working in a small town in another midwestern state he said was quite conservative. Brandon described his coworkers in the town as particularly homophobic, and the only gay man he knew there left due to harassment. Interestingly, while the town was in a clearly midwestern state, he connected the homophobic violence there to the South:

> I moved with my fiancée to there; [it was] very conservative. It's the middle of nowhere; it's BFE. I mean, it's Springfield-tucky;

you get all the inbred people from Kentucky come up. It's horribly conservative; it's gross.

He said that due to his fear he did not tell many people there he was transgender. Through using a crude generalization, he alluded to the image of the poor rural southern white, the redneck man, as the source of the conservatism and violence he feared. Thus, even though Brandon had a more nuanced spatial distribution of fear than that of men who lived in major cities, the idea of the South as a source of intolerance still permeated his understanding of danger.

Southeast

Men in the Southeast agreed the West and East Coasts were generally safer than the South; however, they identified and sometimes lived in the same kinds of tolerant areas that men in the West and Midwest described. These safer areas were usually major cities or liberal enclaves in college towns. For example, Bert, a white man, found a tremendous amount of support in the college town in North Carolina where he lived when he was raising money for chest reconstruction surgery:

> The community are so supportive, and my sense of what happened around my fundraiser was that people just really wanted to help. There was just a lot of love, and people were like, "Well, we just love you, and we want whatever you want," you know, "Here." . . . Maybe other areas aren't quite like that. I get the sense that they're not. Particularly like, you know, small towns in this state. I mean twenty miles from here, it's a different world.

Bert, like other men living in the areas of the Southeast they characterized as safer, marked out distance between where he lived and more dangerous nearby places.

The story of Alan, a white gay man living in urban Kentucky, fit the metronormative narrative of moving from a dangerous small town to a more accepting city, though he challenged the idea that all places in the Southeast are inherently dangerous.

> You'd think in a place like this where we're not exactly the most tolerant atmosphere, you'd think it would be more hoop jump-

ing [for medical and legal transition], but, no. This city is unique from the rest of the state in that we do that here and we're pretty understanding. If you tried to do that in, say, that small town a few hours away, you'd have an issue. This city is definitely unique, and a lot of people come here because they know they're gonna have a safe environment here. People flock here.

He went on to say he was one of the people who had flocked to the city from a small Appalachian town. Describing the area where he grew up, he said:

Awful. It's a small town in the backwater of the state. And just to give you an idea, we had evangelists who'd get on the radio on Sunday morning, and they would give you sermons about how homosexuals should kill themselves so they wouldn't be tempted to hurt children. I went to band camp, and we actually had someone that was outed during the camp, and we were all forced to line up while this kid was dragged bodily out of the camp and thrown out. He didn't do anything to anybody; they just found out he was gay. So not exactly the most tolerant environment. They have the hate down there quite a bit, so I was very, very happy to leave. I was terrified of myself being down there because if anybody even suspected, then, you know, something bad was gonna happen to me.

Alan felt as though he had to leave his small town for the more accepting city. He did appreciate certain aspects of small-town life, but he did not think he would have survived there as a gay or trans man.

Overall, interviewees mapped their fears spatially, relying on region and urban and rural distinctions to locate their fears of violence. No matter their own location, individual men tended to use their local knowledge to articulate a more detailed understanding of where was safer and less safe. Men who lived in the West tended to think everywhere outside coastal cities was unsafe, whereas men who lived in the Midwest and the Southeast made finer distinctions between and within regions. Overall, men across the three regions viewed the South and most rural places as less safe. While their sense of vulnerability as trans people heightened their fears, the intolerance they actually reported seeing was most often about homophobia and racism. The fears that trans men attach to particular spaces, whether realized or not, do not just exist inside their thoughts but also shape how they interact in those spaces.

RURAL CONTEXTS AND CONFORMITY

It is clear that trans men's geographies of safety influence how they think about where they want to live and the places they would consider traveling. In addition, other people might evaluate their masculine practices differently depending on the gender, racial, class, and sexual norms of a place. Men's fears of violence tied to those evaluations affected the masculinities they practiced and how they interacted in the places. These shifts in masculinities, both how men practiced them and how others evaluated them, occurred both where trans men felt safe and where they feared violence. In dangerous places, interviewees used shifting interactional practices to try to avoid violent victimization.

Rural spaces provide a particularly telling example of how the gendered, raced, classed, and sexualized features connected to place shaped both these shifting masculine practices and evaluations by others. Across the interviews, fear of homophobia, racism, and transphobia was higher in rural places than in most urban or suburban places. Yet instead of transphobic violence, for the most part interviewees reported experiencing or witnessing explicit evidence of homophobia, the attendant enforcement of normative masculinity, and racism in rural places.[29] Due to these fears and this knowledge of violence, men were more likely to conform to local expectations for gender and sexuality and, for white trans men, to participate at least passively in systems of racial domination when interacting in rural settings.

Again, Brandon Teena's story came up frequently and tied the men's fears to rural spaces, which made for a heightened fear of vulnerability to transgender-based violence overall. Holden, a white man living in suburban Wisconsin, described the difference in his fear when interacting with other men in the large college town where he lived versus interacting with white rural men nearby:

> I guess for me I would feel more safe in a group of college-town guys than in a group of redneck guys. Um, you know, like the whole Brandon Teena story . . . definitely that's like, it makes me uncomfortable. I guess because I feel like I don't fit the typical

male stereotype that's kind of in place in that type of culture. So yeah, so it makes me feel really uncomfortable, and if I were to be confronted or something, that would be a scary situation.

Holden believed that because his masculinity did not line up with the hypermasculinity of redneck men, he might face violence like Brandon Teena. Holden's narrative intimately connected the violence that Teena experienced to the violence of the controlling image of the redneck man—this was a fear of white heterosexual violence. Thus, to avoid potential violence, he avoided interacting with such men and modified his own behavior when he could not avoid them.

Because others recognized the majority of these men solely as men in most everyday situations, a fear of transgender violence was not usually at the forefront of their minds. Rather, it was not being properly masculine, being perceived as a gay man, or being marked as a person of color that triggered trans men's fears in most settings. For example, Jason, a white man living in suburban Ohio, found that as his sexuality and gender presentation changed he had new fears.

> Coming out as a lesbian and being able to hold my girlfriend's hand walking down the street never once was an issue, never, not once. When I began my transition and I was married to a woman, holding her hand obviously, we were every other straight couple on the planet. But once I transitioned and really started dating men is when that fear of [pause] "Am I gonna get my ass kicked for holding my husband's hand?" Really . . . that was something that scares the shit out of me. You know. Transition never. It didn't scare me. Being a gay man scares me.

When Jason was partnered with women—read as a lesbian when he was living as a woman and as straight when living as a man—he was not afraid. But once partnered with men as a man, he was afraid. Thus, the fear of homophobia, which was even more dangerous because being a gay man is often considered an affront to normative masculinity, was particularly heightened for Jason. In general, there is greater tolerance for the female masculinity associated with lesbians than the effeminacy associated with gay men in rural places.[30] Although this may be true of urban places as well, it reflects the more flexible gender expectations for women in rural places.

While Jason had a heightened fear of homophobic violence in rural spaces, his ability to be read by others as a cisgender straight man—and particularly as a white man—offered him access to the rural space and a relative sense of safety. Jason went on to say that although fears of homophobic violence were often present in the back of his mind across spatial contexts, he and his husband had not experienced any problems in their midsized Ohio city with a sizeable gay population. When I asked if there was anywhere he would feel less safe holding hands with his husband, he described the very small town in another Midwest state where his family lived and said, "Never, never, never, never, never, never . . . no, never in a million years" would he hold his husband's hand there. In the small town, he feared physical violence against himself and his husband as well as problems for his family in the community. Public affection between gay men was certainly not "in place" in the rural space. Jason's heightened awareness of the potential for transgender violence in rural settings sharpened his fear of homophobic violence in the town, even though no one outside his family knew he was transgender.

Again, trans men living in rural areas, especially in the Southeast, mapped their fears of social violence, like transphobia, racism, and homophobia, in more specific terms than men who saw everywhere outside Chicago or San Francisco as unsafe. According to their stories, this mapping and the shifting behavior that went along with it were crucial for their survival. For example, Jack, a white man living in rural Tennessee, was early in his physical transition, and he had fears about transphobic violence because he worried he was not recognized reliably as a man, although others read him as a man in most situations. He said:

> I don't wanna be a freak. Because, again, they're not as accepting here. . . . You know, of cross dressers and drag queens or whatever. Coming from the Albuquerque area, you see that all the time. . . . But, here? You'll get shot and thrown in a holler.

I asked if that danger was true for the whole area, and he replied:

> I think it's a little bit more accepting in the city. I think the lesbian, gay, transgender, [but] as you get further into rural, it's definitely

not. I mean you still see KKK signs. . . . Uh, no, they don't take kindly to Hispanics or blacks or any of that.

Since Jack was not secure in the recognition as a man that made other men feel safer in rural settings, he had heightened levels of fear. This fear made it particularly important to Jack to fit in and not be seen as a "freak."

Yet what did it mean to be a "freak" and not to fit in these rural spaces? Like several other interviewees, Jack went from talking about potential violence for sexual or gender transgression to discussion of racist violence against people of color. This suggests a conflation in these narratives of different forms of bigotry. In some senses, even white respondents, who were quite unlikely to experience racist violence, feared people they thought were racist because they thought individual racist attitudes were likely to be accompanied by transphobic, sexist, and homophobic attitudes. These combined fears encouraged men to be complicit in some forms of intolerance in order to protect themselves from the bigotries that could be directed at them. Again, these fears are sincerely felt, but when fear narratives work to center white men's own marginality in the face of racism, they are also moves to innocence from complicity in white supremacy. Nearly all of the men I interviewed who lived in rural places were white and described particularly high levels of racism in their rural communities. Though these fears of transphobic violence were very present in Jack's mind, like other white working-class rural trans men in this study, he gained acceptance in the community where he lived through being read as a white straight man doing masculinities in line with rural community ideals. In other words, these men were "in place" due to their apparent race, masculinities, sexuality, and class in rural spaces. Fitting in, in this sense, is not just being seen as "normal" but rather conforming to the dominant gendered and racialized ideals of the local community and even, at times, leaving the racism of other whites unchallenged.

Conforming to these local ideals of gender, sexuality, and race was not something an individual could necessarily control. Gabriel, a multiracial man living in a Deep South suburb, echoed the sentiment about the strong racial divisions of rural communities. When I asked him about his sense of safety when he would visit his black family members in a rural southeastern community, Gabriel said:

> Most of my concerns when traveling through that area is making it from pocket to pocket of black communities. I get very uncomfortable in a racial sense. I'm not actually too concerned with being perceived as queer, 'cause that usually isn't the first thing that comes to mind in those areas. At this point I'd have to be like on top of a dude making out for them to notice that there was something queer about it. So, that usually isn't the first thing. I'd be more concerned about the white communities in those areas. My family is from that area, but there that line between black and white is way broad, like it's a thick, thick line that isn't often crossed.

Even though he had relationships with people in that area, those prior relationships would not break the line of white supremacy. He felt that because he could fairly easily shape stranger's perceptions of him as a heterosexual cisgender man, he did not worry about transphobic and homophobic violence among strangers—only racist violence. He could escape this feared racial violence only by avoiding predominately white rural spaces. Notably, Gabriel did not mention the same strong fears of transphobic or homophobic violence that were so prominent in white men's narratives of safety and space.

Sean, a white man living in the rural upper Midwest, reiterated the role of whiteness in surviving and claiming belonging for people living in predominately white rural communities, particularly since race was understood here as a fixed visible marker of difference:

> If you're of another race, you're not going to fit in here. The people that have money and power are white around here, and if you can't figure out how to get in with that, you're not going to get anywhere. I mean, I don't feel like I have a lot in common with most people in this town, but I feel like I can pass. I do what I can with that, but I realize that it's a gift I've been given. Race makes a huge difference because it's so obvious that you're an outsider.

Unlike men of color, white trans men can find a measure of acceptance and space from transphobic violence in rural communities by taking part in systems of racial subordination and division. As Andrea Smith explains, it is common for marginalized people to gain a little space from their own oppression through actively or passively taking part in other systems of domination.[31] This clearly illustrates how even when men acknowledge their white privilege and their distaste for racism, their narratives of transphobic fear become a move to innocence because they feel they cannot challenge the racism of other whites.

There was an underlying assumption in many of these narratives of rural fear and rural life that it was crucial to protect oneself by avoiding rural places or at least engaging in more conforming behavior when one was there. Further, avoiding victimization was central to being a regular guy and achieving a Goldilocks masculinity. As in the earlier discussion of Brandon Teena, this had the effect of blaming victims of violence and was a way to narrate innocence and respectability for trans men who could or did conform to these expectations. While these strategies might have offered some protection, taken as a whole this projection of rural vulnerability encourages men to conform to local normative masculine ideals and to avoid intervening or challenging these and other inequalities. At the same time, these narratives of rural danger reproduce the image of rural spaces as backward, premodern, and in need of a civilizing force. By both avoiding victimization and framing others as violent, some trans men protected their safety, established their innocence, and maintained a Goldilocks masculinity.

By examining fears and experiences of violence as they are mapped onto rural spaces, we see how fears of transphobic, homophobic, and racist violence act as powerful forms of social control in this particular spatial context. Rural contexts are one site where these processes transpire, but these same dynamics happen across a range of specific contexts and scales. It appears that these fears, whether realistic or not, encourage conformity to local expectations of sexuality and gender, which is a form of complacency and even participation in systems of social domination over others—all of which depends on the social location of the man and how others recognize him in the given place. Thus, contexts seen as more inherently dangerous are more likely to produce social control and to reproduce systems of domination through both everyday social interactions and narrative moves to innocence.

CONCLUSION

Narratives of trans vulnerability to violence, more than experiences of physical violence, produced heightened fears for trans men. They mapped their fears not just on certain neighborhoods but drew on their geographic imaginaries of region and of urban, rural, and suburban spaces. These spatially based fears centered on classed and racialized controlling masculine images, like the thug and the redneck, in a way that reproduced the innocence of other gendered, racialized, and classed men. Both the narratives about feared perpetrators, like the redneck, and victims, like Brandon Teena, reproduce a notion of respectability and proper masculinity for some men through social distance from those who commit violence and those who are victimized. These moves to innocence and attempts to avoid experiencing violence also lead to conforming masculine practices in interactions and complicity with systems of domination, such as white supremacy. Rural spaces and the image of violent hypermasculine rednecks in them were particularly associated with danger in trans men's narratives and thus elicited strong pressures for conformity in everyday interactions. Therefore, fears of spectacular violence, not just experiences of violence, operate as disciplinary mechanisms that keep existing social categories in place.

These findings suggest our understandings of men's fears and other gendered fears are inadequate unless they are understood through an analysis of race, sexuality, class, region, and other aspects of difference. We could not comprehend Ethan's experience, described at the outset of the chapter, of being frequently stopped by the police or of white women seeing him as threatening without an analysis of how race, class, and masculinity, embodied in the thug ideal, shape how others see him as dangerous in urban space. At the same time, we cannot understand Sean's lessened fear in rural spaces without understanding how whiteness and rural working-class masculinities make him "in place" in his rural area.

Discourses of vulnerability based on fears of spectacular violence in public places, even when not born out in experience, encourage conformity in everyday interactions and lead to the reproduction of systems of social domination based on gender, race, and sexuality. Even if fears are based on statistically unlikely events, pervasive narratives of fear of extreme violence are heightened by the cumulative effect of other experiences of violence, such as the many incidents of violence interviewees reported in medical and other institutional contexts. These interactional moves certainly reproduce masculine conformity and complicity with white supremacy, as well as a form of victim blaming through notions of respectability, but they simultaneously offer some protection for individuals as they deploy them. It is unclear if white, normatively masculine, straight, class-privileged trans men would face more frequent violence if they did not engage in conforming practices. The trans men with the most nonconforming gender presentations did report higher incidences of physical violence, and black trans men reported more severe discrimination and violence from police. Thus, there is likely a penalty for straying from normative masculinities. All of this still leaves the question of the broad effects of this ubiquitous understanding of transgender vulnerability. What are the implications of these displays of vulnerability and innocence, as well as fear and violence, for political efforts to better the lives of transgender people?

One likely outcome of trans men's fears is an increased support for politics and policy that actually perpetuate structural and state violence against some of the most marginalized trans people. Scholars such as Kay Whitlock, Dean Spade, and Christina Hanhardt agree that LGBT antiviolence work often relies on a narrow vision of law-and-order policy and a politics of respectability, which further endangers LGBT people who are poor and people of color.[32] Law-and-order policy uses a framework that attributes violence primarily to individual actions and neglects structural sources of violence and inequality. This limited view of violence produces partial and possibly ineffective solutions to these social problems. The effects of the production of fear and moves to innocence that come from the frequent recitation of stories like Brandon Teena's and, sometimes overstated, statistics of violence against transgender people are part of an overall pattern of highlighting trans vulnerability to extreme acts of violence and premature death.[33] It is important to put a spotlight on these heinous acts of violence, but we must simultaneously understand that one of the effects is to increase feelings of hopelessness and despair for young people, which could possibly increase their risk of suicide.[34] While these discourses of vulnerability help draw attention to real problems and act as rallying cries for action, other kinds of effects hinder actually addressing the violence. Events like TDOR serve an important purpose, such that those who no longer have a voice are not forgotten. At the same time, a proliferation of images and understandings of transgender people's potentials for life in addition to their vulnerabilities might be more effective at addressing the needs of transgender people.[35]

There are elements of resistance even in men's stories of fear. One potential avenue for change is trans men and cisgender men pivoting away from narratives of vulnerability and moves to innocence. As a start, this resistance means being careful about furthering narratives of vulnerability that reproduce vulnerable subjecthood and developing better perspective on the distribution of risk and security intertwined with various social locations. Jackie Wang suggests that to truly end racial violence we must reject "a politics of innocence that reproduces the 'good,' compliant citizen." This approach shifts focus away from evaluations of the moral character of individual victims or perpetrators as well as discourses that mark some individuals as "innocent," undeserving victims, all of which in turn constructs some racialized and classed people as criminals or degenerates who deserve violence.[36] This also suggests focusing on an expansive coalitional politics. To go back to Brandon Teena, the frequent recitations of his tragic death often leave out or minimize the other victims killed that night, including Phillip Devine, a black man who was visiting the area and had been dating Teena's friend. C. Riley Snorton recovers a new life for Devine, but not to create another martyr like Teena. Instead, Snorton suggests that in addition to efforts like TDOR the rubric of Black Lives Matter and, specifically, Black Trans Lives Matter holds potent possibilities for reimagining a past and bringing forth a future where those lives actually matter.[37]

The next chapter continues the analysis of spatially produced violence by focusing on how particular institutions, public bathrooms and medical settings, promote fear, violence, and the perpetuation of social inequality. The interactional rules and structures of these institutional spaces generate further narratives of fear for trans men but also more frequent experiences of violence.

5
Institutional Contexts of Violence
HETEROSEXISM AND CISSEXISM IN EVERYDAY SPACES

Public bathrooms and medical settings, such as hospitals, clinics, exam rooms, and therapist's offices, are key sites through which modern techniques of power form and control populations through ideas of sanitation and public health. As trans men's narratives illustrate, these institutions are also important spaces where we see Michel Foucault's idea of disciplinary power working through the enforcement of norms.[1] This enforcement comes both from others, through the disciplining practices of the people with whom trans men interact, and from themselves, when they engage in self-discipline. Whether trans men conform to these norms or resist them, the norms are embedded in interaction. Gender and sexuality and, to varying extents, class, race, and ability are particularly salient for trans men in these institutional spaces because they are largely structured around these social categories. Trans men's experiences in these institutions illustrate what Petra Doan refers to as the "tyranny of gendered spaces," and this chapter expands on this idea to illustrate the multiple intersecting effects of these two particular contexts.[2]

I continue examining fear and violence in trans men's lives through an analysis of the ways that public bathrooms and medical settings provoke fears and actual experiences of violence. Building on the analysis of both spatially based fears and experiences of violence in the production of inequality, this chapter centers on understanding how particular features of institutions promote specific patterns of social domination. I use public bathrooms and medical settings as case studies because they are the institutional spaces where trans men reported the most heightened fears and actual experiences of violence. First, I use an analysis of trans men's accounts of fear and violence in public gender-segregated bathrooms to show how the bathroom is a site of the production of heterosexism and gender conformity. Next, I turn to analysis of trans men's experiences of violence in medical contexts to illustrate how the authority of physicians and other medical personnel in healthcare settings reproduce cissexism and enforce gender conformity. While these patterns of domination are created in each institutional context, their effects likely reverberate across individuals' lives by reinforcing sexist, heterosexist, and ableist norms, as well as contributing to the narratives of fear and innocence that make for complicity in larger structures of violence.

These institutional settings are what I call "amplified sites" of gender and sexuality, as well as ability, race, class, and other dimensions of difference and domination. Amplified sites are spaces structured such that processes of categorization for gender, sexuality, and race, as well as the norms and social actions that reinforce them, play out in heightened ways when people interact in them. The effects move beyond these contexts and then reverberate or ripple across our social lives, whether through their effects on individuals and groups or broader beliefs and ideologies. In other words, they are nodes or sites where these processes are reinforced, created, and incubated. However, these effects do not just stay in those spaces, because they have consequences when people move out of them, from the way individuals move their bodies in interaction to the larger truths we understand about differences of gender, race, and sexuality. Through these two case studies, it becomes clear that the structural arrangements of the spaces foster the production of fear and violence in interaction. These sites are politically important because transforming the underlying organization of these institutions is key to combatting social inequality.

BATHROOMS

On the night of July 28, 2001, Willie Houston, his fiancée Nedra Jones, and another couple enjoyed a night on a riverboat cruise in Nashville, Tennessee, to celebrate Houston and Jones's recent engagement. A series of mundane actions that conflicted with the gender and sexual rules of the public restroom turned a celebration of the pinnacle of heterosexuality into a tragedy of homophobic violence. This incident illustrates how a cisgender person, Willie Houston, came to be memorialized on Transgender Day of Remembrance.[3]

At the end of the evening cruise, Houston and his party stopped to use the restroom before disembarking from the boat. Jones handed her purse to Houston to hold as she headed to the women's room. Melvin Holt, Houston's friend who was visually impaired, also needed to use the bathroom. Houston escorted his friend to the men's room while still holding his fiancée's purse. In the bathroom, Houston and Holt encountered Lewis Davidson III and a friend who started harassing Houston with homophobic remarks. Apparently, Houston's mild-mannered effort to establish his heterosexuality with the protest that his "honey," a woman, was right outside could not override the presence of the purse and his helping another man. Davidson and his anti-gay remarks followed Houston outside the bathroom, and the verbal altercation continued to the Opry Mills parking lot where Davidson fatally shot Houston. As one news account described:

> Willie Houston was shot with his hands in the air, raising his palms in front of his chest and reasoning with the gunman: "Man, we had a good time, and I'm just ready to go home and go to bed."[4]

Though Willie Houston was both cisgender and heterosexual, the root of the events that led to his death was homophobia connected to gender transgression. What role might the interactional rules of the men's bathroom have had in this tragic event? Why in this institutional context might the presence of a purse and the feminized act of caring for another man lead to murder?

Up until that night, visits to public bathrooms had probably been an unremarkable feature of Willie Houston's everyday life. For most cisgender, heterosexual, able-bodied people, their use of public restrooms becomes a topic of conversation only when one is commenting on the availability or cleanliness of a particular bathroom. Yet gender-segregated public bathrooms are a common topic in transgender writing and activism because gender and sexuality are so heightened in these spaces.[5] Unknowingly, Houston had entered a volatile site of contestation where fears and anxieties about gender, heterosexism, and sex play out.

The 2010s have seen much public controversy about trans people's access to bathrooms in the United States. However, this is not the first era when contests over public bathrooms have emerged in the public sphere. Bathroom fears have been used to promote conservative social agendas and maintain the racial and gender status quo in the United States since at least the 1940s. In the post–World War II era, public bathrooms were a visible site of racial segregation. In the face of the civil rights movement, white segregationists argued that racially mixed bathroom facilities would endanger white women through contracting diseases from black women. In the 1970s, as feminists worked to pass the Equal Rights Amendment, strikingly similar language to what we have seen in the past few years was used by conservative groups to stoke fears that the ERA would endanger women by outlawing gender-segregated bathrooms.[6] All of these fears are, of course, unfounded, but as Laurel Westbrook and Kristen Schilt illustrate, fears and policy decisions about spaces like gender-segregated public bathrooms are tied to larger cultural anxieties about the maintenance of gender and sexual difference.[7] To understand why this institutional context is prominent in the lives of trans people, I give a brief overview of research on public restrooms and then analyze their role in trans men's fears and reported experiences of violence in those spaces.

Public Toilets

Public gender-segregated bathrooms are an invention of the eighteenth century linked to urbanization, sanitary reform, and a separate spheres ideology.[8] Segregation in public facilities mirrored the eighteenth- and nineteenth-century white middle-class ideal that men and women should inhabit different domains of daily life. On the surface, public bathrooms are an effort at maintaining public health and hygiene, but on an institutional level, they have their own interactional rules and norms.[9] Behaviors in the public areas of the bathroom largely resemble those in other public spaces, except for what David Inglis refers to as "fecal habitus."[10] This habitus denotes both designations about what is clean and what is dirty and the embodied sets of behaviors around defecation and bathrooms. The rules of fecal habitus tend to be more restrictive for heterosexual men than for women and nonheterosexual men.[11]

In addition to their hygienic and interactional functions, public toilets are also a "tool for keeping existing social categories in place."[12] According to Jacques Lacan, public restrooms are a site of "urinary segregation," in that the gender-segregated nature serves as an everyday reinforcement of gender difference.[13] Erving Goffman wrote in the late 1970s, "The functioning of gender-differentiated organs is involved, but there is nothing in this functioning that biologically recommends segregation; that arrangement is totally a cultural matter.... Toilet segregation is presented as a natural consequence of difference ... when it is rather a means of honoring, if not producing, this difference."[14] This marking of difference is particularly important, as few areas of public life are gender-segregated for men and women in the current era. The retreat into segregated spaces reinforces difference periodically during everyday life.[15] Sheila Cavanagh builds on this idea further by finding that public bathrooms reinforce sexuality, race, and class as well as gender. The modern public restroom is particularly a place of gender and sexual surveillance where "gaps between the perceived sex of the body, gender identity, and the insignia on the toilet doors are subject to inquiry. The space is designed to authorize an invasive and persecutory gaze. Mirrors, fluorescent lighting, and metallic surfaces all invite voyeuristic attention."[16] Kyla Bender-Baird extends this to note these segregated bathrooms are a "technology of disciplinary power" that reinforces a gender binary.[17]

The surveillance function of public bathrooms is evident in the proliferation of accounts of what Jack Halberstam calls "the bathroom problem,"[18] meaning the problem of harassment and violence against gender-nonconforming and transgender people when using public bathrooms. In a range of settings, such as work, school, and public spaces, transgender and gender-nonconforming people report being denied access to safe and appropriate bathrooms through both institutional policy and individual harassment.[19] The continuing relevance of bathrooms as a key site of social control is clear in recent attempts by conservatives in a number of U.S. states to restrict transgender people's access to bathrooms.[20] HB2, a bill passed by the North Carolina legislature in 2016, required transgender people to use the restroom that matched the sex listed on their birth certificate, regardless of their appearance and identity. Along with religious freedom laws, the conservative activism represented by these bills is a clear reaction to increasing liberal equality gains for LGBT people. The denial of access has a variety of negative psychological and physical consequences for transgender and gender-nonconforming people, including avoiding public space altogether or planning out routes and destinations based on the availability of accessible bathrooms.[21]

Public bathrooms are an important site where transgender and disability politics intersect. Access to bathrooms is a central issue in both transgender and disability justice movements because being unable to take care of toilet needs when out in public can limit access to public space in general.[22] In fact, disability can mark particular bodies as already gender and sexually nonconforming and the construction of public bathrooms for only a narrow range of bodies marks other bodies as disabled and nonconforming.[23] For example, narrow stall doors in multiuser bathrooms disable wheelchair users, whose chairs might not fit the entrance. On the other hand, the single-user bathrooms often marked for disabled people and, frequently, used by transgender and gender-nonconforming people provide crucial access at the same time that they suggest bodies marked as disabled and, thus, queer should be kept away from normative bodies.[24] Thus, the use of public bathrooms is central to disability and transgender movements and to the people who live at the intersections of these subjectivities.

I focus primarily on public gender-segregated multiuser bathrooms, where interviewees interacted mostly with strangers. By public I mean bathrooms outside private homes and readily used by multiple people as they move through their everyday lives. These bathrooms might be in privately owned spaces, such as a retail store or a restaurant, or they might be public accommodations, like in a public park or an airport, but they all offer a space for what Harry Molotch calls "doing the private in public." In this sense, public bathrooms not only offer both physical and psychological relief for those who can access them—and thus have larger access to public space—but also produce the vulnerability and anxiety that comes from exposing one's body and its most private functions with perhaps only a stall door for separation. By focusing on trans men's accounts of interactions with strangers in bathrooms, we learn how, in these amplified sites of gender and sexuality, sex categorization shapes the larger interactional rules of spaces that are so crucial for accessing public space in everyday life.

More than two-thirds of the sixty-six trans men I interviewed mentioned the institutional context of the gender-segregated public bathroom as a source of fear. Across these accounts, interviewees had very different fears of and experiences in the public bathrooms marked for men and those marked for women, and there was a disjuncture between trans men's fears and actual experiences in public bathrooms. They feared harassment and the possibility of being perceived as threatening in women's bathrooms, and they did experience harassment there. Conversely, though they feared violence in men's rooms, they actually reported very few experiences of violence in that space. However, these fears of violence in men's public restrooms and locker rooms encouraged a general adherence to the homophobic rules of men's restrooms. Both these fears and experiences of violence are powerful forms of social control that reinforce domination and subordination in particular regard to gender and sexuality in the institutional context of the bathroom. Women's bathrooms are a place of gender policing that punishes nonconformity, whereas men's bathrooms are a site of reestablishing heterosexism and masculinity throughout daily life. Over time, these rules become embodied and like second nature, which shows how the enactment of systems of domination are imbued in the seemingly banal rituals and actions of everyday life.

Managing Bathroom Fears

Interviewees most feared gender-segregated public bathrooms when they were early in their transition or being read as between genders. They feared they would no longer fit in in the women's room but would not be accepted in the men's either. Josh, a white man living in rural Northern California, who did not think he was recognized reliably as a man early in transition, explained:

> If I can help it, I don't use bathrooms, public bathrooms. Because I don't want to get hassled in the women's bathroom, yet I don't want to get beat up in a guys' bathroom.

Due to this potential for violence, trans men like Josh had to decide whether they could risk accessing one space or the other or whether they should avoid using bathrooms altogether.

Early in transition, trans men often risked harassment in women's bathrooms, a space that reinforced gender conformity through punishing nonconformity, if they could not avoid bathrooms altogether. In fact, a number of the interviewees had experienced years of harassment in women's bathrooms, some long before they even thought of transitioning. This harassment occurred because others read them as men or because they did not conform to expectations of how women should look. James, a white man living in urban California, was fearful of using men's bathrooms, but when I asked if he ever had any bad experiences, he said:

> The only problems I've ever had is just when I go into the women's bathroom, you know. . . . And the first incidence was over ten years ago, actually, where the police came and they were surrounding the bathroom, and they were like, "What are you doing in here?"

James's story illustrates that this harassment by other bathroom users, bystanders, workers, and even the police stems from others believing they, or at least their gender nonconformity, did not belong in that space. Sam, a Latinx man in urban California, said, "I remember being kicked out of the [women's] bathroom, too, and that was before I transitioned." In many ways, the experiences of trans men prior to and early in transition mirror Kath Browne's findings regarding the gender policing, or genderism, that women who were often mistaken for men experienced when accessing public bathrooms.[25]

The violence trans men experienced in women's bathroom effectively punished gender nonconformity, regardless of whether the harassers read interviewees as men or as gender-nonconforming women. Trans men's fears that stemmed from repeatedly experiencing this harassment were heightened in rural areas. For Finn, a white man living in urban Minnesota, finding a bathroom that felt safer was a constant worry when he presented as a butch woman or early in his transition, especially in rural places:

> I was very fearful any time [using the bathroom]. I would just not go to the bathroom. I mean, I'm sure this is a story you hear all the time, but you plan your whole day around when you can use a bathroom, and it's all about, "Where are there unisex bathrooms? Where can I safely pee? When can I make a stop at home so that I don't have to use one if I can't find a unisex bathroom?" And that's probably the biggest danger that I always felt in bumble-fuck Wisconsin was this, "Can I use the bathroom safely?"

The consequences of recognition and misrecognition became fraught in the gender-segregated context of the bathroom as opposed to nonsegregated settings. It is also likely his whiteness made him less of a threat. Jack, a white man living in rural Appalachia, was particularly worried using segregated bathrooms when driving around rural areas all day as part of his job because his chest did not conform to normative standards for men, even if the rest of his appearance did:

> I was afraid to go into the men's room, 'cause I didn't want the shit kicked out of me. But, literally, every time I go into the women's bathroom, I'm getting, "Aah! There's a man in here." Okay, so then you hold it, you know, hit a dumpster with a napkin. I still have bathroom phobia because I still have breasts.

This fear did not stop Jack from living and traveling in rural spaces in general, but his gender nonconformity in the gender-segregated spaces of the public bathroom made for potentially frightening consequences for gender recognition or misrecognition. As with Finn and Jack, avoiding public bathrooms in order to prevent harassment and other forms of violence was common among interviewees. Being unable to comfortably use public bathrooms led to less access to public space, emotional and psychological stress, and potential health issues, such as dehydration and urinary system problems from holding it.[26]

Disability and particular medical conditions could make it even more difficult to find accessible bathrooms and also to avoid using public bathrooms. For instance, foregoing bathrooms altogether was not an option for an interviewee whose diabetes made it a particularly urgent issue to use public bathrooms frequently. Thus, the punishment of gender nonconformity was both potentially disabling, by causing health issues, and exacerbated by certain disabilities. Whether it was their general appearance, the shape of their body, or a disability, trans men were punished for their nonconformity through harassment and the threat of more violence from others in the bathroom.

Though interviewees reported problems across rural, urban, and suburban spaces when trying to access women's bathrooms, they often invoked racialized and classed notions of masculinity when they imagined the consequences might be worse in rural places and the South. Trans men worried both rednecks and regular guys would use violence to protect threatened women in the bathroom, since protection was a core component of these ideal types and a legitimated expression of aggression. Yet in some instances, such as traveling through airports in the South, it was difficult to avoid using a gender-segregated bathroom. This made for tough choices for trans men who did not feel like they were reliably recognized as men. Andrew, who lived in suburban Tennessee, described his decision process for which bathroom to use when traveling while presenting as a man:

> About half the time, I'll go into the men's bathroom, and half the time I'll go in the women's. And I think it's a decision that I don't know until I get up there and walk through the door. Predominantly, what keeps me from going into the men's bathroom is where I am. And I think to myself, "You know if somebody's gonna look at me sideways and wonder what I'm doing in the bathroom." I would rather get "caught" in the women's bathroom than I would in the men's. Because I can prove that I'm supposed to be in the female bathroom. You know I've got the ID for that. I don't have the ID for the other. And I don't want to get caught in, you know, Georgia with Bubba in the bathroom [*laughter*].

Invoking the controlling image of the redneck is shorthand for Andrew's spatially based fear and also reinforces the image of the classed, racialized violent hypermasculinity inherent to this controlling image.

Further, Andrew's story also illustrates how whiteness and citizenship can act to reduce fear of violence. Having government-issued identification provided Andrew with legally based gender recognition when his recognition in interaction was uncertain. This same proof would not necessarily be available to trans men who were undocumented immigrants. This demonstrates the importance of this kind of legal recognition in situations where official proof that they belong is crucial. In addition, men of color, who may have identification that matches the bathroom they are trying to use, may be concerned that any interaction with institutional authorities, for instance the police, might be more dangerous for them. It is likely that race, gender, and sexuality are intertwined in these bathroom experiences, as shown by David Eng and Alice Hom's analysis of a Korean American dyke's interactions with white women in a women's restroom.[27] The white women believed the Korean American woman was in the wrong bathroom and attributed this to an inability to read English. Thus, race, gender, ability, and sexuality are all at play in these spaces, even if gender is often the most salient.

Trans men's accounts make it clear that gender nonconformity, intertwined with race, sexuality, and ability, is strictly policed in most women's bathrooms. For many interviewees, this frequent harassment was a sign that they did not fit in the space and that they must use the men's room, even with their fear of physical violence in that space. The potential of using men's restrooms offered the possibility of relief from harassment in the women's.

Going by the Rules

The men's public bathroom is a major site of trans men's fear and anxiety because it is the gender-segregated space they encounter most frequently in their everyday lives and they have had very little experience with the interactional rules of that space before transition. When interviewees first started regularly using men's public bathrooms, their fears were heightened. For most trans men like Henry, a white man in suburban Indiana, learning the rules of the men's bathroom was an important part of facing this fear:

> You have to learn bathroom etiquette. Men don't talk in bathrooms. The ladies' room is a social gathering place. They'll talk about everything. Men don't. They go in; they do their thing; they get out. You don't look at 'em if you don't absolutely have to, you know?

As has been noted by Halberstam and others, these rules of most men's public bathrooms are based on maintaining heterosexuality.[28] In contrast to women's restrooms, the general rules of men's bathrooms suggest, as Henry said, there should be little conversation or eye contact and certainly no looking at other bodies. Men should also grant each other plenty of physical space to avoid contact. The heightened worry about transphobic violence in these spaces is linked to not properly performing normative gender as it reflects ideas about sexual nonconformity. The concern is that by breaking the rules one might be read as a gay man or sexually deviant and then physically assaulted. Only amid this conflict based on sexuality did trans men worry they might experience further violence due to being transgender.

The possibility of violence made it feel particularly important for trans men to follow the homophobic rules of men's restrooms. Andrew, a white man who was living in suburban Tennessee, described his fears early on when he visited a busy public bathroom on a trip to Chicago:

> I remember standing in line waiting for the stall, because I have to go in the stall. The urinals are over here to my right; the sinks are back over here behind my left shoulder. There were men in there everywhere, and I remember there was some teenage kid standing over at the urinal, and I was standing in line staring straight ahead thinking to myself, "Don't look at that kid. Don't look at that kid. Don't look at that kid." Because I thought if I look at him and I get caught looking at him, somebody's gonna think I'm a pervert or a weirdo. "What are you starin' at this young kid for? He's using the bathroom." And I just remember standing stock still staring straight ahead like I was watching paint dry waiting for my turn.

This example illustrates the tension that stems from the fear of violating the rules by appearing to be gay or sexually deviant. Like other men, learning the rules of the bathroom offered some protection for Andrew in general, and he began to feel more comfortable as he became more accustomed to following those rules. He continued:

> If I go into the men's bathroom, 99 percent of the time nobody's gonna look at me one way or the other. Why? Because they're probably not gay, you know? And I don't mean to be, you know, stereotypical, but the idea is that if a guy is lookin' at you in the bathroom, then he's probably wanting something more.

Thus, Andrew internalized not just the rules themselves but the sexual logic behind the rules—that a stray glance signaled homoerotic desire. Whether internalizing this homophobic reasoning or not, trans men counted on it to allow them to use the restroom in peace. They were able to access the space by following the rules and making sure they were not perceived as gay. Thus, the rules of the space reinforced compulsory heterosexuality.[29] While men's public bathrooms can be homoerotic spaces, none of the interviewees mentioned this.[30] For trans men, recognition by others as men, through appropriate behavior that marked them as properly heterosexual, allowed them to use these gender-segregated spaces without violence. Following the rules was a further way to distance themselves from the controlling image of the faggy man, even if it was also a strategy to protect themselves from violence.

As the men confronted their fears of men's public bathrooms and had few negative experiences, using the men's restroom became more routine, and fears faded. Most men reported their fears in bathrooms significantly diminished as they were further in their transition. In fact, Wesley, a white man living in a midsized city near the Appalachian region, had become so comfortable in the men's bathroom that he would purposely take a long time in the stall to get a break from work. For Wesley the bathroom turned from a place of fear to one of comfort as his body and actions had become habituated to the gendered space.

Changing in the Locker Room

Interviewees were often especially fearful of gender-segregated settings where one's full body was potentially exposed, such as a locker room. However, men managed their fear by following the rules, learning to adjust their routines, protecting sensitive bodily areas, and even reframing parts of their bodies as authentically male. Jacob, a white man living in urban Minnesota, described his fears using the men's locker room:

> I used to have that feeling when I walked in there. I'm like, "I don't have a penis. Anybody could figure out something." And I actually figured out a way to take a shower. And so, I would go in there, shower and come out, and they wouldn't know. But I was terrified. I'm like, "Somebody easily could figure this out." So yeah, I feel more scared in the locker room than I do anywhere.

By choreographing his movements, such as turning his body at particular angles, he was able to protect parts of his body from view and thus manage his fear.

Over time, interviewees embodied the rules of the space and became accustomed to masking body parts that might mark them as outsiders in the space. The experience of Woody, a white man living in urban California, exemplifies this pattern:

> I mean, I get changed in a locker room full of guys every single day.... And the great thing about sexism and homophobia is that guys do not check each other out in locker rooms, unless you go to like the big gym in the gay neighborhood, where they'll

definitely check you out. But, when it's a bunch of straight guys, they're not checking each other out, because they're afraid that someone's gonna think that they're gay. And if there's a gay guy there, he is definitely not checking anybody out, 'cause he's afraid that you're gonna know that he's gay. So it's like I turn around. All they're pretty much seeing is my butt, but I'm not as like freaked out about it as I used to be. Like now, I'm just kind of like, "Whatever," and nobody's fucking looking at me, like I'm not even worried about it. I'm not nervous.

In fact, over time, access to the space also changed the way they thought about parts of their body. This experience of being in the locker room without a problem helped Woody to normalize the size and shape of his own genitals, which had previously been a source of fear:

I almost am kind of like, "This is completely normal male genitalia." I'm totally comfortable with it. I don't know if that makes much sense, and it might kind of sound a little weird, but it's like, "This is male. This is normal male genitalia," 'Cause it feels completely male to me, and it's not like I'm trying to envision it a certain way.

Thus, accessing the space helped him recognize his body in a new way, while becoming more confident with his body as authentically male made him even more comfortable in the space. This naturalization into the space did not just affect trans men's level of fear but changed how they moved through the world and understood their own bodies.

In sum, when interviewees first started regularly using men's public bathrooms, their fears were heightened, yet very few actually reported experiencing any problems in the men's room. Their experiences of harassment and violence in women's bathrooms may have heightened their initial fears of men's bathrooms, but these heightened fears never materialized. This is because they participated in the homophobic rules of the men's room, and the rules themselves prevented a lot of scrutiny from other men. As the interviewees became more familiar with the gender-segregated space, they learned how to use the interactional rituals of the men's bathroom to increase their sense of safety. Over time, they developed a male-socialized gendered habitus, which conveyed a comfort that marked them as "natural" inhabitants of that space. Thus, both the understanding that the rules protected interviewees from scrutiny and the repeated experience of accessing the bathroom with no issues created a sense of safety over time. Being able to access the men's bathroom without any notice was a confirmation of their recognition as men. By being confident in this recognition, the experience of accessing the gender-segregated space became an unremarkable part of their everyday routine, and they were less likely to make decisions about bathroom use based on their geography of safety.

The homophobia of the men's bathroom creates a form of gendered safety and encourages conformity at the same time. Adhering to the rules of this gendered space becomes like second nature for trans men over time, and following the rules allows others in the space to read them as men. For all men, the space reinforces the naturalness of "urinary segregation" and reinforces the homophobia of the interactional rules of the bathroom. Trans men should not be singled out in particular for reinforcing these norms. Rather, the interactional rules of the bathroom promote binary understandings of gender and homophobia. Surely, most men do not fear every public bathroom they enter, but that is the point: those rules become incorporated into how one just is in those situations.

Nowhere to Go

Though most of the interviewees eventually started using men's bathrooms without problems, the men who had the most visually gender-nonconforming appearances reported experiencing ongoing harassment and violence no matter what space they entered. Julian, who lived in a Midwest Rust Belt city, a white and indigenous trans man who also identified as genderqueer, had what he described as a flamboyantly feminine personal style that continually shaped how he accessed a variety of spaces:

> I usually don't go to places like straight bars, 'cause they're just really not good spaces for me—if I did, I would go with women and go into the women's room. It confuses people a lot, but I know how to walk the walk, because I was socialized to be feminine, and so it's an easier space for me to be in. I look femme enough that people just get weirded out, but they don't

like scream at me, at least at this point. I get in more trouble in the men's room where people question whether or not I should be in there, which is unusual [for trans men]. Like several, where like people'd be like, "Hey, you!" Everything from like "Hey, you know this is the men's room?" to like "What the fuck—this is the men's room" to people like wanting to debate with me about whether or not I should be in there or like wanting to see my ID.

These ongoing incidents of harassment meant that Julian avoided men's bathrooms overall, especially when traveling through rural areas or other places he felt less safe. His story illustrates nonconformity is not welcome in either space. He felt more able to fit in the interactional rules of the women's space, but his nonconformity meant he could not gain the comfort other trans men eventually found in the men's room. Gender-nonconforming trans people experience more violence in bathrooms than other trans people, which mirrors the fact that they experience more harassment overall.[31]

Disability, another kind of nonconformity, also made it difficult for some men to go by the rules. For example, Michael, a white man living in urban California, found himself positioned in his wheelchair at the crotch level of men at urinals in an airport bathroom by an attendant.[32] Another interviewee had trouble attending classes at his university because a medical condition forced him to use the bathroom frequently and there were no nearby bathrooms where he felt comfortable. Ability also figured in Willie Houston's story, since he was likely targeted for assisting another man in addition to carrying a purse. Each of these instances illustrates bathrooms are an amplified site of disability as well as gender and sexuality.

Thus, adhering to the rules of the bathrooms, having a conforming gender presentation, and having an able body allowed for the comfort over time experienced by most interviewees. In the sense that being left alone in the men's room for most of the men is a form of social honor, those who are visibly nonconforming do not receive that honor and, instead, become abject. In the end, most trans men go through the process of being stigmatized when they experience harassment in women's public restrooms to receiving social honor through the interactional rituals of the men's bathroom, whereas gender-nonconforming people continue to be stigmatized.

For the most part, trans men reported fewer incidents of harassment and violence in men's bathrooms versus women's public bathrooms, which was more about the underlying rules of each space than men as a whole being more accepting than women. Gender-segregated public bathrooms continue to create gender difference for all and, in a particularly salient way, for transgender people. The difference in interaction between the two settings has less to do with plumbing and more about broader notions about the protection of women and the shoring up of men's masculinities. The women's bathroom is a site for the active policing of gender normativity that both protects women from the heterosexual threat of a "man in the bathroom" and reinforces normative ideals of feminine appearance. Though gender is policed in the men's room, the men's room is primarily a sexual space,[33] as evidenced by the centrality of heteronormativity to its interactional rules, whereas the women's is based on gender, as shown in the enforcement of gender conformity in the space. The interactional rules of the men's bathroom, based on strictly heterosexist ideals, may serve a function similar to what Goffman found regarding gender, as a regular reminder of the regulation of sexuality as part of masculinity.[34] Actual experiences of violence mark that gender nonconformity, along with disability, does not belong in the women's or men's public bathroom. With the advent of formal LGBT rights victories and potential shifts in normative ideals of masculinity, the men's public bathroom functions as a regular reminder of the dominance of heterosexuality and gender normativity. With this background, the murder of Willie Houston becomes less shocking and is an extreme outcome of the reproduction of gender and sexual domination through the everyday rules of this institutional context.

In bathroom and locker room experiences, we see another disjuncture in fear and experiences of violence. The salience of fears for trans men in the amplified site of bathrooms decreases over time, which is less a reflection of a misreading of the potential for danger in these spaces than an example of how the microprocesses that create and maintain heterosexism and cissexism (through reinforcing gender conformity) happen rather powerfully as unremarkable quotidian practices. Gender and sexuality are amplified in these sites for everyone who enters, but that amplification becomes part of the background noise and does not register once they are habituated to the rules. Bathroom experiences demonstrate not only how varying fears shape processes of social domination and subordination but also how sometimes one must, usually unthinkingly, partake in these rules in order to accomplish everyday bodily functions and survive in a particular social context. Following the rules reduces fear and minimizes interactional difficulties. In other words, going by the rules makes it possible to care for basic biological needs without being hassled or threatened with violence.

MEDICAL INSTITUTIONS

Waiting for a nurse or doctor while sitting on the crinkly white paper covering an exam table can make one feel quite vulnerable. Depending on the reason for the visit, you might be wearing a paper or cloth gown that does not quite close in the back, and this exposes you to the chill created by the ventilation system and limits your movement without exposure. With the closed door or, perhaps, just a curtained-off area in a space shared with strangers, it can be hard to tell if seconds or minutes have passed while you wait for medical care. Perhaps you feel fear that you will get bad news or that you will not be able to pay for whatever procedures the people in white coats deem necessary. Will you be deemed sick or healthy? Normal or not? Some of us might feel even more vulnerable in that moment depending on the experiences we, or people like us, have had in this context. As we sit there waiting, we work hard to push down that nagging fear rooted in the question of whether this visit will cause us more harm than healing.

That feeling of vulnerability is especially heightened for trans people trying to access medical care, where doctors, nurses, and therapists often see them as oddities, attention seekers, mentally ill, or perhaps duplicitous. In fact, it was in these hospitals, doctor's offices, and clinics where trans men's fears of violence were often realized. For example, Jason, a white man who lived in suburban Ohio, shared a particularly harrowing recent story of seeking care for a severe bladder problem and being physically assaulted and refused proper care because he was transgender:

> It got to the point where I was in so much pain that I went to a Catholic hospital here in town. I have never in my life been treated like such a subhuman, ever. The nurses were rude. They were like, "What do you want us to do? Put a catheter in you? What do you want?" And I was like, "Make it stop hurting." I was like, "I'm not

here looking for pain drugs. I want you to figure out what the hell's going on." The doctor literally was in and out of the room, like just didn't wanna deal with me. They ordered a CAT scan.

During the CAT scan, the nurse he was left alone with physically assaulted him:

> I mean, why would anybody do that, but it hurt and I screamed. And ever since then, I will not go see a doctor by myself. Later, they literally kicked me out of the hospital, and I was in agonizing pain, so I was like down by the parking garage, and I was just kind of lying there holding my gut, and nurses walking by, nobody paying any attention. Eventually, I got out of the garage [when his partner came to pick him up]. That was quite possibly the most horrific experience I've ever had in my life.

This story illustrates that some of the worst violence trans men experience is when they are at their most vulnerable in medical contexts. For Jason it was not just his illness that made him vulnerable but the authority of doctors and nurses who could decide whether to treat him and were in the position to assault him in the exam room. It was clear to trans men in incidents like this that they were literally being punished with poor care and physical violence due to their gender and bodily nonconformity.

This extreme example of violence illustrates the vulnerability in the medical exam room that is part of a typical experience in medical and psychiatric settings where the patient is subject to the provider's authority. In the contemporary United States, doctors and other medical or psychiatric personnel hold the authority to determine who is physically or mentally ill and who is healthy and, thus, who is considered a normal citizen of the society. Medical institutions and doctors as institutional authorities are, at their core, supposed to heal people from illness, yet this was the primary site where trans men reported experiences of violence directed at them primarily because they were transgender. Having less power in these institutional contexts and the focus on their bodies made trans men particularly vulnerable in these settings. The mistreatment and discrimination they feared actually occurred and caused physical, psychological, and financial harm. Medical contexts were also often the sites of more subtle forms of violence that caused small, often psychological, injuries that had a large cumulative negative effect over time.[35] The various forms of violence trans men experienced in medical contexts not only were enactments of cissexism and transphobia but also punished gendered bodily nonconformity. These types of incidents are common and widespread in research, activist, and personal accounts of trans people's efforts to access healthcare.[36] Trans people's pervasive experiences of violence illustrate the particularly negative effects of the gender and sexual logics of theses amplified sites when coupled with medical authority.

While certainly not all transgender people need or want medical interventions as part of a transition, most of the trans men I interviewed saw access to a variety of medical procedures as absolutely crucial to living in their bodies and everyday social worlds in a way that lined up with their gender identity. Transgender people in the United States have sought medical transitions since at least the second quarter of the twentieth century and have consistently had to negotiate with medical practitioners to access care.[37] As many trans scholars and activists, such as Vivian Namaste and Dean Spade, have shown, transgender people often have considerable knowledge of proper medical procedures and technological advancements. In contrast, while many doctors have limited knowledge, they hold the authority to grant access to medical procedures and decide who should and should not receive treatment. Doctors, therapists, and other medical and psychiatric authorities act as gatekeepers, such that transgender patients often feel they have to present themselves as model patients in order to be granted access to medical transition.[38] All of this is premised on the medicalization of trans bodies as "abnormal" and "pathological" and a set of medical standards in transgender healthcare that tend to recommend a slow and controlled set of steps to access care.[39]

Dean Spade established that the medical construction of this ideal patient, which dates from this early struggle between knowledge and authority, is a "reification of the violence of compulsory gender norm compliance."[40] Being the model patient requires transgender people to present themselves as having mental health issues that need to be cured, produce a narrative of being "trapped in the wrong body," and express a desire to enact normative gender practices and be heterosexual after transition.[41] In addition, they need to present themselves as wanting to engage all aspects of medical and legal transition as well as present themselves as gender-conforming men or women.[42] Thus, medical gatekeepers enforce a range of gender norms through granting or denying access to healthcare based on this model, and this enforces the violence of gender-norm conformity.

Trans people today do not always have to fit the mold of the ideal patient to access care, but they still have to navigate widely varying medical standards and provider practices that present different notions of patient autonomy and medical gatekeeping. More restrictive guidelines prescribed a period of psychotherapy and required trans people to demonstrate "lived experience" in order to access medical transition, but many guidelines have become more flexible in recent years.[43] Due to longtime activism by transgender people and allies, the pathologizing and normalizing medical models have begun to shift.[44] Yet many of the variations of this medical model employed by individual practitioners still hold trans people accountable to "born this way" and "wrong body" narratives in order to access care.[45] In addition, transition-related care can be prohibitively expensive, especially given that trans people often face economic marginalization stemming from employment discrimination and family rejection.[46] There are exceptions to these archaic restrictions on care, such as clinics that provide low-cost care and employ informed-consent models that seek to shift authority and control away from providers and toward patients. While there are a number of different models for transgender healthcare, few if any regulatory mechanisms require doctors, therapists, or others to follow one model or another.[47] Indeed, the trans men I interviewed articulated a wide range of acceptance and rejection of various models of transition-related care. They were active in seeking the care they needed, even as economic factors and convenience led some to make do with what care they could find in their local area.

Blocking access to transition through gatekeeping can cause a range of physical and emotional harm for trans people, and importantly, it can take what could be a joyful process and turn it into one rife with challenges and pain. Jacob, a white man living in urban Minnesota, described how the local university-based gender clinic changed significantly with a new director from an empowering approach to a restrictive approach:

> The old director supported trans people. The new director, you had to do it his way. That's when the whole gatekeeping thing started. It wasn't like that before, because the old director was trans, so

she knew the psychic thing that people were going through. That's the very awful thing about the universities is they take the joy out of our transitioning. They don't get it, because they make us go through all this shit that I'm sure you've heard a million times from people. So that was the biggest thing. They took the joy out of transition. Not only did they take the joy out of it, but you had to [deal with] their abuse. And then you still had to deal with your own gender stuff. So it was a huge difference. . . . So basically, the biggest thing is that it should be a joyful transition; it should not be a painful transition. It's their pain. And if you have the proper support and stuff, it doesn't hurt. It does hurt before that time, but once you start to transition, it's really truly a joyful thing. It makes us happier than hell. It doesn't cause pain.

Thus, as Jacob explains, restrictive medical processes not only cause various forms of harm but also take away the potential for expressing a range of emotions and responses to transition, including both ambivalence and happiness. While this analysis focuses on instances of violence, it is worth noting the goal is not just accessing medical transition or general healthcare without violence but allowing this to be a process of joy and celebration.

Searching in Local Contexts

For many interviewees, the first jump through the hoops of medical gatekeeping was simply finding medical professionals willing to provide transition-related care. Men living in major cities such as San Francisco, Chicago, and Minneapolis were usually able to find transition-related care fairly easily. However, those living in rural areas or in smaller and less cosmopolitan cities often had difficulty finding local medical providers willing to prescribe hormones or provide additional care. Henry, a white man in suburban Indiana, wanted to find transgender-related care in his local area:

This area right here, it's very hard to find doctors who will help you get started. The one that was in this area has stopped doing that. The doctor I have now, she's good. I was her first transgender patient, and she was about number twenty-five I called after getting a "Nope. Nope. Absolutely not [from other doctors]." I had one doctor tell me . . . , "Absolutely not! And any doctor who does should have his license revoked."

Henry eventually found a willing doctor, but the process of calling twenty-five providers was time consuming and subjected him to the derision of transphobic providers. Ethan, a black man living in a mid-sized Michigan city he described as fairly conservative, said it took some time for his primary care doctor to understand he was serious about starting testosterone therapy. When she finally referred him to an endocrinologist that would work with him, he had to join a year-long waiting list for his first appointment.

Men living in rural areas who could not find a willing local doctor often had to travel to the closest metropolitan areas, though not every doctor in a given city would provide care. Like Henry, Jack, a white man living in rural Appalachia, found abuse when seeking care from practitioners in his rural area:

> I'm way out in the country. In the hills, mountains, however you wanna say it. Um, the rednecks. So, I talked to my OB-GYN about it. Taboo situation. "No. We're not gonna discuss that." You know, "You were born a female. God made you a female. God doesn't make mistakes. Maybe you need to go to church."

After being rebuffed by the transphobic OB-GYN, Jack spent about five months chasing down leads in his local area and finally found a support group in a midsized city where he received information about willing doctors, but it was about fifty miles away.

Despite Jack's characterization of his rural area, it was not that all urban doctors were more accommodating to their trans patients but that trans men had more options in urban rather than rural locales. Josh, who lived in rural Northern California, was encouraged by his local doctor to travel to San Francisco for transition-related care, with the assumption doctors there would be experienced and supportive. However, all was not rosy even for the men who actually lived in San Francisco. For example, Drew, a white man living in San Francisco, had trouble getting his doctor to prescribe hormones:

> My doctor wasn't down either. She was a butch dyke, and she was like, "Oh, you don't want to take that stuff. It's going to make you

get all hairy, and it's going to make your clit get big; your voice is going to drop. You don't want to take that." and I was like, "Yes I do! That's exactly what I want." Then she told me that I would have to go to like therapy for six or seven months, and I went and saw my therapist once, and I had my therapist call her and just tell her to put me on the stuff. My therapist lied, because I used to go to her all the time. She lied and said I had been going for the whole time. You know what I mean? So then she gave me the goods.

Drew was clearly confident in what he required, but he needed the help of a sympathetic therapist who was willing to bend rules and advocate on his behalf to get the care he needed. Eventually, the physician refused to help him with a legal gender-marker change, and he left her care. Drew had experiences of dissatisfaction in accessing care from his physician similar to those of rural men or men living in metropolitan areas with few providers, but he could easily find a different provider with little hardship because of his location. Unlike Henry, Drew did not have to call twenty-five different doctors to find a replacement. Even for men who had few financial resources, there were free or low-cost clinics in San Francisco and other major cities that provided both transition-related and routine primary care. Thus, trans men in resource-rich major cities had many more options to choose from when a specific provider denied them care.[48]

Most of the trans men I interviewed understood the denial of care when seeking transition-related services as a form of transphobic violence.[49] There are a number of medical needs for which one's primary care physician may not have the expertise or the willingness to provide the treatment requested by a patient. It is certainly possible some physicians felt like they could not provide proper care and, without malice, recommended trans men seek care elsewhere. Yet from these men's accounts, it was clear most physicians denied treatment and particular courses of care because the patient was a trans man, not because they did not have the proper expertise to treat them. For example, physicians regularly prescribe testosterone to men whose hormone levels fall below the typical range, yet trans men are often considered a special case and denied this care.[50] It is notable how reluctant many physicians are to assist trans people in their medical transitions in a time when doctors prescribe all sorts of pharmaceuticals and perform a variety of medical procedures that significantly alter individuals' bodies and have potential negative side effects (e.g., medication for toenail fungus that may cause liver failure). This hesitance is also a testament to how providers themselves are embedded in the gender and sexual logics of the space. The frustration this reluctance causes for trans people has been widely noted in scholarly and activist discourses around transgender medicine and was present throughout interviewees' accounts. The threat that doctors might deny treatment set up the conditions under which trans men were more vulnerable to abuse from the providers who did provide care.

Tap Dance for Care

Phillip, a white man, could not find a willing provider in his midsized North Carolina city, so he regularly traveled about seventy miles to a university town to visit an endocrinologist who would continue his hormone prescription. In describing his interactions, he said:

> The one guy at the endocrinology specialty clinic, he [*pause*] I had never felt uncomfortable with the doctor at all [before]. He actually asked to see my breasts, and I was like, "I'd never had that with my gyno." I was seeing a gynecologist 'cause a gynecologist can prescribe the testosterone, too, and he never had to see anything like that. And I'm thinking, "That's kind of weird." But I showed him because, you know, you do your little dance, you do your little tap dance in front of these people. You know, the red tape. But I was just like, "What the hell?"

Though he felt violated, Phillip had to delicately negotiate his interactions with the doctor in order to maintain access to hormone therapy. As a gatekeeper, the doctor had far more control over the situation and could treat patients inappropriately with few consequences.

What care trans men receive and how they receive it is often up to the discretion of the doctor, who sometimes relies on whether the patient fits the ideal model of the transgender patient and how compliant the individual is rather than on established medical protocols.[51] Thus, when interviewees were able to locate willing providers, they often had to manage inappropriate and damaging behavior in order to get the care they needed. These incidents illustrate how medical contexts are sites where gender and sexuality are amplified, with particularly negative effects for trans people. Josh, who lived in rural Northern California, shared a story about a local endocrinologist, one of few providers in his rural county who would prescribe testosterone, who would frequently ask trans people to remove their clothes and would otherwise behave inappropriately. She was "talked to" by administrators, but the doctor continued to use her authority, as ensured by the structure of the medical context, to treat transgender patients inappropriately. Even if the administrators and policy of the particular hospital or clinic do not condone this behavior, the practitioner's authority is difficult to contest in the exam room. Patients like Phillip feel like they really only have the option to suffer this treatment or restart the arduous process of finding more competent care elsewhere. Josh noted that due to these experiences "a lot of trans people, they don't go to doctors because they are afraid of being treated badly." Thus, this conduct by medical providers means that trans people avoid accessing all kinds of healthcare, which can have major repercussions for their overall health.

The subtler incidents of abuse trans men experienced from providers were made even worse when they happened in front of an audience. Gavin, a white man living in a major city in the Midwest Corn Belt, could find reliable health providers only through the university hospital in the town where he lived early in his transition, which happened to be the most politically liberal town in the state:

> He was prescribing my testosterone, and he also did some of these yearly pelvic exams. That was uncomfortable. I feel like it's always going to be awkward, but he always had some student. Like, an intern just like seeing how it worked. How that office works. And he would ask, "Is it okay if so-and-so is in the room there?" You know, "Seeing how it goes?" That always felt strange to me. That felt kind of uncomfortable to me. Just thinking about these sorts of histories of displaying nonnormative bodies in this educational, sort of medical setting.

Thus, Gavin felt his body being displayed for others was a form of exploitation, which was likely heightened by the general discomfort Gavin experienced during the pelvic exam. Again, though the doctor did not physically assault or yell at Gavin, the exam with audience still made Gavin feel like an oddity and marked his body as nonnormative. Even though the care he was getting was not ideal, when the doctor left the medical center Gavin was unable to find a new doctor for gynecological care and had not had an exam since.

Transgender people with the means to do so have traveled, sometimes even internationally, to access medical care since transition technologies have existed.[52] Interviewees went to Thailand or Serbia for some surgeries, though most men accessed transition-related procedures and care domestically. At the same time, interviewees often had to travel far within their region to access competent trans healthcare. For instance, it was unsurprising that interviewees in Chicago and surrounding areas traveled to Howard Brown for care, a clinic in Chicago that offers care on a sliding scale and utilizes a patient-centered informed-consent model, but it was striking how many interviewees from much farther away traveled to the clinic. Men came from Wisconsin, central Illinois, Indiana, Michigan, and as far as the three-hundred-mile, five-hour drive from Cincinnati to go to Howard Brown. For these men, it was worth traveling to find quality care, especially from providers who had less restrictive ideas about the transition process. Similar patterns emerged in other cities, such as Minneapolis and Atlanta, though interviewees on the West Coast were less motivated to travel.

Trans men in all three regions sought providers who were convenient, affordable, and, if possible, didn't make them do any kind of dehumanizing "tap dance" to receive care. Thus, traveling for less restrictive forms of care was an effort to break free from the regulatory effects of more restrictive standards of care. Interviewees were more likely to easily get transition-related care on the West Coast than in the Midwest or South, though major cities provided the most options. The ability to travel for care was limited by available funds to pay for travel and lodging and to take time off work, but many of the men who traveled did not have many financial resources. Rather, they relied on family support and informal networks to pool resources. Location and resources both encouraged and limited mobility as trans men sought humane care. Some men even moved, like Ben, an Asian American man who moved to a major midwestern city to access care after he could not find a doctor who was willing to prescribe testosterone in his previous home in a small city in Indiana. Further, Ben and his fiancée were hoping to move to the Southeast for better weather and job opportunities, but he would have had to have a prescription set up with an online pharmacy because he did not trust there would be reliable care there.

Violence While Getting Medical Care

The most jarring violence interviewees experienced was being subjected to harm from medical practitioners when trying to access medical care to heal from injury or illness. This transphobic violence occurred regularly when trans men were addressing general health needs and ranged from subtle annoyances, such as doctors making inappropriate jokes or dealing with bureaucracies where they were illegible, to abuse and physical violence at the hands of medical personnel. This violence caused a range of reported harm from less intense psychological effects to physical trauma. Each incident of violence made it clear that these were amplified sites of gender and sexuality and that trans men's bodies and gendered histories were not in place in medical contexts.

Some of the most common issues trans men reported when seeking general medical care were structural issues with policy and forms, as well as being misgendered by personnel. Michael, a white man living in urban California, had to make frequent visits to the local medical center for disability-related medical issues and found the limited and binary options on the forms themselves did not provide categories that reflected his gender, sexuality, or intimate and romantic relationships:[53]

> There's no space for being queer, let alone for being trans in the paperwork. And I'm an advocate for trans competency and queer competency, and I go in to get my own care, and it sucks.

It can be difficult to always be an activist or advocate, especially when one is in the more vulnerable role of patient. The mundane experience of filling out forms becomes problematic when the forms and procedures do not have space for gender and sexual diversity. These forms, often one of the first things one sees when seeking care, are a reminder to trans men that their bodies, identities, and histories are out of place in the gendered logic of the medical institution.

Like the forms, having staff call them by the wrong name and pronouns—a commonly reported microaggression—was a particularly jarring experience as they were trying to access care.[54] Cooper, a white man who lived in a rural area on the border between Minnesota and Iowa, said, "It wasn't like they refused me service or anything, but when I told them that I preferred male, they just kept calling me female." When the hospital was absorbed into a larger medical system, his care improved because they had better training and policies regarding the treatment of transgender people. Though relatively minor when taken as individual incidents, at least in comparison to the reports of psychological, verbal, and physical violence in the rest of this section, these instances of violence add to the marginalization of trans men and increase their feelings of powerlessness in an institution where they seek healing.

Trans men frequently found their transgender history would come up when visiting the doctor for unrelated issues. Many healthcare providers would then focus on this information rather than the problem at hand by asking invasive and irrelevant questions about their transition history, performing unnecessary examinations, and deciding hormones and other aspects of transition must be the cause of clearly unrelated conditions. This phenomenon is widespread and colloquially referred to as "trans broken arm syndrome," meaning that a trans person seeking care for a broken arm is grilled by physicians and medical staff about their transgender history and, perhaps at the same time, the broken arm is somehow blamed on their being transgender.[55] For example, interviewees reported seeking medical care for issues like seasonal allergies and being asked by doctors for a lengthy recounting of their transition history. Both misgendering and invasive questions are examples of what stef shuster names "discursive aggression." These verbal acts of violence in everyday talk enforce normative gender structures.[56] The majority of interviewees found the reminder of their transgender status and medical personnel's lack of training in transgender-related health issues made their transgender identities and histories salient in situations where it would not have been otherwise, which caused unnecessary discomfort and stress while trying to access care.

Being transgender and vulnerable to a physician's authority in medical institutions made trans men subject to violations of the privacy of their bodies at a time when they were especially vulnerable. Similar to the abuses suffered when trying to seek transition-related care, trans men experienced inappropriate and invasive surveillance of their bodies during regular medical care. During a serious illness, Aaron, a white man who lived in Chicago, was hospitalized:

> My endocrinologist at the hospital pulled down my pants without my consent to look at my genitalia. She kept going, "Just checking." Now, what was she "just checking"? She never said. And it's not like I was there for some related issue. I was there for new-onset diabetes.

In the midst of dealing with serious illness and hospitalization, Aaron was at his most vulnerable to the strange and abusive behavior of the physician. In another example, an interviewee sought care for strep throat, and the physician demanded to perform a pelvic exam—an invasive demand that is certainly not the standard examination for strep throat. In yet another example, Chris, a white man living in urban Northern California, illustrated the vulnerable position of the sick patient in this incident when he sought care for sleep apnea:

> I've never had bad experiences, because I'm just a people person. Except with doctors because I'll tell them. I told one doctor, and he didn't want to touch me after he found out. That's horrifying. It's just awful when you feel sick that you're so despised just because of who you are, and it's not even who, it's what you are, because he liked me before. He grabbed my tongue and looked down my throat, and he said, "Not a problem. You have this thing. We can do surgery; it'll clear it right up." Then, I don't know why, I told him. I think I did because I didn't want it biting me in the ass somewhere. And that's when he said, "Oh! You have mental problems. It's obvious you have mental problems." So it went from there.

The doctor's reaction sent Chris a message that he was mentally, physically, and morally deficient right when he was most vulnerable. Again, those trans men who have short- or long-term disabilities must more frequently access medical spaces where their bodies are judged normative in regard to gender and ability.

The image of transgender people as duplicitous and mentally unstable may have made hospital personnel more hostile to trans patients and their families, as well as more likely to suspect them of drug-seeking behavior.⁵⁷ Sean, a white man living in the rural upper Midwest, described his own painful experience of receiving transphobic care at the closest hospital:

> I had a horrible kidney stone. I didn't know what was going on, and I went in there, and you know, after a while I had to tell them, "Well, it could be a pelvic problem or something." And I had to tell them my deal, and boy, were they nasty to me, and they got rid of me. They were like, yeah, bad gas. Go home; you'll be fine. And so then, I came back the next day in horrible pain and screaming in pain, and I'm not a noisy person. And had this dry heaving and just sick as could be. And finally they did a CT scan. Okay, you have a kidney stone; here's some pain medication. And luckily I passed it, so I didn't have to go to any other doctor. They were pretty nasty to me and weird with me.

While Sean had no desire to return to that hospital after this physically and emotionally painful experience, it was the only one in his area, and he found himself back there soon after:

> Two weeks later, we had to go in for my wife; she had broke her face [from a fall], and they remembered me. And then I think that got passed around because I heard people talking in the hallway. And she had to get surgery for that. Well, they didn't give her antibiotics after surgery, and I don't know if that's because they didn't like me or they were giving her substandard care or not. I won't go that far, but she ended up getting a bone infection, which was really serious. It ended up where she had to get IV antibiotics every twelve hours for, like, I think it was four or five months. And she had to go down and sit in a hyperbaric chamber and get oxygen once a day down in [a major city a few hours away] for months. So that really sucked. And then she had to get another surgery at the end of it all. But when we kept trying to go back to the surgeon saying, "You know, she's still in a lot of pain," they were really dismissive of us and acted like we were just there to get attention.

Sean believed the medical personnel's knowledge of his transgender status had some effect on both his and his wife's care at the local hospital; however, it was difficult for Sean to avoid the hospital, since there were few options for medical care in his rural area.

These experiences of violence in accessing all sorts of medical care often led to avoiding healthcare altogether and filled the men I interviewed with dread when they had to enter these institutions. This is one arena where trans men's fears and their experiences lined up and resulted in tragic consequences. If anything, their experiences of violence often exceeded their fears. The disjuncture here is that medical institutions, which are supposed to help all people and encourage health, end up as the main perpetrators of violence in the lives of trans men. Further, this violence can be even more jarring when it occurs in the professionalized atmosphere of the exam room, with its attachment to white-collar physicians and other practitioners, as opposed to the common fears of transphobic violence, which are linked to racialized and classed masculine images like the thug and the redneck. Since avoiding victimization is central to the normative regular guy ideal, these experiences of violence made it difficult to achieve the standard of Goldilocks masculinity. These experiences in the medical context likely increased both trans men's fear of violence in spaces like bathrooms and their spatially based fears overall. If they experience pervasive violence at the doctor, then they might anticipate it in other settings.

Where they lived mattered in interviewees' ability to seek out competent and humane medical care. Though men experienced violence across geographic contexts, those in large urban centers, particularly in the West, had many more options for accessing care. Since many of the trans men of color lived in urban centers (likely due to histories of racial segregation and migration), their ability to find care was similar to urban white men I interviewed. At the same time, racial disparities in access to healthcare were likely to affect care, but this too was not evident in these narratives. In general, those with financial means and family support had the most success in getting medical care without violence. They used knowledge of their local areas to find competent care, though options were limited, as in Sean's example, or emergency situations, such as in Jason's and Aaron's cases, made them particularly vulnerable and unable to avoid medical violence. Disabled men and those with serious health issues tended to interact with medical systems more often, along with the attendant violence produced in those institutional spaces.

Crucially, the medical context itself makes gender and other categories of difference salient through the collection of information about gender and also due to the assumptions about sex and gender difference that underlie much medical knowledge. Thus, this makes gender and the sexed body, and a transgender history, amplified in these settings. The gendered effects of the underlying structure of the institution are particularly visible for trans people, but every person who moves through medical contexts experiences this, even if they are not fully conscious of it. The unequal power relation between doctors and patients inherent in the medical context made trans men particularly vulnerable to abuse by medical personnel. In addition, medical institutions were a particular site of transphobic violence because trans men's bodies were often exposed and it was difficult to hide their transgender status or history. The power imbalance made trans men want to appear compliant so that they fit provider's idea of a person who deserved care.

Though I have not detailed it extensively here, medical contexts produced not only diverse forms of violence but also an array of resistance to this violence among trans men. Some of it is evident in the accounts in this chapter, such as maneuvering to seek different care providers and helping new doctors understand how to treat trans patients with respect and dignity. Many of these men engaged in resistance through organizing and educating in their local communities and at regional and national levels. For example, after his horrific experience, Jason started speaking at trainings at other local hospitals in an effort to educate medical practitioners so that his experience would not be repeated. Although resistance is not the focus of this analysis, it is important to recognize that trans people are not dupes of the medical system, as some authors have argued.[58] Dean Spade remarks, "Sexual and gender self-determination and the expression of variant gender identities without punishment (and with celebration) should be the goals of any medical, legal, or political examination of or intervention into the gender expression of individuals and groups."[59] One important way to reach the goals of gender expression without abuse and with joy is to properly train a range of medical and mental health practitioners to offer trans-competent care. Yet if the problems in medical contexts are rooted in the structure of the institutions, it is questionable if this violence will really cease without significantly changing the structure that makes gender and the sexed body and, perhaps more important, gender and sexed difference so amplified. Whether individual providers are overtly transphobic, they are still embedded in the rules and logic of the institution, similar to public bathroom users. Clearly, many of these medical contexts do not support trans people's joy in their everyday lives or when accessing medical care. At the same time, in the face of structural conditions of unequal power in these institutions, trans people actively undertake a myriad of approaches to create justice and, perhaps, joy in this context.

CONCLUSION

The specific institutional arrangements of bathrooms and medical contexts produce particular forms of fear and violence that reinscribe patterns of social domination through both mundane everyday activities and clear acts of intentional violence. Men's bathrooms provoked a particularly strong set of fears that were not realized by most men, while women's bathrooms were more common sites of harassment and the enforcement of gender conformity. Over time, men became habituated to the homophobic interactional rules of the men's bathroom, which reproduced heterosexism through unremarkable everyday practices. Lastly, medical violence was the most common form of transgender-related violence in interviewee's lives. Interviewees faced difficulties accessing healthcare without being subjected to transphobic violence. Experiences of violence in medical settings illustrate that the structures of these institutions and the salience of gender in them set the stage for punishing gender and bodily nonconformity. Each institutional space by centering gender and sexuality as underlying organizing principles furthers trans men's vulnerability to violence.

The relationship between fear, violence, and masculinity weaves throughout trans men's narratives of public bathrooms and medical institutions. Like so many other spaces and places trans men encounter in everyday life, the regular guy ideal and Goldilocks masculinity figured into each of these settings. To achieve a Goldilocks masculinity, one should not commit unjustified acts of violence (too hard), but one must also avoid being victimized by violence (too soft). Beyond just preventing the harm of violence itself, through avoiding victimization some men could reach toward achieving this masculine ideal. Thus, by not using women's public bathrooms and following the rules in the men's, most trans men could also maintain a properly masculine sense of self. Yet the structure of medical contexts made it difficult to avoid victimization. Trans men made efforts to find regular care where they would not experience violence, but there was little choice when sudden and severe illness overcame them. Thus, this is a context where this group of men has particular difficulty maintaining a Goldilocks masculinity.

Trans men's narratives of using gender-segregated public bathrooms and accessing medical care show how relations of domination of sexuality and gender are produced in everyday interactions based on the structural arrangements of particular institutions. This gives evidence of the diffuse and diverse ways that inequality and power are produced in social life and how specific institutions produce particular forms of inequality. If public bathrooms were not gender-segregated, would men be as likely to reproduce heterosexism and gender conformity in them? Would medical contexts produce transphobic violence if they were structured around empowering patients rather than reifying doctors' control? The answer in both cases is likely no. However, while these relations of domination are produced in particular sites, they are not limited to them. We can see how in the case of bathrooms this reminder of heterosexism, which is likely below the level of consciousness for most men, is peppered throughout men's days as they enter these spaces. This homophobia surely followed Willie Houston, whose murder is described at the outset of this chapter, out of the bathroom. Though Houston's case is clearly an extreme example, it does show how transgressions of heterosexist rules of the bathroom do not stay in those contexts. The same can be said for trans men's experiences of violence in medical contexts, as this violence causes physical and psychological harm that carries into the rest of their lives. In the face of increasing formal legal equality for gays and lesbians as well as transgender people, these contexts reaffirm that cissexism and heterosexism have not gone away but still persist in the fabric of the institutions people encounter in their everyday lives.

In the case of public bathrooms, we see another example where fears are potentially protective, and at the same time, the expression of these fears also acts as a move to innocence in the reproduction of heterosexism and gender conformity. The anxieties that trans men felt early in their transitions, which for some did not go away if they had a particularly nonconforming presentation, reflect the political and cultural tensions evident in contemporary bathroom debates. Whether it is yet another bathroom bill introduced into a state legislature or a vote over a city ordinance, these debates are not really about transgender people, though they do have real effects on the fears and experiences of trans people. Rather, these bathroom and locker room spaces are symbolically important as one of the last explicit vestiges of gender segregation, made even more meaningful because they are tied to notions of privacy and sanitation. What is lost in this focus on the symbolic importance of these spaces is the work that actually happens in the amplified site of bathrooms and locker rooms to shore up gender and sexual normativity. This work goes beyond just the sorting that happens when individuals decide to enter one door or another. The interactional rules in the women's allow communication and scrutiny as an enforcement of normative femininity and binary gender and also maintain a sense of heterosexuality. Men's bathrooms and locker rooms are a site of the shoring up of the link between heterosexuality and masculinity through the interactional rules of the space. Thus, in the policy debates over bathrooms and locker rooms, it is important to go beyond the symbolic effects and understand these spaces are sites where disciplinary norms are not just enforced but amplified in ways that reverberate beyond the tiled bathroom walls.

Medical contexts are, perhaps obviously, key sites of the reinforcement of scientific and medical authority that has material effects on trans bodies and minds. This is evident in the structures of the institution that disempower the patient under the medical gaze. The violence trans men and other trans people experience in these settings are likely due to explicit transphobia on the part of individual practitioners, but this does not fully explain the harms done in these settings by sometimes well-meaning physicians, nurses, and staff. As in bathrooms, a larger form of gendered work happens in medical settings. The structure of the institution reifies not only scientific authority but also medical knowledge that is deeply informed by a logic of essentialized biological gender difference. Thus, it is not just the authority of medical and psychiatric providers to decide who is to be labeled sick that is reproduced in these contexts for cisgender and transgender people alike. It is also the authority to enforce essential gender difference as it plays out on bodies and minds for all under the medical gaze.[60] The violence of these gendered processes might be particularly visible for trans or disabled people, but it is an underlying logic that structures the institution in mundane everyday practices and processes—from filling out forms to treatment decisions based on deep assumptions of gender difference. Like bathrooms, this amplified site of the sometimes explicitly violent but often mundane reinforcement of a logic of essential biological difference ripples out beyond the walls of hospitals and exam rooms. These ripples and reverberations are carried with individuals in their bodies not only as physical and emotional scars but also in the ways they move through spaces. The symbolic and ideological aspects of these logics also carry away from these sites and join with the ripples from other sites to form and reshape broader ideologies.

Fear and violence are particularly visible means of enforcing the norms and ideologies produced within institutional contexts because they show who is most out of place in those spaces, but that is not the only means through which they are reproduced. In fact, it may be those unremarkable routinized everyday practices that are both the most effective in keeping existing social categories in place and the most difficult to change in combatting inequities. In other words, it is crucial to look at not just how the extreme is produced but also how what is normal and everyday is fashioned. Locating these amplified sites and the particular ways they discipline difference and normativity is a key tactic in addressing everyday inequality, especially when the sites act as barriers to accessing public space, health and well-being, and the material resources to live livable lives. This view of structural inequality as produced in institutions has the potential to inform a broad politics focused on institutional change rather than individual perpetrators.

Conclusion
CONTEMPORARY MASCULINITIES AND TRANSGENDER POLITICS

This research journey started amid the dark-green forests and rolling farmlands of Oregon's Willamette Valley and moved down to the gleaming San Francisco Bay and on to the golden hills of rural California. Next, after picking up a rental car amid the hot concrete of Atlanta, the journey continued surrounded by buzzing cicadas and through the granite cliffs of Tennessee and the drifting country music of Nashville. Then, it went up through Kentucky to the Ohio River and home of the Derby, back down to Berea and then Knoxville, and across the rolling Smokey Mountains to the warm waters of the Carolina coast. The journey picked up again among the skyscrapers of Chicago and wound around the states that touch the Great Lakes, through the farmlands and the rusting but striving cities of Michigan as the leftovers from Hurricane Sandy pelted the area with wind and rain. Heading back down to the flat farmlands of Ohio, it caught another glimpse of the Ohio River and then went back up through the brown fall cornfields lining the highways of Indiana and Illinois. Heading farther north, the journey returned to the shore of Lake Michigan, and as the winds started whipping small accumulations of snow across the interstate, it went on to the shining lakes of Madison. As ice started to accumulate on the landscape, another push led to the Twin Cities of Minneapolis and St. Paul. From there, more long hours of driving led far outside the orbit of the cities. I completed the sixty-sixth interview in a Minneapolis suburb over four years after starting the first. Finally, the last rental car was returned after clocking thousands of miles, and a flight was made back to the gray skies and damp of the Pacific Northwest.

All of this was done in an effort to understand what it means to be a man and to be masculine in the United States in the second decade of the twenty-first century. These are the questions that Seth asked in the introduction: "What does it mean to be man?" And why does he sometimes "give in to the pressures of masculinity in America"? Through the stories of a diverse group of trans men, gathered via that journey across three regions, I found there are many meanings to being a man and ways to embody that social category. Indeed, men's expressions of masculinity and experiences as men depended on the spaces and places they lived in and moved through during their everyday lives.

Men in Place focuses on the ways gender, race, class, sexuality, ability, and their intersections are perpetuated in social interaction in order to understand how social inequality persists across a range of spaces that are quite different from one another. The comparative analysis of the narratives of trans men who live in geographically dispersed spaces and come from a range of social locations brought to light insights more broadly about contemporary U.S. masculinities and more specifically about the particular experiences of this group of men. These men's stories show that discourses of gender, race, and sexuality form our ideas about particular spaces and shape our practices within them.

One of the most important insights that emerged from trans men's stories is that the contemporary model of masculinity in the United States is a Goldilocks masculinity, embodied in the regular guy. This regular guy ideal, which most closely aligns with white, suburban, middle-class normalcy, varies across places. However, in each space the ideal is always somewhere in the middle between hypermasculinity on one end, embodied by the controlling images of the thug and the redneck, and femininity and effeminacy, women and faggy men, on the other. Using racial formation theory, I show that racialized hypermasculinities, such as the thug and the redneck, are racial, gender, class, and sexual projects that contain racism in rural spaces and assign blame for both black and white men's poverty to individual rather than structural characteristics. This adds a spatial understanding to Pierrette Hondagneu-Sotelo and Michael Messner's proposition that privileged men construct themselves as more enlightened in contrast to the hypermasculinity of racialized groups, which allows more privileged men to pose themselves as comparatively egalitarian.[1]

Goldilocks masculinity is about finding that just-right spot in the middle of the continuum of masculine ideals, which marks the people at each end as lacking the positive traits of rationality, control, and situationally appropriate flexibility that form this contemporary ideal of the regular guy. This dynamic was particularly clear in trans men's narratives of spatially appropriate expressions of emotion, especially anger and aggression. Regular guys could be soft when they need to be and hard when they need to be. In contrast to hypermasculine men's inability to cry and uncontrolled sexuality, as well as narratives of faggy men and women not being able to control their emotional displays, the regular guy is a combination of properly in control but expressive when the situation calls for it. Further, interviewee's narratives of spatially based fear demonstrated that the lack of control evident at both ends of this spectrum also means that the thug and the redneck are to be feared because of their anger and violence and that the faggy man is constructed as a victim of violence. Indeed, these fear narratives suggest men should avoid being perceived as a faggy man. This imperative is particularly strong in amplified sites like men's public bathrooms, where the rules of the space reestablish heterosexism in daily life. Here, self-disciplining practices to avoid victimization become unremarkable routine ways of moving through an everyday space. By actively avoiding victimization amid the threat of multiple forms of violence and simultaneously distancing themselves from the kind of men who commit violence, regular guys narrate their own innocence while they participate in, or are at least complicit in, the perpetuation of social disparities. Displacing the blame for inequality allows some men to maintain their privilege and appear more egalitarian at the same time.

Men in Place also contributes insights about trans men as a group of men to scholarship on men and masculinities, where their lives are often left out due to a cisgender and essentialist bias. Foremost, the analysis woven through this book points to the importance of an intersectional perspective to understanding difference among men, as well as the experiences of groups of men who share a particular aspect of social location, such as having a transgender history. We need to better understand the differences and similarities among the bodies subsumed under the category of man. It is time to move beyond the usually unspoken assumption that trans men are not fully men that underlies much masculinities research, as well as theorizing of trans men's experiences as somehow always separate from those of cisgender men. My analysis of recognition demonstrates neither trans men nor cisgender men are born men but become them through processes of social recognition that reflect spatially based gender, sexual, and racial knowledge and by encountering the social interactions resulting from that recognition. While certain aspects of gender transition are unique to trans men, both trans men and cisgender men share the broader cultural scripts about testosterone and bodily affect that permeate age-based bodily transitions for men, such as the narrative of adolescent boys transitioning into men. Further, as my analysis of fear and violence shows, both trans and cisgender men map their fears spatially as they navigate a complex relationship between fearlessness and avoiding victimization. Beyond, perhaps, the experience of being raised as a girl, trans men have a few distinctive experiences as men that include managing particular forms of legal and social misrecognition, fears of violence heightened by possibilities of transphobic violence, and transphobic violence in medical and psychiatric spaces. Future research on both cisgender and trans men will benefit from further exploring similarities among and differences between groups of men.

Across trans men's stories, it was clear that those who did not fit normative standards for men in regard to gender, sexuality, race, and ability were "out of place" in many spaces. They stood out as the group of men who experienced the most policing of their bodies and actions from others. This was evident when their bodies did not fit rigid notions of sex difference in medical contexts or when their visual nonconformity made neither the men's nor the women's bathroom a safe choice. Nonconforming men's experiences show that it is particularly difficult if individuals try to express nonbinary identities in interaction. Trans men's fears of being perceived as gay men in public bathrooms and rural spaces illustrate the overlap of gender and sexual nonconformity connected to the image of the faggy man, who is especially threatening and threatened in these spaces. The analysis also makes clear that black men do not fit in public spaces where the police constantly harass them and that state-sponsored violence for being perceived as a thug is a very real possibility.

SPACE IN INTERACTION AND INEQUALITY

We often look at images of politicians or men in popular culture to understand contemporary masculinities. Indeed, these references are peppered throughout the book. However, none of the men I interviewed were politicians, and none were famous actors, musicians, or even popular internet personalities. Despite having many impressive qualities, in most senses these were everyday men. The slices of their lives they shared in their narratives provided snapshots of the ways that gender, sexuality, race, ability, and class operate in the contemporary United States. This book follows the tradition in sociology of making the everyday world problematic, as Dorothy Smith would say, and focusing on the minutiae of social interactions and behaviors that construct the social world, following Erving Goffman or Harold Garfinkel.[2] This lens roots an understanding of social inequality in what people do with one another not just in the spectacular moments of life but in the everyday. The occurrences that are usually unremarkable or just how things are reveal much about how embedded and long-standing social relations of dominance and subordination are constantly re-created and adapt to changing historical and social contexts.

Not only do race, gender, sexuality, class, and other aspects of difference both shape and are shaped by different spaces and places, but they intermingle differently in each context. Without centering the analysis on intersectionality and multiplicity, I would have missed the full picture of what was occurring in trans men's experiences and missed how these narratives speak to men's experiences of masculinity more broadly. Thus, an intersectional analysis that is attentive to multiplicity must not just go beyond the mantra of race, class, and gender but further break down categories like gender. In this case, it means that to analyze gender we must think not just about women and men but about nonbinary people, cisgender and transgender people, and masculinity and femininity. While the group of trans men in this study is somewhat more racially diverse than most previous research, an even more racially diverse sample would help push the analysis further past a black/white binary or a white men/men of color binary. An increased focus on the experiences of Asian, Latinx, Native, and other trans men and, importantly, a more nuanced comparative analysis of racialization and transgender experiences would deepen this analysis in significant ways.

Men in Place also points to the ways an intersectional lens can be used to highlight how certain aspects of inequality become heightened in particular spaces and places at certain historical moments. For example, men's bathrooms are central sites of the reproduction of heterosexism in the contemporary United States, but if we studied public bathrooms in the Jim Crow era in the U.S. South, we might conclude that race was clearly one of the main organizers of access to bathrooms. This does not mean that sexuality did not shape the bathrooms then and race does not shape them now. Rather, this point suggests that what is closer to the surface in one time gives us insight into the particular role of that space in the creation of power and resistance in that moment and location.

Understanding the spaces interactions occur in, as well as collective ideas about space and place, is absolutely crucial for uncovering the organization of social life. Urban, rural, or suburban location, along with region and institutional contexts, offer different levels of analysis to focus on and compare across. These spatial contexts condition the social expectations and the structural conditions that individuals negotiate, reproduce, and resist in their everyday lives, especially at the level of interaction. Though some sociological research does attend to space and place at times, it is usually treated as a background characteristic. For example, Candace West and Don Zimmerman certainly point to the importance of context in their understanding of the role of situated gender expectations, but this aspect of the theory is often not actively addressed in the voluminous scholarship that uses this perspective.[3] The analysis in this book also suggests how the doings that are products of this negotiation are repeated and become routinized, such as in men's bathrooms. This repetitive nature of gender has been theorized by others, but it is usually absent in work that uses the doing gender perspective, which at times treats actors as if they had no prior history coming into a particular interaction.[4] By bringing together these perspectives with an understanding of the disciplinary mechanisms of particular spaces and the self-disciplining practices individuals engage in, we get a better view of how these social relations are created, re-created, and resisted as individuals move between spaces in their everyday lives.

This book shows the value of foregrounding space and place through comparative work across spatial contexts, such as regions or urban and rural spaces, and across institutions. Through these comparisons, we can understand how individual, interactional, and structural conditions all come into play to shape people's behavior as they move about their lives. Dominant discourses of rural queer and transgender life make rural trans men's lives seem unlivable. It is important to go beyond the narrative that trans people do not exist in rural places or that their only chance of having a livable life is to follow the metronormative narrative and move to the city. Instead, a comparative approach shows that rural trans men may have particular needs or experiences related to place, as do their urban counterparts. For example, trans men in both urban and rural contexts have received inadequate care from medical providers. Yet they differ in that urban trans men have less difficulty finding new providers, especially in major cities. This suggests that rather than building another trans healthcare center in a major city (even if it is needed), some resources should be directed to smaller cities or for doctors with expertise in trans healthcare to travel to underserved areas for regular clinics. It is difficult to counter metronormative and other geographic narratives when little research focuses on transgender and queer lives outside the cities of the East and West Coasts. Fortunately, there is increasing scholarly and popular interest in LGBT lives outside coastal cities, and this study complements that work.[5] In sum, the proliferation of research and understanding of transgender lives should aim at matching the diversity and complexity of those lives.

TRANSGENDER VIOLENCE

In recent years there has been a surge in visibility of trans people and issues in the U.S. popular media as well as major reforms to trans policy and legal rights. The speed of these changes was unimaginable when I completed the first interview for this project.[6] At the same time, these changes have been even more amplified by a highly visible social and political backlash from conservative activists, with bathroom bills being the most visible example. Further, some of the formal gains that came during President Obama's second term, including supportive federal education policy and transgender access to military service, have been reversed by the Trump administration as of 2018. Yet what is often missing from these heated mainstream debates are questions about which trans people will benefit most from these reforms and how the underlying logics and unintended consequences of these changes might actually negatively affect some trans people. Dean Spade argues that "legal equality goals threaten to provide nothing more than adjustments to the window-dressing of neoliberal violence that ultimately disserve and further marginalize the most vulnerable trans populations."[7] In this light, do efforts at attaining legal equality actually hurt the most marginalized trans people rather than produce substantive change? If Spade is correct, why are these reforms the focus of most mainstream transgender rights organizations and larger political efforts?

The answer lies in the kinds of fears and explanations for violence I have detailed throughout *Men in Place*. One thread running through interviewees' narratives was the idea that most inequality and social violence is the product of individual actions by bad, violent, or hateful people. By posing transphobic, racist, homophobic, and sexist violence as the property of bad individuals, particularly connected to rural men in the South, this violence becomes a problem of individuals who cannot control their aggressive urges and ignores the structural arrangements that limit the life chances of trans people. The fears at the base of this way of thinking are affirmed through vulnerability rituals, such as Transgender Day of Remembrance, where individual trans people are memorialized for the crimes committed against them by these bad individuals. Yet for all of the fears of violence presented across the trans men's stories, most were not realized, except in medical spaces. In fact, these mostly unfounded fears act as powerful forms of social control that encourage conformity and complicity in relations of social domination. Race, gender, sexuality, class, and ability shape who is blamed for violence and who can profess innocence while simultaneously reaping the limited benefits that stem from mainstream political efforts.

Transgender activism and political efforts in the mid to late 1990s often focused on the inclusion of transgender people as a protected group in hate crimes legislation, organized around the horrific acts of violence committed against trans people such as Brandon Teena and Marsha P. Johnson.[8] These efforts were a victory for transgender people in terms of recognition, but at the same time they supported a legal and legislative solution to the problem of transgender marginalization. Dean Spade uses the insights of critical race theorists to show that these approaches to legal reform focus on a victim–perpetrator model, which assumes violence against transgender people happens solely because bad transphobic people do it, in line with the fear narratives of trans men.[9] In a neoliberal framework, social problems are solved through an emphasis on personal responsibility rather than systemic or transformative tactics. In fact, legal reforms focused on hate crimes and antidiscrimination are not actually effective at deterring incidents of violence and bias. Whether through formal policy or grassroots organizing, these approaches, under the guise of increasing safety, work to direct further resources to the criminal justice system.[10] Lisa Duggan argues that these neoliberal law-and-order politics of increased policing and imprisonment have become the primary methods of containing the poverty produced by the economic effects of neoliberal policy.[11] In the case of transgender violence, these law-and-order politics lead to further violence against the poor trans women of color who are also most at risk of being victimized by the spectacular violence imagined in narratives of transgender vulnerability. Thus, these approaches are most likely to strengthen the institutions, such as police and prisons, which visit incredible structural violence against poor and racially marginalized trans people, including the kind of violence black trans men experience from the police and the criminal punishment system. This structural violence increases the marginalization that makes trans women of color more vulnerable to the acts of interpersonal violence that actually occur.

Transgender antidiscrimination laws in employment, housing, and education did make most trans men I interviewed feel safer in particular geographic locations, but laws based on single identities are quite limited. Kimberlé Crenshaw, in her work that coined the term *intersectionality*, makes clear that legal strategies that focus on only one aspect of identity or social location will necessarily leave out those who simultaneously experience multiple forms of social marginalization.[12] Thus, legal efforts must be combined with measures to address the poverty, racism, and other forms of structural inequality that make particular trans people more vulnerable. Further, in order to combat the structural violence perpetuated by the state, one must consider solutions outside the logic of the state itself and away from a liberal-rights framework.[13]

Legal and political efforts would best focus on reforms targeted toward the most common sources of violence faced by transgender people at the same time as measures aimed at bettering the lives of the most economically and socially marginalized trans people. We could imagine a TDOR that goes beyond making sure the dead are not forgotten or increasing police attention to transgender people to cataloging the less spectacular abuses that transgender people suffer in medical contexts, in prisons, and otherwise at the hands of the state and other institutions. The solutions stemming from this wider focus might shift the blame from individuals and onto the structures that make individuals vulnerable in the first place.

Trans men's narratives show that public bathrooms and medical institutions are crucial sites for this institutional change. Increased numbers of the single occupancy–style gender-inclusive bathrooms can be a welcome refuge for a person who fears harassment or violence because others think they might not belong in the women's or men's bathrooms. They are also often accessible to people with a wide range of disabilities.[14] The more radical change would be to abolish gender-segregated bathrooms altogether.[15] This idea creates quite a bit of fear and is a frequent touch point for gender panics, but gendered bathrooms, a thoroughly modern invention, did not exist in this form until the past two centuries. The change not only would add to transgender and gender-nonconforming people's comfort and health in everyday life but also has the potential to disrupt the production of homophobia and gender conformity in these institutional settings. In fact, all-gender multiuser bathrooms are being installed across the United States, including at my own university, and people seem to be using them together with few problems. At the very least, institutions can establish policies that all new or remodeled buildings have gender-inclusive bathrooms, as well as changing existing single-user and multiuser gender-segregated bathrooms.

Bathrooms are a potentially fruitful site for coalition building between transgender and disability movements and furthering the shared goals of each movement. In order to make public bathrooms truly accessible, as Alison Kafer argues, disabled people should not just seek access to the institution of the gender-segregated bathroom but should be part of a larger demand "to undo the gendered conventions of the toilet as part of our larger struggles for access to public space."[16] This would make for a more radical accessibility for cisgender, transgender, and gender-nonconforming people whose bodies are marked as disabled and not. Accordingly, this would also help to recognize that trans and gender-nonconforming activists are also disability activists and vice versa, as were several interviewees.

It will take a combination of approaches to reduce the multiple forms of violence trans people encounter. One of the core aims of transgender sociology should be to expand understanding of transgender people's lives in multiple locations and to address the many forms of violence against them. It is clear in this arena, too, an analysis of power and domination that moves toward liberation must remain thoroughly intersectional by attending to multiplicity at the individual and group level, as well as recognizing interlocking systems that differently affect the life chances of transgender people.

MASCULINITIES AND INEQUALITY

This book speaks to a central contemporary debate in the field of men and masculinities about the meanings of hybrid masculinities.[17] The Goldilocks masculinity of the regular guy ideal is clearly a hybrid masculinity. The prevalence of the mobilization of hybrid masculinities from various groups of men means the hypermasculinity central to some scholars' understanding of hegemonic masculinity is no longer as widely acceptable and, most important, no longer serves to legitimate patriarchy. Instead of rejecting everything about subordinate masculinities, such as those associated with gay men, this hybrid formation allows for incorporation of some of these formerly subordinated practices. Yet the following questions remain about the meaning of these hybrids: Are they a sign of more egalitarian gender relations and decreasing homophobia?[18] Are they solely local variation?[19] Or are they superficial rather than substantive changes that repackage hegemonic masculinity without upsetting relations of power in any significant way?[20] Clarifying the role of hybrid masculinities is crucial to a better understanding of the persistence of social inequity.

The answers to these questions about the significance of the Goldilocks masculinity as a normative masculinity rest on what effect it has on the persistence of inequality between men and women and among men. First, the differing treatment and often privilege that most trans men report experiencing when others socially recognize them as men signals inequality between women and men is very much alive. Second, the fact that men of color, particularly black men, did not experience these same privileges and that narratives of emotion tied their affect to aggression and violence shows intersecting racial and gender hierarchies among men are still present. Further, homophobia and heterosexism are still embedded in social relations, as evidenced by narratives of participation in the everyday homophobic rules of the men's bathroom as well as descriptions of heterosexual dyads as the proper place for emotional romantic relationships. Thus, the fact that interviewees agreed overt acts of homophobia were unacceptable and only enacted by hypermasculine men does not erase the hold heterosexism has over everyday life. With this evidence, the position that there is a general decline in homophobia and increasing egalitarian gender relations appears to be overly optimistic.

The remaining two positions in this debate are similar in their understanding that hybrid formations do not necessarily signal substantive changes in gender relations, but they differ in that Raewyn Connell and James Messerschmidt see them as only local variations, whereas Tristan Bridges and C. J. Pascoe argue they reflect wider-reaching dynamics.[21] Since hybridity is a strategy to respond to feminist and other challenges to the gender order through the appropriation of aspects of subordinated and marginalized masculinities, hybridity would likely emerge in the spatial contexts where these challenges are the most intense. Urban spaces, particularly major cities, are far less homogenous than rural spaces in terms of large communities of color and large visible queer populations. Thus, the realities of major cities in the early twenty-first century may mean hegemonic masculinity might not be as sufficient for legitimating patriarchy and the gender order. In contrast, masculinities in rural spaces were marked with more rigidity than flexible urban ideals. This urban and rural difference may be a sign of the coming of a particular historic bloc or a shift in hegemonic power relations. Rural spaces are inherently associated with whiteness, whereas that is not possible in urban spaces in the same way because of concentrations of people of color—though there may be more men of color in rural spaces than in the past.[22] Thus, different strategies to maintain the gender order become necessary as power becomes unstable with historic change in particular spaces and places. The change over time in major cities is evident when comparing men who transitioned in the 1980s with those in the 2010s; furthermore, there was some evidence of the growing ascendance of hybridity in less progressive cities and rural places. While these do represent local variation, it is an important kind of variation that should command the attention of those who are interested in upending social inequities of gender, race, class, and sexuality.

Taken in sum, this discussion points to the importance of locating the spatial dimensions of hybridity and shows their rise signals something greater than just local variation. In fact, the way these hybrid formations both emerge in and refer to particular spaces and places shows how they aid in maintaining the gender, racial, and class order in spite of surface-level changes. The spatial construction of hybridity that emerged from interviewee's stories suggests good men are in the cities and bad men are in rural spaces, regardless of continuing evidence of inequalities in both places. The racial, gender, and sexual projects of the thug and the redneck protect the regular guy from being implicated in unacceptable violence, homophobia, sexism, and racism. This spatial construction illustrates how distancing oneself from culpability in continuing inequalities works to further legitimize social dominance. Thus, spatially locating hybrid masculinities, as well as understanding their intersecting gender, racial, class, and sexual dynamics, is key to evaluating the effects of changes in contemporary masculinities and social relations.

Even though these hybrid formations do not necessarily represent substantive change, I should note it is positive that men want something more than a narrow range of masculine practices, even if expressed only on the surface. Many of the men who participated in this study truly wanted to be good men, whatever their version was, and quite a number wanted to combat their privilege directly. Part of this desire to be a good man stemmed potentially from their time being treated as women or their intersecting sexual, class, and race social positions. Certainly not all trans men took on these projects, but more than a few were committed to both substantive everyday change and broad political transformation. For some this meant committing to antiracist practice in an overtly racist community; others fought for improvements in trans healthcare access through education and advocacy; and still others worked in coalition with other feminists on issues that affect transgender and cisgender women alike. These men demonstrate it is crucial to go beyond surface-level changes and commit to actions that actually break down gender, racial, sexual, and class relations.

Changes in style could gesture toward real change, but it takes much deeper collective work and the transformation of structural relations to make changes in social relations a reality. If we focus on individual actions, progressive men show the best avenue for change through constant critical reflection and a sustained commitment to social justice that highlights people who experience multiple marginalizations rather than just recentering privileged men, but this is no easy task. In all, it would be best to exercise caution at every surface change in privileged men's practices and every iteration of the new man. The attendant celebrations of these small superficial changes often obscure continuing systemic inequities. It bears repeating here that the burden of combatting social inequality based on race, gender, and sexuality should not fall most heavily on a group of men who experience quite a bit of marginalization for their gender status, even if they are unlikely to experience spectacular transphobic violence outside medical settings. Trans men's stories illustrate that resistance, too, must be contextual and that effective strategies for change must take into account both the specific spaces and places where power relations are created and re-created and how these contexts fit into the larger landscape of social life.

Acknowledgments

I am first and foremost deeply grateful to the men who shared their stories with me. Their incredible insights along with their encouragement to continue this work have truly fueled the project from start to finish. I am grateful to the many listserv administrators, activists, and friends who connected me to these men.

Thanks go to the Center for the Study of Women in Society at the University of Oregon for financial support through graduate research grants and the Jane Grant Dissertation Fellowship. CSWS director Carol Stabile and staff Peggy McConnell, Shirley Marc, and Alice Evans provided crucial support and encouragement. This project was supported financially at the University of Oregon through the Department of Sociology's Wasby-Johnson Dissertation Research Award, the Center on Diversity and Community's Summer Research Award, and funding from the College of Arts and Sciences. The departments of Ethnic Studies and Women's and Gender Studies gave vital support through graduate teaching fellowships and were places both to feel at home and to push myself intellectually. I would not have been able to finish the book without an American Association of University Women American Fellowship Short-Term Publication Grant.

I first started thinking about this project in my sociology classes at San Francisco State University. I thank Andreana Clay, Chris Bettinger, and Karen Hossfeld, who helped me see I might have a place in academia. Without their encouragement and support, I would not have thought of applying to PhD programs.

I could not have asked for a better dissertation committee. My gratitude for Jocelyn Hollander and Ellen Scott, coadvisors extraordinaire, is boundless. Thank you for giving me the latitude to fulfill my vision and for never letting me rest on easy arguments or unclear writing. Your continued mentoring and friendship have been invaluable. I thank Lynn Fujiwara, who introduced me to the perspectives that have shaped my best work and showed me how to push past the boundaries of sociology. Thanks go to C. J. Pascoe for providing invaluable insight and energy for my work, which has solidified my confidence as a scholar. Thanks go to Lizzie Reis for her intellectual generosity. There is nothing better than knowing a group of tough feminists have your back. I thank other faculty at the University of Oregon who supported me over the years, including Daniel Martinez HoSang, Yvonne Braun, and Eileen Otis. Friends and fellow graduate students provided support and camaraderie, including "Accoutabilla-buddies" Lauren Bratslavsky and Katie Rodgers, Matt Friesen, Chris Hardnack, Sarah Ray Rondot, Megan Burke, and too many others to name. Sarah Cribbs, Ryanne Pilgeram, and other SSFN-RIG members provided important encouragement, community, and laughter. Thanks go to transcriptionists Ellen Taylor, Wesley D. Shirley, Paula Wilson, Kim Barker, and Meghan Morgavan.

Many people at Portland State University helped make this book a reality. I thank my supportive colleagues in Women, Gender, and Sexuality Studies, including Sally McWilliams, Eddy Alvarez, Stephanie Lumsden, and Lisa Weasel. Staff members Sarah Curtis and Darrow Omar have been indispensable. The writing groups, retreats, and resources provided through the Jumpstart Writing Program, thanks to the work of Danelle Stevens, Janelle Voegele, and Kristie Kolesnikov, were instrumental in helping me squeeze out time for writing between service, teaching, and other obligations in my first years at PSU. Christina Gildersleeve-Neumann, as well as Greg Pugh, Vicki Reitenauer, and Hyeyoung Woo, have provided accountability and friendship in our Jumpstart writing group. Elena Aviles and Xia Zhang provided essential feedback on my work, inspiration from their incredible scholarship, and mutual support at our migrating weekly group. I thank Tristen Kade for being a stellar research assistant. Thanks go to Craig Leets and the QRC staff. The feminist sociology feedback group started by Maura Kelly provided intellectual community to a lonely sociologist across the Park Blocks. My heartfelt gratitude goes to Maura, Amy Lubitow, Emily Shafer, JaDee Carathers, MacKenzie Christensen, Amanda Hendrix, and Erin Savoia for giving essential feedback on the first full draft of the book.

This book benefited from the input of numerous scholars and writers, including Amy Stone, Beth Hutchison, Catherine Connell, Derrais Carter, Erica Rand, Jessica Fields, Laurel Westbrook, Naomi Adiv, and stef shuster. Thank you all so much. Thanks go to Tristan Bridges for incisive comments and enthusiasm for the manuscript. I thank Cooper Lee Bombardier for his kindness and critical feedback. Thanks go to anonymous reviewers from two presses for their insights. I thank Ben Anderson-Nathe, Emily Kazyak, and D'Lane Compton for advice and intellectual engagement. Shannon Elizabeth Bell has been an incredible friend and inspiration for how to be the best kind of sociologist and human. I thank Carter Sickels for writing encouragement. Thanks go to excellent new writing buddy Sara Jaffe. I thank Adam Morehouse for insightful conversation and keeping me looking sharp. Thanks go to my editor at the University of Minnesota Press, Jason Weidemann, as well as Gabriel Levin, Rachel Moeller, Wendy Holdman, and Mike Hanson.

I am fortunate to have many longtime friends who are the best kind of family and who have always been there for encouragement and distraction, including Ryan Edward Scott, Kristina Cervantes-Yoshida, Deez Davidson, Molly DeCoudreaux, Tamara Llosa-Sandor, Sam Luckenbill, Laura Mason, Derek Schmidt, Kevin Seaman, and Elijah Weiss. I have a wonderful community of friends in Portland, including the Wood-Walshes, the Robinsons, Jose Cruz, Avi Brockman, Katie Carter, Erin Fairchild, and Amie LeeKing. I thank my parents, Janet and Howard Abelson, my siblings, Rachel, Joel, Ruthie, and Sarah, and all my nieces and nephews. Thanks go to Marsha and Ron Grosjean for all kinds of support. Don Barrett was an incredible cheerleader and an inspiration for living a good and just life. I wish he could have seen this book in print. Thanks go to Lori Teachout for helping me figure out how to be an adult. There are too many friends, neighbors, and family members that sustained me to list here. I thank you all.

My deepest appreciation goes to Shelley Grosjean. Thank you for reading every word (multiple times), talking me down and boosting me up, keeping the household reproduction going, and being a lovely, creative, and smart girlfriend. Like all good things, we did this together.

Appendix A
INTERVIEWEE DEMOGRAPHICS

West Interviewees

PSEUDONYM	DENSITY	AGE	TRANSITION (YEARS)	RACE	SEXUAL IDENTITY
Sam	Urban	34	3.5	Latino	Heterosexual/Queer
Mario	Urban	31	4.5	White	Bisexual
Saul	Urban	47	14	White	Queer/Heterosexual
Levi	Urban	40	8	White	Queer
Alec	Urban	25	4	White	Queer/Gay
Oscar	Suburban	19	1	Asian/White	Bisexual
Drew	Urban	37	2	White	Queer
Chris	Urban	48	13	White	Heterosexual
Casey	Urban	36	2	Asian/White	Bisexual
Ken	Urban	29	7	White	Queer
Leo	Urban	36	5	Black	Straight, Bi Questioning
Joel	Urban	49	22	White	Attracted to Women
Paul	Rural	30	7	White	Maybe Bisexual
Josh	Rural	43	5	White	Mostly Heterosexual
Tom	Suburban	28	.5	White	Straight
Michael	Urban	40	2	White	Queer
James	Urban	39	1	White	Straight
Woody	Urban	32	7	White	Queer
Jeffery	College Town	25	4	White	Queer
David	College Town	41	9	White	Bisexual
Robert	College Town	41	10	White	Mostly Straight/Bi

South Interviewees

PSEUDONYM	DENSITY	AGE	TRANSITION (YEARS)	RACE	SEXUAL IDENTITY
Anthony	Suburban	24	In process	White	Polysexual
Tim	Suburban	22	6	Latino/White	Gay/Queer
Diego	Urban	21	In process	Latino	Gay
Andrew	Suburban	43	part time	White	Heterosexual
Mason	Urban	21	5	White	Queer/Mostly Straight
Aidan	Urban	21	1	White	Pansexual
Alan	Urban	32	5	White	Gay Male
Bobby	Suburban	31	1.5	White	Straight
Jack	Rural	49	1	White	Straight Male
Simon	Urban	49	11	White	Primarily Straight
Wesley	Urban	44	20	White	Pansexual
Doug	Urban	24	7	White	Straight
Bert	College Town	49	3	White	Sexy, Flexible
Morgan	Rural	43	10	White	Straight
Phillip	Suburban	28	3	White	Bisexual
Malcolm	Urban	22	2	White	Gay/Queer/Bisexual
Gabriel	Suburban	21	2	Multiracial	Queer

Midwest Interviewees

PSEUDONYM	DENSITY	AGE	TRANSITION (YEARS)	RACE	SEXUAL IDENTITY
Ben	Urban	28	4	Asian	Heterosexual/Queer
Raphael	Urban	38	1.5	Mexican	Queer
Aaron	Urban	24	5	White	Asexual
Henry	Suburban	49	7	White	Attracted to Women
Dominic	Rural	27	2	White	Pansexual
Brandon	Suburban	20	1.5	White	Straight
Ethan	Suburban	38	9	Black	Heterosexual
Eric	Urban	22	3	White	Asexual
Dylan	Suburban	36	6	White	Asexual, Leaning Bi
Jason	Suburban	36	12	White	Gay Male
Julian	Urban	28	7	White	Queer/Pansexual
Luke	Rural	47	5	White	Pansexual
Gavin	Urban	27	7	White	Gay Mostly
Wyatt	Urban	20	2	White	Homosexual
Owen	Suburban	18	5	Mixed Race	Queer
Steven	Rural	22	2	Latino	Open
Silas	College town	19	1	Black	Queer
Logan	College town	21	2	White	Gay But Fluid
Sebastian	Urban	40	.5	White	Pansexual
Holden	Suburban	26	5	White	Queer
Colton	Suburban	38	3.5	White	Attracted to Men
Ian	Urban	27	6.5	White	Gay
Sean	Rural	34	11	White	Straight
Felix	Urban	33	8	White	Queer
Cooper	Rural	26	4	White	Omnisexual
Finn	Urban	26	3	White	Queer
Jacob	Urban	55	13	White	Bi
Seth	Urban	23	1	Black/White	Straight

Appendix B
A NOTE ON METHODOLOGY

When I started doing interviews for this project, I did not think of myself as a person from Oregon. I had lived here for less than a year when I did the first interviews in the San Francisco Bay Area, which had been my home for the first three decades of my life. While the Bay Area will always be home, now that I have lived in Oregon for almost ten years it too is home. Yet I was an object of curiosity for interviewees—a curiosity that became stronger as I traveled to the South and Midwest. Who is this person from Oregon? A few men said they decided to participate because they were just so curious about who I was and why I was coming from so far away. This is only one way that I, as the researcher, became an object of scrutiny and how it changed me—I became a person from Oregon.

In each interview, I learned anew how I was both an outsider and an insider and that the power dynamics of the interview setting were far more nuanced than I could have imagined while in a classroom studying researcher positionality. Though I was a cisgender person doing research with transgender people, that has never been adequate for wholly defining myself or the interviewees and the relations between us. I was a woman interviewing men, though some interviewees assumed that I, too, was a trans man. In fact, people assuming that I am a man, whether transgender or cisgender, is an everyday occurrence for me. Interviewees' stories of the different treatment they received when they were recognized (or in my case misrecognized) as a man by others and the difficulties using gender-segregated public bathrooms resemble, though not identically, my own everyday experiences.[1] In the San Francisco Bay Area some interviewees recognized me, and I them, from local queer spaces. As a queer woman and a feminist butch dyke, I shared understanding of particular cultural aspects of queer experience with some interviewees, which helped build rapport but simultaneously made me an object of suspicion to men who did not trust lesbians. At times, I became uncomfortable when interviewees occasionally said denigrating things about women and queer people and about other marginalized identities I do not hold. My whiteness and middle-class background also contributed to a complex relationship in the interview setting. On the whole, the greatest commonality between participants and myself was our shared commitment to increase knowledge of a wide range of trans men's experiences and to better the lives of trans people.

The roots of this project came from what was happening around me in the Bay Area and Portland in the 1990s and 2000s. The queer communities I came up in, where butch dykes, genderqueers, and trans men (to name a few) often mixed and mingled in the same spaces (and still do in my world), were where I started thinking about the core issues of this book. There have been many overlaps, tensions, and coalitions among these groups in various spaces and places, constituting a sort of borderlands.[2] I am often struck that my younger queer and trans students seem baffled by the contours of these borderlands, just as I have to work to learn about the different terrains that constitute their lives. Further, the landscape of transgender representation and community has changed rapidly in the more than twelve years since I first started thinking about these issues in an academic context. All said, I did not feel like much of an outsider when I started down the path of this research, but as I have gone along the differences and similarities between myself and the men I interviewed became clearer and also showed their many intricacies.

Overall, my interest in masculinity came from my experience as a masculine woman. I wanted to know more about trans men because they were part of my social world. As a feminist, I was critical of some of the masculinities around me, including my own, and found crucial analytic lenses in critical men and masculinities studies and intersectional perspectives from women of color feminisms. Yet in reviewing scholarship on men and masculinities, I found that the lives of trans men, as a group of men, were mostly missing from this field. A major goal of this research project has always been to include trans men, as an understudied group of men, in the field of men and masculinities and to join in the new field of transgender studies that rejected the medicalization and other problematic discourses of transgender experience I found when initially looking for research about trans people. Following Viviane Namaste, my work is most concerned with documenting the everyday lives of transgender people rather than focusing on the etiology of transgender or highlighting the discovery of transgender selves.[3] When I explained these goals during recruitment and the interviews themselves, the men were supportive and eager to share their stories.

Amid all of this complexity, I have constantly tried to sensitize myself to issues of power by following Jacob Hale's suggestions to approach the topic with a sense of humility and interrogate my own subject position.[4] Rather than assuming my own expertise, I worked to elicit trans men's own knowledge. At the same time, I often shared resources and other information with interviewees, when appropriate, that I had gathered from earlier interviews or background research. The interviewees who had little contact with other trans people, whether due to living rurally or because they had been unable or unmotivated to find in-person community, mentioned they appreciated sharing their stories and talking with someone who was knowledgeable about transgender issues. In these senses and others, there were many moments of reciprocity beyond things like participation incentives.

Regardless of our commonalities and nuanced power dynamics, I have tried to be ever conscious of the historical and current problematic relationship between researchers and trans people throughout the research and writing process by being up front about my motivations and by privileging interviewee's understandings of their own lives and actions. I acknowledge, however, that as the researcher I have final say and interpretive voice in this book. I see part of my work as an ongoing negotiation and evolving conversation on how best to show my commitment to transgender people, which extends far beyond this project. I offer these ruminations as part of my reflexive practice as a feminist researcher, but this more sustained discussion is in this appendix and not in the main text of the book because I also wanted to avoid centering myself to the extent possible. Doing this research with trans men has changed me in innumerable ways, not the least of which is deepening my understanding of how our liberation is tied up with one another.

RECRUITMENT AND STORIES AS EVIDENCE

Recruitment was limited to trans men age eighteen and over who were living or were in the process of transition to live socially as men.

This included a range of people with various gender identities (e.g., genderqueer or transmasculine), but they shared a preference to be recognized as men in most settings. My aim was to form a sample that was diverse in terms of race, class, sexuality, and urban/rural location. I continued recruitment until no new stories or explanations were emerging from further interviews. This told me I had reached theoretical saturation and had completed enough interviews.[5] I have been asked why I did not include trans women, particularly butch trans women, in this research focused on trans masculinities. This decision stemmed from a mostly practical consideration to narrow the scope of the project with a focus on men. Trans women are not men, so it did not make sense to include them.

In each region I gathered a snowball sample with multiple starts. I found initial interviewees through personal contacts with friends and acquaintances, postings to online communities and email lists, and fliers posted at community centers and medical clinics. I posted calls for participants in the volunteer section of Craigslist in each of the Midwest states I planned to visit.[6] The men I recruited through Craigslist ranged from being leaders in their local trans community to never having met another trans person before but overall showed no obvious differences from other participants. Trans men can be difficult to find, since some blend into the larger society after transition and maintain little contact with transgender communities, but I found the snowball sampling method was effective in finding less visible men through their acquaintances who were more visible.

These interviews represent many miles of travel, as well as several thousand pages of interview transcripts. A systematic analysis of these transcripts allowed me to draw out the patterns and themes across the interviewees' narratives. Sixty-six men is a small portion of trans men and an even smaller proportion of men overall living in the United States.[7] All that said, this kind of in-depth qualitative analysis focuses more on understanding the nuance of individual lives and the workings of everyday interaction than is possible with more close-ended interviews or surveys. Thus, while this is not a generalizable sample per se, it would be difficult, if not impossible, to get at these nuanced accounts with a larger sample. As it stands, these men's stories and my analysis of the patterns and themes that emerged across them offer suggestive evidence for the larger workings of gender inequality, masculinities, and transgender experience.

Notes

INTRODUCTION

1. I use the phrase "live as men" to distinguish the time in each interviewee's life after he began to present and live his everyday life being known to himself and others as a man. This is not meant to imply that trans men are somehow not fully men at any point in their lives, to the extent that anyone is solidly living in that social category, but to try to reflect their own varying understandings of their social experience. For some men their lives included periods of time living as a nonbinary person or a woman prior to living as a man.

2. "Trans men" refers to people whose bodies were assigned female at birth and who have transitioned socially and perhaps medically and legally to live as men. Not all of the people who fit this description would identify with this term, but among the research participants I found, this was less controversial than other options. For a discussion of debates around terminology, see Susan Stryker, *Transgender History: The Roots of Today's Revolution* (New York: Seal Press, 2017).

3. Others have used the phrase "Goldilocks masculinity," though in slightly different ways than I do here. Peter Hennen, *Faeries, Bears, and Leathermen: Men in Community Queering the Masculine* (Chicago: University of Chicago Press, 2008); Michael S. Kimmel, *Angry White Men: American Masculinity at the End of an Era* (New York: Nation Books, 2013).

4. Patricia Hill Collins, *Black Feminist Thought: Knowledge, Consciousness, and the Politics of Empowerment* (New York: Routledge, 2000); Kimberlé Crenshaw, "Demarginalizing the Intersection of Race and Sex: A Black Feminist Critique of Antidiscrimination Doctrine, Feminist Theory and Antiracist Politics," *University of Chicago Legal Forum*, 1989, 139.

5. Michael Hames-Garcia, *Identity Complex: Making the Case for Multiplicity* (Minneapolis: University of Minnesota Press, 2011), 12.

6. Bonnie Thornton Dill and Ruth E. Zambrana, *Emerging Intersections: Race, Class, and Gender in Theory, Policy, and Practice* (New Brunswick, N.J.: Rutgers University Press, 2009).

7. Joan Acker, "Inequality Regimes: Gender, Class, and Race in Organizations," *Gender & Society* 20, no. 4 (August 1, 2006): 441–64; Collins, *Black Feminist Thought*; Audre Lorde, *Sister Outsider: Essays and Speeches* (Trumansburg, N.Y.: Crossing Press, 1984).

8. Hames-Garcia, *Identity Complex*, 13.

9. Evelyn Nakano Glenn, *Unequal Freedom: How Race and Gender Shaped American Citizenship and Labor* (Cambridge, Mass.: Harvard University Press, 2002). For a discussion of regional differences shaped by capital and industry in the United Kingdom context, see Doreen Massey, *Space, Place, and Gender* (Minneapolis: University of Minnesota Press, 1994).

10. Chandra Talpade Mohanty, *Feminism without Borders: Decolonizing Theory, Practicing Solidarity* (Durham, N.C.: Duke University Press, 2003).

11. The classic texts influencing the intersectional framework throughout the book include Combahee River Collective, "Combahee River Collective Statement," in *Home Girls: A Black Feminist Anthology*, ed. Barbara Smith (New York: Kitchen Table Women of Color Press, 1983); Cherríe Moraga and Gloria Anzaldúa, eds., *This Bridge Called My Back: Writings by Radical Women of Color* (New York: Kitchen Table Women of Color Press, 1984); Lorde, *Sister Outsider*; Gloria T. Hull, Patricia B. Scott, and Barbara Smith, *All the Women Are White, All the Blacks Are Men, but Some of Us Are Brave: Black Women's Studies* (Old Westbury, N.Y.: Feminist Press, 1982).

12. Michael Omi and Howard Winant, *Racial Formation in the United States*, 3rd ed. (New York: Routledge, 2014); Patricia Yancey Martin, "Gender as a Social Institution," *Social Forces* 82, no. 4 (2004): 1249–73; Cecilia Ridgeway, "Interaction and the Conservation of Gender and Inequality: Considering Employment," *American Sociological Review* 62, no. 2 (1997): 218–35; Cecilia L. Ridgeway and Lynn Smith-Lovin, "The Gender System and Interaction," *Annual Review of Sociology* 25, no. 1 (1999): 191–216; Barbara J. Risman, "Gender as a Social Structure: Theory Wrestling with Activism," *Gender & Society* 18, no. 4 (2004): 429–50.

13. The Pat character from *Saturday Night Live* in the early 1990s is one example where much of the joke is based on the confusion others experience when they cannot easily tell whether Pat is a woman or a man. The "where are you from?" question that people of color often report being asked is another example. The question is often an attempt by the person asking it to ascertain the racial, ethnic, or national background of the individual, which is simultaneously othering because it assumes that the person is not a full citizen and from "here," meaning the United States. For how this dynamic operates through language, see Jocelyn A. Hollander and Miriam J. Abelson, "Language and Talk," in *Handbook of the Social Psychology of Inequality*, ed. Jane McLeod, Ed Lawler, and Michael Schwalbe (New York: Springer, 2014), 181–206.

14. Candace West and Don H. Zimmerman, "Doing Gender," *Gender & Society* 1, no. 2 (1987): 125–51; Martin, "Gender as a Social Institution"; Barbara Poggio, "Editorial: Outline of a Theory of Gender Practices," *Gender, Work & Organization* 13, no. 3 (2006): 225–33. Some scholars have at-

tempted to use the doing gender perspective to understand race and other aspects of social location, such as Candace West and Sarah Fenstermaker's work, but this approach has been arguably less accepted in understanding race. See "Doing Difference," *Gender & Society* 9, no. 1 (1995): 8–37.

15. Jocelyn A. Hollander, "'I Demand More of People': Accountability, Interaction, and Gender Change," *Gender & Society* 27, no. 1 (2013).

16. Judith Butler, *Gender Trouble: Feminism and the Subversion of Identity* (New York: Routledge, 1990).

17. Michael Omi and Howard Winant, *Racial Formation in the United States from the 1960s to the 1990s* (New York: Routledge, 1994), 60.

18. Ruth Wilson Gilmore, *Golden Gulag: Prisons, Surplus, Crisis, and Opposition in Globalizing California* (Berkeley: University of California Press, 2007), 37.

19. Racial formation theory, especially in its original articulation, lacks an understanding of the co-constitutive nature of race with gender and sexuality. Priya Kandaswamy demonstrates, however, that the theory is improved by a more intersectional understanding and that racial formation theory can and should be incorporated into intersectional approaches. "Gendering Racial Formation," in *Racial Formation in the Twenty-First Century*, ed. Daniel Martinez HoSang, Oneka LaBennett, and Laura Pulido (Berkeley: University of California Press, 2012), 23–43.

20. George Lipsitz, *The Possessive Investment in Whiteness: How White People Profit from Identity Politics* (Philadelphia: Temple University Press, 2006).

21. West and Zimmerman, "Doing Gender"; Omi and Winant, *Racial Formation in the United States from the 1960s to the 1990s*.

22. Mary McIntosh, "The Homosexual Role," *Social Problems* 16, no. 2 (1968): 182–92; Kenneth Plummer, *Sexual Stigma: An Interactionist Account* (London: Routledge, 1975); Michel Foucault, *The History of Sexuality*, vol.1 (New York: Pantheon Books, 1978).

23. Cathy J. Cohen, "Punks, Bulldaggers, and Welfare Queens: The Radical Potential of Queer Politics?," *GLQ: A Journal of Lesbian and Gay Studies* 3, no. 4 (1997): 437–65; Eve Kosofsky Sedgwick, *Epistemology of the Closet* (Berkeley: University of California Press, 1990); Adrienne Rich, "Compulsory Heterosexuality and Lesbian Existence," *Signs: Journal of Women in Culture and Society* 5, no. 4 (1980).

24. Foucault, *The History of Sexuality*; Dean Spade, *Normal Life: Administrative Violence, Critical Trans Politics, and the Limits of Law* (New York: South End Press, 2011).

25. Michael Brown, "Gender and Sexuality I: Intersectional Anxieties," *Progress in Human Geography* 36, no. 4 (2012): 541–50; Massey, *Space, Place, and Gender*; Linda McDowell, *Gender, Identity, and Place* (Minneapolis: University of Minnesota Press, 1999).

26. Lynda Johnston, "Gender and Sexuality I: Genderqueer Geographies?," *Progress in Human Geography* 40, no. 5 (2016): 668–78; Lynda Johnston and Robyn Longhurst, *Space, Place, and Sex: Geographies of Sexualities* (Lanham, Md.: Rowman & Littlefield, 2010); Natalie Oswin, "Critical Geographies and the Uses of Sexuality: Deconstructing Queer Space," *Progress in Human Geography* 32, no. 1 (2008): 89–103.

27. Japonica Brown-Saracino, "How Places Shape Identity: The Origins of Distinctive LBQ Identities in Four Small U.S. Cities," *American Journal of Sociology* 121, no. 1 (2015): 1–63; Thomas F. Gieryn, "A Space for Place in Sociology," *Annual Review of Sociology* 26, no. 1 (2000): 463–96; John R. Logan, "Making a Place for Space: Spatial Thinking in Social Science," *Annual Review of Sociology* 38, no. 1 (2012): 507–24.

28. Tim Cresswell, *In Place/Out of Place: Geography, Ideology, and Transgression* (Minneapolis: University of Minnesota Press, 1996).

29. Brown-Saracino, "How Places Shape Identity."

30. George Chauncey, *Gay New York: Gender, Urban Culture, and the Makings of the Gay Male World, 1890–1940* (New York: Basic Books, 1994); John D'Emilio, *Sexual Politics, Sexual Communities: The Making of a Homosexual Minority in the United States, 1940–1970* (Chicago: University of Chicago Press, 1983); Gayle S. Rubin, "Thinking Sex: Notes for a Radical Theory of the Politics of Sexuality," in *Pleasure and Danger: Exploring Female Sexuality*, ed. Carole S. Vance (Boston: Routledge, 1984), 267–319.

31. J. Jack Halberstam, *In a Queer Time and Place: Transgender Bodies, Subcultural Lives* (New York: New York University Press, 2005); Kath Weston, "Get Thee to a Big City: Sexual Imaginary and the Great Gay Migration," *GLQ: A Journal of Lesbian and Gay Studies* 2, no. 3 (1995): 253–77.

32. For example, see David Bell and Gill Valentine, "Queer Country: Rural Lesbian and Gay Lives," *Journal of Rural Studies* 11, no. 2 (1995): 113–22; David Bell, "Farm Boys and Wild Men: Rurality, Masculinity, and Homosexuality," *Rural Sociology* 65, no. 4 (2000): 547–61; Scott Herring, *Another Country: Queer Anti-urbanism* (New York: New York University Press, 2010); Colin R. Johnson, *Just Queer Folks: Gender and Sexuality in Rural America* (Philadelphia: Temple University Press, 2013); Emily Kazyak, "Midwest or Lesbian? Gender, Rurality, and Sexuality," *Gender & Society* 26, no. 6 (2012): 828–48.

33. Mary L. Gray, *Out in the Country: Youth, Media, and Queer Visibility in Rural America* (New York: New York University Press, 2009).

34. Emily Kazyak, "Disrupting Cultural Selves: Constructing Gay and Lesbian Identities in Rural Locales," *Qualitative Sociology* 34, no. 4 (2011): 561–81.

35. E. Patrick Johnson, *Sweet Tea: Black Gay Men of the South* (Chapel Hill: University of North Carolina Press, 2008). James T. Sears, *Growing Up*

Gay in the South: Race, Gender, and Journeys of the Spirit (New York: Routledge, 1991).

36. For a narrative of the development of queer theory that centers the contributions of women of color feminists and queer people of color from the beginning, see Michael Hames-Garcia, "Queer Theory Revisited," in *Gay Latino Studies: A Critical Reader*, ed. Michael Hames-Garcia and Ernesto Javier Martinez (Durham, N.C.: Duke University Press, 2011), 19–45.

37. Viviane K. Namaste, *Invisible Lives: The Erasure of Transsexual and Transgendered People* (Chicago: University of Chicago Press, 2000); Catherine J. Nash, "Trans Geographies, Embodiment and Experience," *Gender, Place & Culture* 17, no. 5 (2010): 579–95.

38. Kath Browne, Catherine J. Nash, and Sally Hines, "Introduction: Towards Trans Geographies," *Gender, Place & Culture* 17, no. 5 (2010): 573–77; Petra L. Doan, "The Tyranny of Gendered Spaces—Reflections from beyond the Gender Dichotomy," *Gender, Place & Culture* 17, no. 5 (2010): 635–54; Sally Hines, "Queerly Situated? Exploring Negotiations of Trans Queer Subjectivities at Work and within Community Spaces in the UK," *Gender, Place & Culture* 17, no. 5 (2010): 597–613.

39. Exceptions include Kale Bantigue Fajardo, "Queering and Transing the Great Lakes Filipino/a Tomboy Masculinities and Manhoods across Waters," *GLQ: A Journal of Lesbian and Gay Studies* 20, no. 1–2 (2014): 115–40; Sally Hines, *TransForming Gender: Transgender Practices of Identity, Intimacy and Care* (Bristol, U.K.: Policy Press, 2007); Emily Skidmore, *True Sex: The Lives of Trans Men at the Turn of the Twentieth Century* (New York: New York University Press, 2017).

40. All of the interviewees identified as "a man," "male," or "a guy" of some sort, and several also identified as genderqueer or otherwise outside typical binaries of man/woman and masculine/feminine. Though nonbinary identities are becoming even more prominent at the time of this writing, they did not seem to have a strong effect on the kinds of interactions that are the focus of this book, and so I do not extensively analyze them here.

41. While it is absolutely important to generate more knowledge about a broad range of trans people, it is well beyond the scope and focus of this book to adequately explore the lives of all trans masculine, masculine of center, nonbinary, trans women, trans feminine, and other transgender people. I hope this book is one contribution among many to better understand the full breadth of trans people's identities, subjectivities, and material needs.

42. Dean Spade, "Mutilating Gender," in *Transgender Studies Reader*, ed. Susan Stryker and Stephen Whittle (New York: Routledge, 2006), 315–32.

43. For a thorough discussion of Janice Raymond's effects on transgender health policy in the United States, see Monica Roberts, "TransGriot: Why The Trans Community Hates Dr. Janice G. Raymond," *TransGriot* (blog),

September 20, 2010, http://transgriot.blogspot.com; Cristan Williams, "Fact Checking Janice Raymond: The NCHCT Report," *The TransAdvocate* (blog), September 18, 2014, http://transadvocate.com.

44. For a comprehensive overview of this pattern of the use of transgender women as objects of both queer and sociological research, see Namaste, *Invisible Lives*. See also Raewyn Connell, "Transsexual Women and Feminist Thought: Toward New Understanding and New Politics," *Signs* 37, no. 4 (2012): 857–81; and Talia Mae Bettcher, "Trapped in the Wrong Theory: Rethinking Trans Oppression and Resistance," *Signs* 39, no. 2 (2014): 383–406.

45. Susan Stryker, "(De)Subjugated Knowledges: An Introduction to Transgender Studies," in *The Transgender Studies Reader*, ed. Susan Stryker and Stephen Whittle (New York: Routledge, 2006), 1–18. For another discussion of the shift from trans people from objects to subjects in sociology, see Kristen Schilt and Danya Lagos, "The Development of Transgender Studies in Sociology," *Annual Review of Sociology* 43, no. 1 (2017): 425–43.

46. Raewyn Connell, "Accountable Conduct: Doing Gender in Transsexual and Political Retrospect," *Gender & Society* 23, no. 1 (2009): 104–11; Namaste, *Invisible Lives*; Jay Prosser, *Second Skins: The Body Narratives of Transsexuality* (New York: Columbia University Press, 1998).

47. micha cárdenas, "Trans of Color Poetics: Stitching Bodies, Concepts, and Algorithms," *S&F Online*, no. 13.3 (2016); C. Riley Snorton and Jin Haritaworn, "Trans Necropolitics: A Transnational Reflection on Violence, Death, and the Trans of Color Afterlife," in *Transgender Studies Reader 2*, ed. Susan Stryker and Aren Z. Aizura (New York: Routledge, 2013), 66–76.

48. C. Riley Snorton, *Black on Both Sides: A Racial History of Trans Identity* (Minneapolis: University of Minnesota Press, 2017).

49. Raewyn Connell, *Masculinities* (Berkeley: University of California Press, 1995). The following discussion of Connell's theory comes from this text.

50. Raewyn Connell, *The Men and the Boys* (Berkeley: University of California Press, 2000), 29, emphasis in original.

51. Douglas Schrock and Michael Schwalbe, "Men, Masculinity, and Manhood Acts," *Annual Review of Sociology* 35 (2009): 277–95.

52. Kath Browne, "Stages and Streets: Reading and (Mis)Reading Female Masculinities," in *Spaces of Masculinities*, ed. Bettina van Hoven and Kathrin Hörschelmann (New York: Routledge, 2005), 219–30; J. Jack Halberstam, *Female Masculinity* (Durham, N.C.: Duke University Press, 1998); C. J. Pascoe, *Dude, You're a Fag: Masculinity and Sexuality in High School* (Berkeley: University of California Press, 2007). See also James W. Messerschmidt, *Gender, Heterosexuality, and Youth Violence: The Struggle for Recognition* (Lanham, Md.: Rowman & Littlefield, 2012).

53. Lucas Gottzén and Wibke Straube, "Trans Masculinities," *NORMA*

11, no. 4 (2016): 217–24; Henry Rubin, *Self-Made Men: Identity and Embodiment among Transsexual Men* (Nashville, Tenn.: Vanderbilt University Press, 2003). For an overview of scholarship that explores the relationships between trans men and lesbians and biographical literature on trans men, see Carla A. Pfeffer, *Queering Families: The Postmodern Partnerships of Cisgender Women and Transgender Men* (New York: Oxford University Press, 2017).

54. Raine Dozier, "Beards, Breasts, and Bodies: Doing Sex in a Gendered World," *Gender & Society* 19, no. 3 (2005): 297–316; Jamison Green, "Part of the Package: Ideas of Masculinity among Male-Identified Transpeople," *Men and Masculinities* 7, no. 3 (2005): 291–99; Kristen Schilt and Catherine Connell, "Do Workplace Gender Transitions Make Gender Trouble?," *Gender, Work & Organization* 14 (2007): 596–614; Salvador Vidal-Ortiz, "Queering Sexuality and Doing Gender: Transgender Men's Identification with Gender and Sexuality," in *Gendered Sexualities*, ed. Patricia Gagne and Richard A. Tewksbury (Amsterdam: JAI, 2002).

55. Kristen Schilt, *Just One of the Guys? Transgender Men and the Persistence of Gender Inequality* (Chicago: University of Chicago Press, 2010).

56. Pfeffer, *Queering Families*. See also Jane Ward, "Gender Labor: Transmen, Femmes, and Collective Work of Transgression," *Sexualities* 13, no. 2 (2010): 236–54; Cameron T. Whitley, "Trans-Kin Undoing and Redoing Gender: Negotiating Relational Identity among Friends and Family of Transgender Persons," *Sociological Perspectives* 56, no. 4 (2013): 597–621.

57. Salvador Vidal-Ortiz, "Transgender and Transsexual Studies: Sociology's Influence and Future Steps," *Sociology Compass* 2, no. 2 (2008): 433–450.

58. Schilt's regional comparison and inclusion of trans men in Texas expands the geographic scope, but as she notes, more regional research on trans men is necessary. Schilt, *Just One of the Guys?* In addition, a racially and geographically diverse sample is crucial in understanding the mutual constitution of gender, race, sexuality, and class. See Kylan Mattias de Vries, "Intersectional Identities and Conceptions of the Self: The Experience of Transgender People," *Symbolic Interaction* 35, no. 1 (2012): 49–67.

59. Connell, *Masculinities*.

60. Michael S. Kimmel, "Masculinity as Homophobia: Fear, Shame, and Silence in the Construction of Gender Identity," in *Theorizing Masculinities*, ed. Harry Brod and Michael Kaufman (Thousand Oaks, Calif.: Sage Publications, 1994); Mairtin Mac an Ghaill, "The Making of Black English Masculinities," in *Theorizing Masculinities*, ed. Harry Brod and Michael Kaufman (Thousand Oaks, Calif.: Sage Publications, 1994), 183–99.

61. Karen D. Pyke, "Class-Based Masculinities: The Interdependence of Gender, Class, and Interpersonal Power," *Gender & Society* 10, no. 5 (1996): 527–49.

62. James W Messerschmidt, *Nine Lives: Adolescent Masculinities, the Body, and Violence* (Boulder, Colo.: Westview Press, 2000), 10.

63. Patricia Yancey Martin, "Mobilizing Masculinities: Women's Experiences of Men at Work," *Organization* 8, no. 4 (2001): 587–618.

64. Michael Kimmel, *Manhood in America: A Cultural History*, 3rd ed. (New York: Oxford University Press, 2012).

65. Raewyn Connell and James W. Messerschmidt, "Hegemonic Masculinity: Rethinking the Concept," *Gender & Society* 19, no. 6 (2005): 829–59.

66. James W. Messerschmidt, "Engendering Gendered Knowledge: Assessing the Academic Appropriation of Hegemonic Masculinity," *Men and Masculinities* 15, no. 1 (2012): 56–76.

67. Demetrakis Z. Demetriou, "Connell's Concept of Hegemonic Masculinity: A Critique," *Theory and Society* 30, no. 3 (2001): 337–61.

68. Steven L. Arxer, "Hybrid Masculine Power: Reconceptualizing the Relationship between Homosociality and Hegemonic Masculinity," *Humanity & Society* 35, no. 4 (2011): 390–422.

69. Demetriou, "Connell's Concept of Hegemonic Masculinity," 355.

70. Tristan Bridges and C. J. Pascoe, "Hybrid Masculinities: New Directions in the Sociology of Men and Masculinities," *Sociology Compass* 8, no. 3 (2014): 246–58.

71. Connell and Messerschmidt, "Hegemonic Masculinity."

72. Eric Anderson, *Inclusive Masculinity* (New York: Routledge, 2009).

73. Jeff Hearn, Alp Biricik, and Tanja Joelsson, "Theorising, Men, Masculinities, Place and Space: Local, National and Transnational Contexts and Interrelations," in *Masculinities and Place*, ed. Andrew Gorman-Murray and Peter Hopkins (Burlington, Vt.: Ashgate, 2014), 27–41.

74. Andrew Gorman-Murray and Peter Hopkins, eds., *Masculinities and Place* (Burlington, Vt.: Ashgate, 2014).

75. Connell and Messerschmidt's use of region in "Hegemonic Masculinity: Rethinking the Concept" is different from the more common use to denote the geographic subdivisions within a nation-state that I also use. The U.S. Census defines *region* as "groupings of states and the District of Columbia that subdivide the United States for the presentation of census data." U.S. Census Bureau, "2010 Census: Geographic Terms and Concepts" (Washington, D.C.), http://www.census.gov.

76. Shannon Elizabeth Bell and Yvonne A. Braun, "Coal, Identity, and the Gendering of Environmental Justice Activism in Central Appalachia," *Gender & Society* 24, no. 6 (2010): 794–813.

77. Sara L. Crawley, "The Clothes Make the Trans: Region and Geography in Experiences of the Body," *Journal of Lesbian Studies* 12, no. 4 (2008): 365–79.

78. Trent Watts, *White Masculinity in the Recent South* (Baton Rouge: Louisiana State University Press, 2008).

79. Jo Little, *Gender and Rural Geography: Identity, Sexuality, and Power in the Countryside* (New York: Pearson, 2002); Edward W. Morris, "'Rednecks,' 'Rutters,' and 'Rithmetic: Social Class, Masculinity, and Schooling in a Rural Context," *Gender & Society* 22, no. 6 (2008): 728–51.

80. John Tomaney, "Region and Place II: Belonging," *Progress in Human Geography* 39, no. 4 (2015): 507–16.

81. Katherine McKittrick, *Demonic Grounds: Black Women and the Cartographies of Struggle* (Minneapolis: University of Minnesota Press, 2006).

82. Kathy Charmaz, *Constructing Grounded Theory: A Practical Guide through Qualitative Analysis* (Thousand Oaks, Calif.: Sage, 2006).

1. MASCULINITIES IN SPACE

1. *Thug, redneck,* and *faggy* came from interviewees' description of these types. While they were primarily affectionate reclaimed terms or self-identified terms, they were occasionally used with derogatory meaning.

2. Patricia Hill Collins, *Black Feminist Thought: Knowledge, Consciousness, and the Politics of Empowerment* (New York: Routledge, 2000), 69.

3. Michael Omi and Howard Winant, *Racial Formation in the United States*, 3rd ed. (New York: Routledge, 2014), 125.

4. While Omi and Winant acknowledge the intersectional relationship and mutual constitution of race, class, gender, and sexuality, they primarily focus on race because they believe race is the essential rubric for understanding inequality and difference in the modern world. Omi and Winant, 106. Women of color feminist scholars, among others, argue this is a fundamental weakness in their approach. For example, Priya Kandaswamy convincingly argues that "racial formation is fundamentally a gendered and sexualized process," but also that incorporating racial formation into an intersectional analysis fundamentally shifts feminist frameworks of intersectionality. Thus, bringing together intersectionality and racial formation builds the analytic power of each. "Gendering Racial Formation," in *Racial Formation in the Twenty-First Century*, ed. Daniel Martinez HoSang, Oneka LaBennett, and Laura Pulido (Berkeley: University of California Press, 2012), 24.

5. Hugh Campbell and Michael Mayerfeld Bell, "The Question of Rural Masculinities," *Rural Sociology* 65, no. 4 (2000): 532–46.

6. Michael Kimmel, *Manhood in America: A Cultural History*, 3rd ed. (New York: Oxford University Press, 2012).

7. Chris Gibson, "Cowboy Masculinities: Relationality and Rural Identity," in *Masculinities and Place*, ed. Andrew Gorman-Murray and Peter Hopkins (Burlington, Vt.: Ashgate, 2014), 127.

8. Kimmel, *Manhood in America*.
9. Gibson, "Cowboy Masculinities."
10. Gibson, "Cowboy Masculinities."
11. Laura McCall, "Introduction," in *Across the Great Divide: Cultures of Manhood in the American West*, ed. Matthew Basso, Laura McCall, and Dee Garceau (New York: Routledge, 2001), 1–24.
12. Victoria E. Johnson, *Heartland TV: Prime Time Television and the Struggle for U.S. Identity* (New York: New York University Press, 2008).
13. This temporarily revived the independence of the heroic artisan. Kimmel, *Manhood in America*.
14. Deborah E. Popper, "The Middle West: Corn Belt and Industrial Belt United," *Journal of Cultural Geography* 30, no. 1 (2013): 32–54.
15. James Shortridge cited in Popper, "The Middle West."
16. Stephen Meyer, *Manhood on the Line: Working-Class Masculinities in the American Heartland* (Urbana: University of Illinois Press, 2016); Popper, "The Middle West."
17. Levi Gahman, "Gun Rites: Hegemonic Masculinity and Neoliberal Ideology in Rural Kansas," *Gender, Place & Culture* 22, no. 9 (2015): 1203–19; Kimmel, *Manhood in America*; David T. McMahan, "Heartland: Symbolic Displays of Aggression and Male Masculinity in Rural America," *Qualitative Research Reports in Communication* 12, no. 1 (2011): 51–59; Adam Ochonicky, "The Millennial Midwest: Nostalgic Violence in the Twenty-First Century," *Quarterly Review of Film and Video* 32, no. 2 (2015): 124–40.
18. Popper, "The Middle West."
19. Carla D. Shirley, "'You Might Be a Redneck If . . .': Boundary Work among Rural, Southern Whites," *Social Forces* 89, no. 1 (2011): 35–61.
20. Trent Watts, *White Masculinity in the Recent South* (Baton Rouge: Louisiana State University Press, 2008).
21. Shannon Elizabeth Bell and Yvonne A. Braun, "Coal, Identity, and the Gendering of Environmental Justice Activism in Central Appalachia," *Gender & Society* 24, no. 6 (2010): 794–813.
22. Watts, *White Masculinity in the Recent South*.
23. Peggy F. Bartlett, "Three Visions of Masculine Success on American Farms," in *Country Boys: Masculinity and Rural Life* (University Park: Pennsylvania State University Press, 2006), 47–66.
24. Gregory Peter et al., "Cultivating Dialogue: Sustainable Agriculture and Masculinities," in *Country Boys: Masculinity and Rural Life* (University Park: Pennsylvania State University Press, 2006), 27–45.
25. Peter et al., "Cultivating Dialogue."
26. Michael Kimmel and Abby L. Ferber, "'White Men Are This Nation': Right-Wing Militias and the Restoration of Rural American Masculinity," *Rural Sociology* 65, no. 4 (2000): 582–604.

27. Raewyn Connell and James W. Messerschmidt, "Hegemonic Masculinity: Rethinking the Concept," *Gender & Society* 19, no. 6 (2005): 829–59.

28. Patrick Huber and Kathleen Drowne, "Redneck: A New Discovery," *American Speech* 76, no. 4 (2001): 434–37.

29. Lucy Jarosz and Victoria Lawson, "'Sophisticated People versus Rednecks': Economic Restructuring and Class Difference in America's West," *Antipode* 34, no. 1 (2002): 8–27.

30. Edward W. Morris, "'Rednecks,' 'Rutters,' and 'Rithmetic: Social Class, Masculinity, and Schooling in a Rural Context," *Gender & Society* 22, no. 6 (2008): 728–51; Jarosz and Lawson, "'Sophisticated People versus Rednecks.'"

31. "Mud bogging" refers to driving trucks and other four-wheel-drive vehicles off road in mud and dirt.

32. Omi and Winant, *Racial Formation in the United States*, 125.

33. Shirley, "'You Might Be a Redneck If....'"

34. Jarosz and Lawson, "'Sophisticated People versus Rednecks,'" 14.

35. Shirley, "'You Might Be a Redneck If...,'" 38.

36. John Hartigan Jr., "Who Are These White People?: 'Rednecks,' 'Hillbillies,' and 'White Trash' as Marked Racial Subjects," in *White Out: The Continuing Significance of Racism*, ed. Ashley W. Doane and Eduardo Bonilla-Silva (New York: Routledge, 2004).

37. Jarosz and Lawson, "'Sophisticated People versus Rednecks.'"

38. Shannon E. M. O'Sullivan, "Playing 'Redneck': White Masculinity and Working-Class Performance on Duck Dynasty," *Journal of Popular Culture* 49, no. 2 (2016): 367–384; Watts, *White Masculinity in the Recent South*.

39. O'Sullivan, "Playing 'Redneck.'"

40. "About," Redneck Revolt, https://www.redneckrevolt.org/about.

41. Patricia Hill Collins, *Black Sexual Politics: African Americans, Gender, and the New Racism* (New York: Routledge, 2004), 56. For further discussion of the brute image, see Ronald L. Jackson, *Scripting the Black Masculine Body: Identity, Discourse, and Racial Politics in Popular Media* (Albany: State University of New York Press, 2006).

42. Calvin John Smiley and David Fakunle, "From 'Brute' to 'Thug': The Demonization and Criminalization of Unarmed Black Male Victims in America," *Journal of Human Behavior in the Social Environment* 26, no. 3–4 (2016): 350–66. For further discussion of the links between policing black masculinity and sexuality in the postslavery era, see Rashad Shabazz, *Spatializing Blackness: Architectures of Confinement and Black Masculinity in Chicago* (Urbana: University of Illinois Press, 2015).

43. Khalil Gibran Muhammad, *The Condemnation of Blackness: Race, Crime, and the Making of Modern Urban America* (Cambridge, Mass.: Harvard University Press, 2011).

44. Michelle Alexander, *The New Jim Crow: Mass Incarceration in the Age of Colorblindness* (New York: New Press, 2010).

45. Travis L. Dixon and Daniel Linz, "Overrepresentation and Underrepresentation of African Americans and Latinos as Lawbreakers on Television News," *Journal of Communication* 50, no. 2 (2000): 131–54.

46. Smiley and Fakunle, "From 'Brute' to 'Thug.'"

47. Natalie P. Byfield, *Savage Portrayals: Race, Media, and the Central Park Jogger Story* (Philadelphia: Temple University Press, 2014).

48. Cathy J. Cohen, "#DoBlackLivesMatter? From Michael Brown to CeCe McDonald on Black Death and LGBTQ Politics" (Kessler Award, New York, December 12, 2014), http://www.racismreview.com.

49. Kimberle Crenshaw and Andrea Williams, "Say Her Name: Resisting Police Brutality against Black Women," African American Policy Forum, 2015, http://www.aapf.org/sayhernamereport/.

50. Kimberle Crenshaw, "Beyond Racism and Misogyny: Black Feminism and 2 Live Crew," *Boston Review*, 1991; Aída Hurtado, *Beyond Machismo: Intersectional Latino Masculinities* (Austin: University of Texas Press, 2016).

51. Raewyn Connell, *Masculinities* (Berkeley: University of California Press, 1995).

52. Derrick R. Brooms and Armon R. Perry, "'It's Simply Because We're Black Men': Black Men's Experiences and Responses to the Killing of Black Men," *Journal of Men's Studies* 24, no. 2 (2016): 166–84.

53. Eduardo Bonilla-Silva, "The Linguistics of Color Blind Racism: How to Talk Nasty about Blacks without Sounding 'Racist,'" *Critical Sociology* 28, no. 1–2 (2002): 41–64.

54. Jackie Wang, "Against Innocence: Race, Gender, and the Politics of Safety," *LIES: A Journal of Materialist Feminism*, no. 1 (2012): 145–71.

55. Larger cultural discussions of both country and rap music as lowbrow and undignified forms of entertainment illustrate a further connection between the thug and the redneck. Nadine Hubbs, *Rednecks, Queers, and Country Music* (Berkeley: University of California Press, 2014).

56. Michael P. Jeffries, *Thug Life: Race, Gender, and the Meaning of Hip-Hop* (Chicago: University of Chicago Press, 2011), 88. For another nuanced discussion of the thug in relation to black masculinity, see Aimé J. Ellis, *If We Must Die: From Bigger Thomas to Biggie Smalls* (Detroit: Wayne State University Press, 2011).

57. Research on the dating preferences of heterosexual black women suggest that they find elements of the thug image attractive, particularly the muscled and dark-complexioned physical ideal, but they desire a man who behaves and dresses like a "nice guy." Kristie A. Ford, "Thugs, Nice Guys,

and Players: Black College Women's Partner Preferences and Relationship Expectations," *Black Women, Gender & Families* 6, no. 1 (2012).

58. C. Mallinson and Z. W. Brewster, "'Blacks and Bubbas': Stereotypes, Ideology, and Categorization Processes in Restaurant Servers' Discourse," *Discourse & Society* 16, no. 6 (2005): 787–807.

59. Tristan Bridges and C. J. Pascoe, "Hybrid Masculinities: New Directions in the Sociology of Men and Masculinities," *Sociology Compass* 8, no. 3 (2014): 246–58.

60. Michael S. Kimmel, "Masculinity as Homophobia: Fear, Shame, and Silence in the Construction of Gender Identity," in *Theorizing Masculinities*, ed. Harry Brod and Michael Kaufman (Thousand Oaks, Calif.: Sage Publications, 1994).

61. C. J. Pascoe, *Dude, You're a Fag: Masculinity and Sexuality in High School* (Berkeley: University of California Press, 2007).

62. Marlon T. Riggs, "Black Macho Revisited: Reflections of a Snap! Queen," *Black American Literature Forum* 25, no. 2 (1991): 389–94. See also Carissa M. Froyum, "'At Least I'm Not Gay': Heterosexual Identity Making among Poor Black Teens," *Sexualities* 10, no. 5 (2007): 603–22.

63. Connell, *Masculinities*.

64. Riggs, "Black Macho Revisited."

65. C. Walter Han, "No Fats, Femmes, or Asians: The Utility of Critical Race Theory in Examining the Role of Gay Stock Stories in the Marginalization of Gay Asian Men," *Contemporary Justice Review* 11, no. 1 (2008): 11–22.

66. For a discussion of contemporary Israeli masculinities, see Varda Wasserman, Ilan Dayan, and Eyal Ben-Ari, "Upgraded Masculinity: A Gendered Analysis of the Debriefing in the Israeli Air Force," *Gender & Society* 32, no. 2 (2018): 228–51.

67. Kathryne M. Young, "Masculine Compensation and Masculine Balance: Notes on the Hawaiian Cockfight," *Social Forces* 95, no. 4 (2017): 1341–70.

68. Kathleen Gerson, *The Unfinished Revolution: Coming of Age in a New Era of Gender, Work, and Family* (New York: Oxford University Press, 2011).

69. For a contemporary analysis of how the notion of the ideal worker can bolster a separate spheres ideology, see Youngjoo Cha, "Reinforcing Separate Spheres: The Effect of Spousal Overwork on Men's and Women's Employment in Dual-Earner Households," *American Sociological Review* 75, no. 2 (2010): 303–29.

70. Karen D. Pyke, "Class-Based Masculinities: The Interdependence of Gender, Class, and Interpersonal Power," *Gender & Society* 10, no. 5 (1996): 527–49.

71. This distinction has become quite popular in psychology to understand

Latinx masculinities. G. Miguel Arciniega et al., "Toward a Fuller Conception of Machismo: Development of a Traditional Machismo and Caballerismo Scale," *Journal of Counseling Psychology* 55, no. 1 (2008): 19.

72. For another complex contemporary approach to the varieties of Latinx masculinities through an intersectional framework, see Hurtado, *Beyond Machismo*.

73. Raewyn Connell, "Politics of Changing Men," *Arena Journal* 6 (1996): 53.

74. Omi and Winant, *Racial Formation in the United States*, 129.

75. Bridges and Pascoe, "Hybrid Masculinities."

76. James W. Messerschmidt and Tristan Bridges, "Trump and the Politics of Fluid Masculinities," *Democratic Left* (blog), July 15, 2017, http://www.dsausa.org/trump_and_the_politics_of_fluid_masculinities.

77. C. J. Pascoe, "Who Is a Real Man? The Gender of Trumpism," *Masculinities & Social Change* 6, no. 2 (2017): 133.

78. Young, "Masculine Compensation and Masculine Balance."

2. ONE IS NOT BORN A MAN

1. I follow Wesley's own naming of his body in referring to his chest protrusions as breasts. Throughout this chapter I use *chests, chest protrusions,* and *breasts* to refer to these areas of the body, but naming these protrusions as *breasts* does not mean that the person themselves is necessarily female, a woman, or feminine. For a discussion of chests on athletes, see Erica Rand, *Red Nails, Black Skates: Gender, Cash, and Pleasure on and off the Ice* (Durham, N.C.: Duke University Press, 2012).

2. For discussion of how whiteness and rural working class masculinities foster acceptance of some trans men in the rural Midwest and Southeast, see Miriam J. Abelson, "'You Aren't from around Here': Race, Masculinity, and Rural Transgender Men," *Gender, Place & Culture* 23, no. 11 (2016): 1535–46.

3. The distinction between sex, sex category, and gender is central to Candace West and Don Zimmerman's formulation. Sex categorization refers to the biological criteria of sex but is not necessarily based on actual bodily sex characteristics. It is also possible for a person to be categorized as not fitting into the category of either man or woman, but this binary is quite persistent in these brief and not fully conscious moments of categorization. "Doing Gender," *Gender & Society* 1 (1987): 125–51.

4. The term *passing* is used at times, and was by some interviewees, to describe when transgender people are recognized in line with their gender identity. *Passing* is controversial when applied to transgender people because, as Talia Bettcher compellingly argues, it can reinforce popular images of trans people as deceptive, a characterization that arguably invites and ex-

cuses violence against trans people. "Evil Deceivers and Make-Believers: On Transphobic Violence and the Politics of Illusion," *Hypatia* 22, no. 3 (2007): 43–65. Moreover, for many transgender people the term suggests that when a trans man is categorized by others as a man and not as transgender, he is being read as something he is not. Instead, it may be more accurate to say they had been "passing" as a woman or girl more than as a man

5. Connell focuses particularly on embodiment and shows that the embodiment of gender is a social rather than fixed biological process. Raewyn Connell, "Accountable Conduct: Doing Gender in Transsexual and Political Retrospect," *Gender & Society* 23, no. 1 (2009): 104–11; see also Carla A. Pfeffer, "'I Don't Like Passing as a Straight Woman': Queer Negotiations of Identity and Social Group Membership," *American Journal of Sociology* 120, no. 1 (2014): 1–44.

6. Judith Butler, *Undoing Gender* (New York: Routledge, 2004). Catherine Jean Nash builds on both Tim Cresswell and Butler to illustrate the spatial nature of these norms and thus recognition. "Trans Experiences in Lesbian and Queer Space," *Canadian Geographer* 55, no. 2 (2011): 192–207.

7. Rebecca J. Erickson, "The Importance of Authenticity for Self and Society," *Symbolic Interaction* 18, no. 2 (1995): 121–44.

8. This approach to identity categories as a collective and inherently social achievement, rather than as a set of individual traits, mirrors much of the thinking in disciplines like sociology and geography and more broadly in cultural studies. For an example of how the collective nature of identity plays out for rural LGBT youth, see Mary L. Gray, *Out in the Country: Youth, Media, and Queer Visibility in Rural America* (New York: New York University Press, 2009).

9. For further description of historically specific norms, see Butler, *Undoing Gender*.

10. Raewyn Connell, "Transsexual Women and Feminist Thought: Toward New Understanding and New Politics," *Signs* 37, no. 4 (2012): 857–81.

11. Jocelyn A. Hollander, "'I Demand More of People': Accountability, Interaction, and Gender Change," *Gender & Society* 27, no. 1 (2013).

12. Public policy regarding the presence of transgender people in gender-segregated spaces, such as bathrooms and locker rooms, are based primarily on bodily criteria, specifically the presence or absence of a penis, and maintain the supposed naturalness of binary sex and gender, as well as heterosexuality. Laurel Westbrook and Kristen Schilt, "Doing Gender, Determining Gender: Transgender People, Gender Panics, and the Maintenance of the Sex/Gender/Sexuality System," *Gender & Society* 28, no. 1 (2014): 32–57. Legal gender classification policies also employ varying ideas of biology and self-knowledge to determine who has access to gender changes on government-issued identification and other documents. Tey Meadow, "'A

Rose Is a Rose': On Producing Legal Gender Classifications," *Gender and Society* 24, no. 6 (2010): 814–37. For further discussion of the complexity of knowledges involved in recognition and misrecognition, see C. Riley Snorton, "'A New Hope': The Psychic Life of Passing," *Hypatia* 24, no. 3 (2009): 77–92.

13. Lise Eliot, *Pink Brain, Blue Brain: How Small Differences Grow into Troublesome Gaps—and What We Can Do about It* (Boston: Mariner Books, 2010); Roderick A. Ferguson, *Aberrations in Black: Toward a Queer of Color Critique* (Minneapolis: University of Minnesota Press, 2003); Rebecca M. Jordan-Young, *Brain Storm: The Flaws in the Science of Sex Differences* (Cambridge, Mass.: Harvard University Press, 2011); Karin A. Martin and Emily Kazyak, "Hetero-Romantic Love and Heterosexiness in Children's G-Rated Films," *Gender & Society* 23, no. 3 (2009): 315–36; Emily Martin, "The Egg and the Sperm: How Science Has Constructed a Romance Based on Stereotypical Male–Female Roles," *Signs* 16, no. 3 (1991): 485–501; Siobhan Somerville, *Queering the Color Line: Race and the Invention of Homosexuality in American Culture* (Durham, N.C.: Duke University Press, 2000).

14. Connell, "Transsexual Women and Feminist Thought," 870.

15. For detailed information on trans people's experiences of violence, see Sandy E. James et al., *The Report of the 2015 U.S. Transgender Survey* (Washington, D.C.: National Center for Transgender Equality, 2016).

16. These hierarchies can vary across time and between transgender communities, but most often, transgender people are most legitimate who have completed or want to access gender-confirming medical care. These hierarchies of legitimacy can also rely on cisnormative standards of presenting oneself as a normative man or woman. In other sites, the most legitimate members of particular trans communities might be transgender people who are the most gender nonconforming. See, for example, Alaina Hardie, "It's a Long Way to the Top: Hierarchy of Legitimacy in Trans Communities," in *Trans/Forming Feminisms*, ed. Kristen Scott-Dixon (Toronto: Sumach Press, 2006), 122–30.

17. Robyn Longhurst, "'Man-Breasts': Spaces of Sexual Difference, Fluidity and Abjection," in *Spaces of Masculinity*, ed. Bettina van Hoven and Kathrin Hörschelmann (New York: Routledge, 2005), 152–65.

18. Moments of misrecognition, and the attendant feeling of dissonance between how one sees themselves and how others see them, are also productive in that the feeling of dissonance can strengthen self-knowledge and produce the ground for resistance. Snorton, "'A New Hope.'"

19. Tim Cresswell, *In Place/Out of Place: Geography, Ideology, and Transgression* (Minneapolis: University of Minnesota Press, 1996).

20. Chandra Talpade Mohanty, *Feminism without Borders: Decolonizing Theory, Practicing Solidarity* (Durham, N.C.: Duke University Press, 2003).

21. Eduardo Bonilla-Silva argues that the United States is moving from a biracial to a triracial pattern of stratification, though he acknowledges local and regional variation. This illustrates national-level disparities and the possibility of change over time. "From Bi-racial to Tri-racial: Towards a New System of Racial Stratification in the USA," *Ethnic and Racial Studies* 27, no. 6 (2004).

22. For discussion of how social status shapes racial perception and vice versa, see Andrew M. Penner and Aliya Saperstein, "Engendering Racial Perceptions: An Intersectional Analysis of How Social Status Shapes Race," *Gender & Society* 27, no. 3 (2013): 319–44. See also Peggy Pascoe, *What Comes Naturally: Miscegenation Law and the Making of Race in America* (New York: Oxford University Press, 2009).

23. Catherine J. Nash, "Trans Geographies, Embodiment and Experience," *Gender, Place & Culture* 17, no. 5 (2010): 579–95.

24. Westbrook and Schilt, "Doing Gender, Determining Gender."

25. Eric Plemons, "Formations of Femininity: Science and Aesthetics in Facial Feminization Surgery," *Medical Anthropology*, 2017, 1–13.

26. Lynda Johnston and Robyn Longhurst, *Space, Place, and Sex: Geographies of Sexualities* (Lanham, Md.: Rowman & Littlefield, 2010).

27. The uproar over the exposure of Janet Jackson's chest during the 2004 Superbowl is another example of this difference. Surely, a similar exposure of Justin Timberlake's chest would not have been memorable or caused controversy.

28. *True Life*, episode 190, "I'm Changing My Sex," directed by Danielle Franco, aired on MTV, September 19, 2009.

29. This is not particularly different for trans men.

30. Andrea Sansone et al., "Gynecomastia and Hormones," *Endocrine* 55, no. 1 (2017): 37–44.

31. Longhurst, "'Man-Breasts.'"

32. S. Lochlann Jain, "Cancer Butch," *Cultural Anthropology* 22, no. 4 (2007): 501–38; Rand, *Red Nails, Black Skates*.

33. Amy Stone illustrates that even in queer spaces where gender and sexual fluidity are emphasized, bodies still matter, and others consider transgender bodies as particularly serious in the otherwise playful context of a queer sexual space. Amy L. Stone, "Flexible Queers, Serious Bodies: Transgender Inclusion in Queer Spaces," *Journal of Homosexuality* 60, no. 12 (2013): 1647–65.

34. Bear communities refer to a gay men's subculture where larger and more hairy men's bodies (like a bear) are highly valued. The masculine appearance of the Bear is often constructed in opposition to the effeminacy of stereotypic depictions of gay men or the clone mentality of gay neighborhoods and circuit parties that value highly sculpted, slim, and youthful

bodies. See Peter Hennen, "Bear Bodies, Bear Masculinity: Recuperation, Resistance, or Retreat?," *Gender & Society* 19, no. 1 (2005): 25–43.

35. This Bear space operated as a queer space similar to Amy Stone's ethnography of The Club, where transgender bodies could be incorporated as sexually desirable queer bodies. "Flexible Queers, Serious Bodies." Bodies still matter in these spaces but are resignified in the context of the particular space.

36. Jane Ward, "Gender Labor: Transmen, Femmes, and Collective Work of Transgression," *Sexualities* 13, no. 2 (2010): 236–54.

37. C. J. Pascoe, *Dude, You're a Fag: Masculinity and Sexuality in High School* (Berkeley: University of California Press, 2007).

38. For similar findings about time since transition, see Raine Dozier, "Beards, Breasts, and Bodies: Doing Sex in a Gendered World," *Gender & Society* 19, no. 3 (2005): 297–316.

39. Erica Rand, "Hips," *TSQ: Transgender Studies Quarterly* 1, no. 1–2 (2014): 98–99.

40. Men's reluctance to dance is a fairly recent gendered and racialized phenomenon in the contemporary United States. Maxine Leeds Craig, *Sorry I Don't Dance: Why Men Refuse to Move* (New York: Oxford University Press, 2013).

41. Douglas Schrock and Michael Schwalbe, "Men, Masculinity, and Manhood Acts," *Annual Review of Sociology* 35 (2009): 279.

42. My findings expand beyond the context of the workplace and illustrate that Schilt's conclusions are still evident in interviews completed nearly ten years later. Kristen Schilt, *Just One of the Guys? Transgender Men and the Persistence of Gender Inequality* (Chicago: University of Chicago Press, 2010).

43. For a discussion of disability and masculinity, see Bo Luengsuraswat, "Proof," in *Gender Outlaws: The Next Generation* (Berkeley, Calif.: Seal Press, 2010).

44. For discussion of backstage and frontstage behaviors, see Erving Goffman, *The Presentation of Self in Everyday Life* (Woodstock, N.Y.: Overlook Press, 1973).

45. Shifts in gender expectations created in one setting, such as women's self-defense classes, can shift individuals' expectations in other contexts. Hollander, "'I Demand More of People.'"

46. Miriam J. Abelson, "Dangerous Privilege: Trans Men, Masculinities, and Changing Perceptions of Safety," *Sociological Forum* 29, no. 3 (2014): 549–70.

47. Schilt, *Just One of the Guys?*

48. Wingfield demonstrates that black men in professions traditionally dominated by women, such as nursing, may not receive the benefits of the glass escalator. Adia Harvey Wingfield, "Racializing the Glass Escalator: Re-

considering Men's Experiences with Women's Work," *Gender & Society* 23, no. 1 (2009): 5–26. For further evidence that black, Asian, and Latinx men do not get the respect at work that white men report, see Schilt, *Just One of the Guys?*.

49. Ann Arnett Ferguson, *Bad Boys: Public Schools in the Making of Black Masculinity* (Ann Arbor: University of Michigan Press, 2000); Victor M. Rios, *Punished: Policing the Lives of Black and Latino Boys* (New York: New York University Press, 2011).

50. According to Westbrook and Schilt, trans men's cisgender coworkers recognize them as men in most situations, but not necessarily when considering trans men as potential sexual partners. "Doing Gender, Determining Gender."

51. Carla A. Pfeffer, *Queering Families: The Postmodern Partnerships of Cisgender Women and Transgender Men* (New York: Oxford University Press, 2017).

52. Cathy J. Cohen, "Punks, Bulldaggers, and Welfare Queens: The Radical Potential of Queer Politics?," *GLQ: A Journal of Lesbian and Gay Studies* 3, no. 4 (1997): 437–65.

53. Carla A. Pfeffer, "'Women's Work'? Women Partners of Transgender Men Doing Housework and Emotion Work," *Journal of Marriage and Family* 72, no. 1 (2010): 165–83; Ward, "Gender Labor."

54. For further discussion of the uneven privileges associated with transition, see Abelson, "Dangerous Privilege."

55. Susan E. Chase, *Ambiguous Empowerment: The Work Narratives of Women School Superintendents* (Amherst: University of Massachusetts Press, 1995).

56. Henry Rubin's study of trans men clearly reflects the promise of self-knowledge. *Self-Made Men: Identity and Embodiment among Transsexual Men* (Nashville, Tenn.: Vanderbilt University Press, 2003).

57. For an analysis of how contests over masculinity on the left and the right reify the contemporary gender order, see C. J. Pascoe, "Who Is a Real Man? The Gender of Trumpism," *Masculinities & Social Change* 6, no. 2 (2017): 119–41.

58. Tryon Edwards, *Dictionary of Thoughts: Being A Cyclopedia Of Laconic Quotations from the Best Authors of the World, Both Ancient and Modern* (Detroit: F. B. Dickerson, 1902).

3. "STRONG WHEN I NEED TO BE, SOFT WHEN I NEED TO BE"

1. Stephanie A. Shields, *Speaking from the Heart: Gender and the Social Meaning of Emotion* (New York: Cambridge University Press, 2002).

2. Michael A. Messner, "The Masculinity of the Governator," *Gender & Society* 21, no. 4 (2007): 461–80.

3. Michael A. Messner, "'Changing Men' and Feminist Politics in the United States," *Theory and Society* 22, no. 5 (1993): 723–37.

4. Sara Ahmed, *The Cultural Politics of Emotion* (New York: Routledge, 2004).

5. Jose Esteban Munoz, "Feeling Brown: Ethnicity and Affect in Ricardo Bracho's *The Sweetest Hangover (and Other STDs)*," in *Gay Latino Studies: A Critical Reader*, ed. Michael Hames-Garcia and Ernesto Javier Martínez (Durham, N.C.: Duke University Press, 2011), 204–19; Danielle Popp et al., "Gender, Race, and Speech Style Stereotypes," *Sex Roles* 48, no. 7–8 (2003): 317–25; Patricia Hill Collins, *Black Feminist Thought: Knowledge, Consciousness, and the Politics of Empowerment* (New York: Routledge, 2000); Adia Harvey Wingfield, "Are Some Emotions Marked 'Whites Only'? Racialized Feeling Rules in Professional Workplaces," *Social Problems* 57, no. 2 (2010).

6. Jessica Fields, Martha Copp, and Sherryl Kleinman, "Symbolic Interactionism, Inequality, and Emotions," in *Handbook of the Sociology of Emotions*, ed. Jan E. Stets and Jonathan H. Turner (New York: Springer, 2006), 155–78.

7. Joyce Davidson, Liz Bondi, and Mick Smith, eds., *Emotional Geographies* (Burlington, Vt.: Ashgate, 2005).

8. Like Deborah Gould, I use both *feelings* and *emotions* to describe instances of affect and emotion. *Moving Politics: Emotion and ACT UP's Fight against AIDS* (Chicago: University of Chicago Press, 2009), 19–20.

9. For a further discussion of affect and emotion, see Brian Massumi, "Navigating Moments," in *Hope: New Philosophies for Change*, ed. Mary Zournazi (New York: Routledge, 2002), 210–42. For a discussion of the difference between affect and emotion as conceptualized in human geography, see Steve Pile, "Emotions and Affect in Recent Human Geography," *Transactions of the Institute of British Geographers* 35, no. 1 (2010): 5–20.

10. Cordelia Fine et al., "Plasticity, Plasticity, Plasticity . . . and the Rigid Problem of Sex," *Trends in Cognitive Sciences* 17, no. 11 (2013): 550–51.

11. Robert M. Sapolsky, *The Trouble with Testosterone: And Other Essays on the Biology of the Human Predicament* (New York: Scribner, 1997); Robert M. Sapolsky, *Behave: The Biology of Humans at Our Best and Worst* (New York: Penguin Press, 2017).

12. John M. Hoberman, *Testosterone Dreams: Rejuvenation, Aphrodisia, Doping* (Berkeley: University of California Press, 2005).

13. Johannes Hönekopp and Steven Watson, "Meta-analysis of the Relationship between Digit-Ratio 2D:4D and Aggression," *Personality and Individual Differences* 51, no. 4 (2011): 381–86; Matthew H. McIntyre et al., "Social Status, Masculinity, and Testosterone in Young Men," *Personality and Individual Differences* 51, no. 4 (2011): 392–96; James W. Pennebaker et al., "Testosterone as a Social Inhibitor: Two Case Studies of the Effect of Tes-

tosterone Treatment on Language," *Journal of Abnormal Psychology* 113, no. 1 (2004): 172–75.

14. Ahmed, *The Cultural Politics of Emotion*.

15. Pierrette Hondagneu-Sotelo and Michael A. Messner, "Gender Displays and Men's Power: The 'New Man' and the Mexican Immigrant Man," in *Theorizing Masculinities*, ed. Harry Brod and Michael Kaufman (Thousand Oaks, Calif.: Sage Publications, 1994), 204.

16. Sapolsky, *The Trouble with Testosterone*.

17. Sapolsky, *Behave*.

18. Scott Schieman, "Anger," in Stets and Turner, *Handbook of the Sociology of Emotions*, 493–515; Shields, *Speaking from the Heart*; Carol Zisowitz Stearns and Peter N. Stearns, *Anger: The Struggle for Emotional Control in America's History* (Chicago: University of Chicago Press, 1986).

19. Arlie Russell Hochschild, *The Managed Heart: Commercialization of Human Feeling* (Berkeley: University of California Press, 1983); Michael D. Robinson and Joel T. Johnson, "Is It Emotion or Is It Stress? Gender Stereotypes and the Perception of Subjective Experience," *Sex Roles* 36, no. 3–4 (1997); Stephanie A. Shields et al., "Gender and Emotion," in Stets and Turner, *Handbook of the Sociology of Emotions*, 63–83.

20. Anger is most closely connected in the cultural imagination to men and masculinity, but research on actual similarities and differences between men's and women's experience and expression of anger is inconclusive. See Richard A. Fabes and Carol Lynn Martin, "Gender and Age Stereotypes of Emotionality," *Personality and Social Psychology Bulletin* 17, no. 5 (1991): 532–40; Schieman, "Anger."

21. This is akin to discursive distancing. Tristan Bridges and C. J. Pascoe, "Hybrid Masculinities: New Directions in the Sociology of Men and Masculinities," *Sociology Compass* 8, no. 3 (2014): 246–58.

22. Hochschild, *The Managed Heart*.

23. Hochschild, *The Managed Heart*.

24. Amy Wilkins, "'Not Out to Start a Revolution': Race, Gender, and Emotional Restraint among Black University Men," *Journal of Contemporary Ethnography* 41, no. 1 (2012): 34–65.

25. Adia Harvey Wingfield, *No More Invisible Man: Race and Gender in Men's Work* (Philadelphia: Temple University Press, 2013).

26. Ta-Nehisi Coates, "Fear of a Black President," *Atlantic*, September 2012, http://www.theatlantic.com/magazine/archive/2012/09/fear-of-a-black-president/309064/.

27. Keegan-Michael Key and Jordan Peele perform an excellent satire of this dynamic through a series of sketches featuring Obama's Anger Translator.

28. Nearly every man who mentioned changes in sexuality with testosterone therapy reported an increase, though this topic did not come up in every

interview. It is common for trans people to report changes in their sexual practices and the meanings of those practices with transition. For example, see Henry Rubin, *Self-Made Men: Identity and Embodiment among Transsexual Men* (Nashville, Tenn.: Vanderbilt University Press, 2003); Kristen Schilt and Elroi Windsor, "The Sexual Habitus of Transgender Men: Negotiating Sexuality through Gender," *Journal of Homosexuality* 61, no. 5 (2014): 732–48.

29. Various hormone therapies have been used over time to increase sexual desire and affect sexual function, yet no causal effect has been proved beyond colloquial reports. Hoberman, *Testosterone Dreams*.

30. Lauren Berlant and Michael Warner, "Sex in Public," *Critical Inquiry* 24, no. 2 (1998): 547–66.

31. Amy T. Schalet, "Raging Hormones, Regulated Love: Adolescent Sexuality and the Constitution of the Modern Individual in the United States and the Netherlands," *Body & Society* 6, no. 1 (2000): 75–105.

32. Jeffery believed men should use a lower dose of testosterone than usually recommended so that bodily changes would occur in the same frame of time that cisgender men usually experienced the changes of puberty.

33. For a discussion of emotional economies of sympathy, see Candace Clark, "Sympathy Biography and Sympathy Margin," *American Journal of Sociology* 93, no. 2 (1987): 290–321.

34. Reflecting homophobia rather than medical evidence, testosterone and other hormones were once used by doctors in efforts to "cure" homosexuality but were ineffective. Hoberman, *Testosterone Dreams*.

35. Sally Hines also found that some trans men wanted relationships with women but only sex with men. *TransForming Gender: Transgender Practices of Identity, Intimacy and Care* (Bristol, U.K.: Policy Press, 2007).

36. Jane Ward, "Dude-Sex: White Masculinities and 'Authentic' Heterosexuality among Dudes Who Have Sex with Dudes," *Sexualities* 11, no. 4 (2008): 414–34. For a discussion of how rural white masculine men interpreted sex with men like them as reinforcing normative masculinity, see Tony Silva, "Bud-Sex: Constructing Normative Masculinity among Rural Straight Men That Have Sex with Men," *Gender & Society* 31, no. 1 (2017): 51–73.

4. GEOGRAPHY OF VIOLENCE

1. Following Mary Jackman, I define violence broadly as "actions that inflict, threaten, or cause injury. Actions may be corporal, written or verbal. Injuries may be corporal, psychological, material, or social." "Violence in Social Life," *Annual Review of Sociology* 28, no. 1 (2002): 405. This definition captures not only the intentionally harmful acts that would be included in

narrower definitions of violence but also the mundane acts that still cause harm. This definition, stemming from the work of feminist theorists and activists, highlights structural and institutional violence in addition to interpersonal violence to capture the range of violence that brings harm to women and other marginalized people. Claire M. Renzetti, "Feminist Theories of Violent Behavior," in *Violence: From Theory to Research*, ed. Margaret A. Zahn, Shelly L. Jackson, and Henry H. Brownstein (Newark, N.J.: Lexis-Nexis Anderson Publishing, 2004), 131–43.

2. Lesley Williams Reid and Miriam Konrad, "The Gender Gap in Fear: Assessing the Interactive Effects of Gender and Perceived Risk on Fear of Crime," *Sociological Spectrum* 24, no. 4 (2004): 399–425.

3. Jocelyn A. Hollander, "Vulnerability and Dangerousness: The Construction of Gender through Conversation about Violence," *Gender & Society* 15, no. 1 (2001): 83–109; Esther Madriz, *Nothing Bad Happens to Good Girls: Fear of Crime in Women's Lives* (Berkeley: University of California Press, 1997); Rachel Pain, "Whither Women's Fear? Perceptions of Sexual Violence in Public and Private Space," *International Review of Victimology* 4, no. 4 (1997): 297–312; Gill Valentine, "The Geography of Women's Fear," *Area* 21, no. 4 (1989): 385–90.

4. C. J. Pascoe, *Dude, You're a Fag: Masculinity and Sexuality in High School* (Berkeley: University of California Press, 2007); Raewyn Connell, *Masculinities* (Berkeley: University of California Press, 1995); James W. Messerschmidt, *Gender, Heterosexuality, and Youth Violence: The Struggle for Recognition* (Lanham, Md.: Rowman & Littlefield, 2012).

5. Petra L. Doan, "Queers in the American City: Transgendered Perceptions of Urban Space," *Gender, Place & Culture* 14, no. 1 (2007): 57–74; Sandy E. James et al., *The Report of the 2015 U.S. Transgender Survey* (Washington, D.C.: National Center for Transgender Equality, 2016); Emilia Lombardi et al., "Gender Violence: Transgender Experiences with Violence and Discrimination," *Journal of Homosexuality* 42, no. 1 (2001): 89–101; Barbara Perry, *In the Name of Hate: Understanding Hate Crimes* (New York: Routledge, 2001); Elizabeth A. Stanko and Kathy Hobdell, "Assault on Men: Masculinity and Male Victimization," *British Journal of Criminology* 33, no. 3 (1993): 400.

6. Reid and Konrad, "The Gender Gap in Fear."

7. Jin Haritaworn, *Queer Lovers and Hateful Others: Regenerating Violent Times and Places* (London: Pluto Press, 2015).

8. Laurel Westbrook, "Vulnerable Subjecthood: The Risks and Benefits of the Struggle for Hate Crime Legislation," *Berkeley Journal of Sociology* 52, no. 3 (2008).

9. James et al., *The Report of the 2015 U.S. Transgender Survey*. For a recent attempt to use various estimates of transgender populations and

homicide reports to better understand the potentially higher murder rate for transgender versus cisgender populations, see Alexis Dinno, "Homicide Rates of Transgender Individuals in the United States: 2010–2014," *American Journal of Public Health* 107, no. 9 (September 2017): 1441–47. For a discussion of the methodological difficulties of making accurate estimates, see Rebecca L. Stotzer, "Data Sources Hinder Our Understanding of Transgender Murders," *American Journal of Public Health* 107, no. 9 (September 2017): 1362–63.

10. J. Jack Halberstam, *In a Queer Time and Place: Transgender Bodies, Subcultural Lives* (New York: New York University Press, 2005).

11. Reid and Konrad, "The Gender Gap in Fear."

12. The official TDOR website listed nearly two hundred events in November 2013 across the globe, from Columbia, South Carolina, to Wellington, New Zealand, though most were clustered in the United States and other Anglophone countries.

13. Dora Silva Santana, "Transitionings and Returnings: Experiments with the Poetics of Transatlantic Water," *TSQ: Transgender Studies Quarterly* 4, no. 2 (2017): 181–90.

14. Sarah Lamble, "Retelling Racialized Violence, Remaking White Innocence: The Politics of Interlocking Oppressions in Transgender Day of Remembrance," *Sexuality Research & Social Policy* 5, no. 1 (2008): 24.

15. Mary Fellows and Sherene Razack, "The Race to Innocence: Confronting Hierarchical Relations among Women," *Gender Race & Justice*, January 1, 1998.

16. Janet Lee Mawhinney, "Giving Up the Ghost: Disrupting the (Re)production of White Privilege in Anti-racist Pedagogy and Organizational Change" (Ottawa: National Library of Canada, 1998), https://tspace.library.utoronto.ca/handle/1807/12096.

17. For a discussion of many of the dynamics of respectability and an overlapping but slightly different use of "innocence" in relation to racist violence, see Jackie Wang, "Against Innocence: Race, Gender, and the Politics of Safety," *LIES: A Journal of Materialist Feminism* 1 (2012): 145–71.

18. There were five incidents of spectacular violence against a person they could name across the interviewees' narratives. Like the women memorialized in TDOR events, these incidents of violence likely had a number of contributing factors, and some occurred before men transitioned. For example, one of the interviewees described an assault he said was targeted at his visible physical disabilities along with his feminine clothing when he was presenting himself as a woman before transition.

19. Fellows and Razack, "The Race to Innocence."

20. Valentine, "The Geography of Women's Fear"; Alec Brownlow, "A Geography of Men's Fear," *Geoforum* 36, no. 5 (2005): 581–92; Miriam J.

Abelson, "Dangerous Privilege: Trans Men, Masculinities, and Changing Perceptions of Safety," *Sociological Forum* 29, no. 3 (2014): 549–70.

21. Movement Advancement Project, *Mapping Transgender Equality in the United States* (Denver, Colo.: Movement Advancement Project, 2017), http://www.lgbtmap.org/file/mapping-trans-equality.pdf.

22. As Talia Mae Bettcher notes, the ability to control one's visibility as a transgender person is classed and racialized. For example, it can depend on being able to afford and access particular medical procedures or legal services. Those who cannot access these resources often have less choice in whether people know about their transgender history and identity. "Evil Deceivers and Make-Believers: On Transphobic Violence and the Politics of Illusion," *Hypatia* 22, no. 3 (2007): 43–65.

23. For a discussion of cisgender gay men's embrace of suburban normalcy, see Wayne Brekhus, *Peacocks, Chameleons, Centaurs* (Chicago: University of Chicago Press, 2003).

24. In fact, female-assigned people may actually have more access to masculine presentations in rural spaces. See Emily Kazyak, "Midwest or Lesbian? Gender, Rurality, and Sexuality," *Gender & Society* 26, no. 6 (2012): 828–48.

25. John Howard, *Men like That: A Southern Queer History* (Chicago: University of Chicago Press, 1999).

26. Michelle Alexander, *The New Jim Crow: Mass Incarceration in the Age of Colorblindness* (New York: New Press, 2010); Angela Davis, "The Color of Violence against Women," *Colorlines,* October 10, 2000.

27. Steven Hsieh, "Trans Activist CeCe McDonald Was Released from Prison Today," *Nation*, January 13, 2014, http://www.thenation.com/blog/177902/cece-mcdonald-was-released-prison-today#; Dean Spade, *Normal Life: Administrative Violence, Critical Trans Politics, and the Limits of Law* (New York: South End Press, 2011).

28. In fact, partly due to the reputation of the area, I planned to stop in Dominic's town just long enough to complete the interview and then travel to the next city on my itinerary. Due to a severe storm, I needed to stay in the town and was both surprised and pleased to find a room at a gay resort. That surprise belied my own geography of safety as a gender-nonconforming, visibly queer woman traveling on my own in an unfamiliar region. This exemplifies the ways my own ideas about geography and safety were consistently challenged during these research trips.

29. Mary Gray also found that racism intersected with sexuality and class in rural communities to offer a measure of acceptance to some white rural queer people. At the same time, there were varying levels of racism across rural spaces and communities. *Out in the Country: Youth, Media, and Queer Visibility in Rural America* (New York: New York University Press, 2009).

30. Kazyak, "Midwest or Lesbian?"

31. Andrea Smith, "Heteropatriarchy and the Three Pillars of White Supremacy: Rethinking Women of Color Organizing," in *The Color of Violence: The Incite! Anthology* (Boston: South End Press, 2006), 66–73.

32. Kay Whitlock, "We Need to Dream a Bolder Dream: The Politics of Fear and Queer Struggles for Safe Communities," *S&F Online*, no. 10.1 (2011); Spade, *Normal Life*; Christina B. Hanhardt, *Safe Space: Gay Neighborhood History and the Politics of Violence* (Durham, N.C.: Duke University Press Books, 2013).

33. Loree Cook-Daniels, "Scaring Ourselves to Death," *My Husband Betty* (blog), 2015, http://www.myhusbandbetty.com/2015/08/27/guest-author-loreecook-daniels-scaring-ourselves-to-death.

34. For a discussion of the effects of these narratives of vulnerability on trans women of color, see Kai Cheng Thom, "Someone Tell Me That I'll Live: On Murder, Media, and Being a Trans Woman in 2015," xoJane, 2015, https://www.xojane.com/issues/someone-tell-me-that-ill-live-murdered-trans-women-2015.

35. There have been numerous recent efforts to shift explicit attention to the extraordinary violence experienced by poor trans women of color at the intersection of white supremacy, capitalism, and transphobia. This includes efforts to show the resiliency of this group of multiply marginalized women, such as the organization Strong Families' Trans Day of Resilience campaign. See http://tdor.co.

36. Wang, "Against Innocence," 170.

37. C. Riley Snorton, *Black on Both Sides: A Racial History of Trans Identity* (Minneapolis: University of Minnesota Press, 2017).

5. INSTITUTIONAL CONTEXTS OF VIOLENCE

1. Michel Foucault, *The History of Sexuality*, vol. 1 (New York: Pantheon Books, 1978).

2. Petra L. Doan, "The Tyranny of Gendered Spaces: Reflections from beyond the Gender Dichotomy," *Gender, Place & Culture* 17, no. 5 (2010): 635–54.

3. Monica Roberts, "TransGriot: The Willie Houston Story," *TransGriot* (blog), 2008, http://transgriot.blogspot.com/2008/08/willie-houston-story.html; David Valentine, *Imagining Transgender: An Ethnography of a Category* (Durham, N.C.: Duke University Press, 2007).

4. Sheila Burke, "Fiancée Describes Houston's Shooting," *Tennessean*, August 1, 2001.

5. Kate Bornstein, "Gender Terror, Gender Rage," in *Transgender Studies Reader*, ed. Susan Stryker and Stephen Whittle (New York: Routledge, 2006), 236–43.

6. Judith Plaskow, "Embodiment, Elimination, and the Role of Toilets in Struggles for Social Justice," *CrossCurrents* 58, no. 1 (2008): 51–64. For a discussion of how access to public toilets affects multiple groups, see Alison Kafer, *Feminist, Queer, Crip* (Bloomington: Indiana University Press, 2013), 154.

7. Laurel Westbrook and Kristen Schilt, "Doing Gender, Determining Gender: Transgender People, Gender Panics, and the Maintenance of the Sex/Gender/Sexuality System," *Gender & Society* 28, no. 1 (2014): 32–57.

8. Olga Gershenson and Barbara Penner, *Ladies and Gents: Public Toilets and Gender* (Philadelphia: Temple University Press, 2009).

9. Sheila L. Cavanagh, *Queering Bathrooms: Gender, Sexuality, and the Hygienic Imagination* (Toronto: University of Toronto Press, 2010); Spencer E. Cahill et al., "Meanwhile Backstage: Public Bathrooms and the Interaction Order," *Journal of Contemporary Ethnography* 14, no. 1 (1985): 33–58.

10. David Inglis, *A Sociological History of Excretory Experience: Defecatory Manners and Toiletry Technologies* (Lewiston, N.Y.: Edwin Mellen Press, 2001).

11. Martin S. Weinberg and Colin J. Williams, "Fecal Matters: Habitus, Embodiments, and Deviance," *Social Problems* 52, no. 3 (2005): 315–36.

12. Barbara Penner, "(Re)designing the 'Unmentionable': Female Toilets in the Twentieth Century," in *Ladies and Gents: Public Toilets and Gender*, ed. Olga Gershenson and Barbara Penner (Philadelphia: Temple University Press, 2009), 141.

13. Jacques Lacan et al., *Écrits* (New York: W. W. Norton, 2006).

14. Erving Goffman, "The Arrangement between the Sexes," *Theory and Society* 4, no. 3 (1977): 316.

15. Marjorie B. Garber, *Vested Interests: Cross-dressing & Cultural Anxiety* (New York: Routledge, 1992).

16. Cavanagh, *Queering Bathrooms*, 43.

17. Kyla Bender-Baird, "Peeing under Surveillance: Bathrooms, Gender Policing, and Hate Violence," *Gender, Place & Culture* 23, no. 7 (July 2, 2016): 984.

18. J. Jack Halberstam, *Female Masculinity* (Durham, N.C.: Duke University Press, 1998), 22.

19. Bornstein, "Gender Terror, Gender Rage"; Cavanagh, *Queering Bathrooms*; Leslie Feinberg, *Stone Butch Blues: A Novel* (Ithaca, N.Y.: Firebrand Books, 1993); Patricia J. Williams, *The Alchemy of Race and Rights* (Cambridge, Mass.: Harvard University Press, 1991).

20. For example, Richard Floyd, HB 2279 Tennessee, Pub. L. No. HB 2279 (2012); Dan Bishop et al., Public Facilities Privacy & Security Act North Carolina, Pub. L. No. HB 2 (2016).

21. Richard Juang, "Transgendering the Politics of Recognition," in

Stryker and Whittle, *Transgender Studies Reader*, 706–20; Shannon Minter and Christopher Daley, *Trans Realities: A Legal Needs Assessment of San Francisco's Transgender Communities* (San Francisco: Transgender Law Center, 2003); National Research Council, *The Health of Lesbian, Gay, Bisexual, and Transgender People: Building a Foundation for Better Understanding* (Washington, D.C.: National Research Council, 2011), http://www.iom.edu/Reports/2011/The-Health-of-Lesbian-Gay-Bisexual-and-Transgender-People.aspx.

22. Simone Chess et al., "Calling All Restroom Revolutionaries," in *That's Revolting* (New York: Soft Skull, 2004), 189–206; Kafer, *Feminist, Queer, Crip*.

23. Miriam J. Abelson, "Night and Day: Gendered Safety and Violence in the Everyday Experiences of Transgender Men," in *Understanding Diversity: Celebrating Difference, Challenging Inequality*, ed. Claire M. Renzetti and Raquel M. Kennedy-Bergen (Boston: Allyn and Bacon, 2014); Eli Clare, *Exile and Pride: Disability, Queerness, and Liberation* (Cambridge, Mass.: South End Press, 2009).

24. Kafer, *Feminist, Queer, Crip*, 155.

25. Kath Browne, "Genderism and the Bathroom Problem: (Re)materialising Sexed Sites, (Re)creating Sexed Bodies," *Gender, Place & Culture* 11, no. 3 (2004): 331–46.

26. Jody L. Herman, "Gendered Restrooms and Minority Stress: The Public Regulation of Gender and Its Impact on Transgender People's Lives," *Journal of Public Management and Social Policy* 19, no. 1 (2013): 65–80.

27. David Eng and Alice Hom, "Q&A: Notes on a Queer Asian America," in *Q&A: Queer in Asian America*, ed. David Eng and Alice Hom (Philadelphia: Temple University Press, 1998), 1–21.

28. See Halberstam, *Female Masculinity*.

29. Adrienne Rich, "Compulsory Heterosexuality and Lesbian Existence," *Signs: Journal of Women in Culture and Society* 5, no. 4 (1980).

30. Lee Edelman, *Homographesis: Essays in Gay Literary and Cultural Theory* (New York: Routledge, 1994); Halberstam, *Female Masculinity*; Laud Humphreys, *Tearoom Trade: Impersonal Sex in Public Places* (Chicago: Routledge, 1975).

31. Daniela Jauk, "Gender Violence Revisited: Lessons from Violent Victimization of Transgender Identified Individuals," *Sexualities* 16, no. 7 (2013): 807–25; Lisa R. Miller and Eric Anthony Grollman, "The Social Costs of Gender Nonconformity for Transgender Adults: Implications for Discrimination and Health," *Sociological Forum* 30, no. 3 (2015): 809–31.

32. Abelson, "Night and Day."

33. Halberstam, *Female Masculinity*.

34. Goffman, "The Arrangement between the Sexes."

35. William A. Smith, Man Hung, and Jeremy D. Franklin, "Racial Battle Fatigue and the 'Mis'Education of Black Men: Racial Microaggressions, Societal Problems, and Environmental Stress," *Journal of Negro Education* 80, no. 1 (2011): 63–82.

36. For example, see Kevin L. Nadal, Avy Skolnik, and Yinglee Wong, "Interpersonal and Systemic Microaggressions toward Transgender People: Implications for Counseling," *Journal of LGBT Issues in Counseling* 6, no. 1 (2012): 55–82; Sonny Nordmarken and Reese Kelly, "Limiting Transgender Health: Administrative Violence and Microaggressions in Health Care Systems," in *Health Care Disparities and the LGBT Population*, ed. Vickie L. Harvey and Teresa Heinz Housel (Lanham, Md.: Lexington Books, 2014), 143–66.

37. Joanne Meyerowitz, *How Sex Changed : A History of Transsexuality in the United States* (Cambridge, Mass.: Harvard University Press, 2002).

38. Viviane K. Namaste, *Invisible Lives: The Erasure of Transsexual and Transgendered People* (Chicago: University of Chicago Press, 2000); Dean Spade, "Mutilating Gender," in Stryker and Whittle, *Transgender Studies Reader*, 315–32.

39. Georgiann Davis, Jodie M. Dewey, and Erin L. Murphy, "Giving Sex: Deconstructing Intersex and Trans Medicalization Practices," *Gender & Society* 30, no. 3 (June 1, 2016): 490–514.

40. Spade, "Mutilating Gender," 329.

41. Talia Mae Bettcher, "Trapped in the Wrong Theory: Rethinking Trans Oppression and Resistance," *Signs* 39, no. 2 (2014): 383–406; Spade, "Mutilating Gender."

42. stef m. shuster, "Uncertain Expertise and the Limitations of Clinical Guidelines in Transgender Healthcare," *Journal of Health and Social Behavior* 57, no. 3 (2016): 319–32.

43. World Professional Association for Transgender Health, *Standards of Care for the Health of Transsexual, Transgender, and Gender-Nonconforming People*, 7th ed. (World Professional Association for Transgender Health, 2012).

44. For a comprehensive overview of standards in transgender medicine, see shuster, "Uncertain Expertise and the Limitations of Clinical Guidelines in Transgender Healthcare."

45. Austin H. Johnson, "Normative Accountability: How the Medical Model Influences Transgender Identities and Experiences," *Sociology Compass* 9, no. 9 (2015): 803–13.

46. Sandy E. James et al., *Report of the 2015 U.S. Transgender Survey* (Washington, D.C.: National Center for Transgender Equality, 2016).

47. As shuster illustrates, part of the difficulty for providers in following these standards is the limited or nonexistent evidence base in support of

these standards. Uncertainty means providers rely on a mix of strictly adhering to guidelines and interpreting them in more flexible ways. "Uncertain Expertise and the Limitations of Clinical Guidelines in Transgender Healthcare." Legal systems and transgender communities also reinforce norms of the proper transgender patient. Johnson, "Normative Accountability."

48. For a discussion of how the needs and resources of trans people can vary between two adjacent cities, see Tooru Nemoto et al., "A Tale of Two Cities: Access to Care and Services among African-American Transgender Women in Oakland and San Francisco," *LGBT Health* 2, no. 3 (2015).

49. Under Mary Jackman's broad definition of violence, the doctors do not have to intend harm for their acts to qualify as violence. Their intentions could be absolutely benign, but it is the harm trans men experience that mark these as acts of violence. "Violence in Social Life," *Annual Review of Sociology* 28, no. 1 (2002): 387–415.

50. See F. Jockenhövel, "Testosterone Therapy: What, When and to Whom?," *Aging Male* 7, no. 4 (2004): 319–24.

51. Meyerowitz, *How Sex Changed*; Spade, "Mutilating Gender"; Jaye Cee Whitehead and Jennifer Thomas, "Sexuality and the Ethics of Body Modification: Theorizing the Situated Relationships among Gender, Sexuality and the Body," *Sexualities* 16, no. 3–4 (2013): 383–400.

52. Aren Z. Aizura, "The Romance of the Amazing Scalpel: 'Race,' Labor, and Affect in Thai Gender Reassignment Clinics," in *Transgender Studies Reader 2*, ed. Susan Stryker and Aren Z. Aizura (New York: Routledge, 2013), 496–511; Susan Stryker, *Transgender History* (Berkeley, Calif.: Seal Press, 2008).

53. Marie-Andrée Jacob, "Form-Made Persons: Consent Forms as Consent's Blind Spot," *PoLAR: Political and Legal Anthropology Review* 30, no. 2 (November 1, 2007): 249–68.

54. Kevin L. Nadal, "Gender Identity Microaggressions: Experiences of Transgender and Gender Nonconforming People," in *That's So Gay! Microaggressions and the Lesbian, Gay, Bisexual, and Transgender Community* (Washington, D.C.: American Psychological Association, 2013), 80–107; Nordmarken and Kelly, "Limiting Transgender Health."

55. Naith Payton, "The Dangers of Trans Broken Arm Syndrome," *Pink News*, July 9, 2015, http://www.pinknews.co.uk/2015/07/09/feature-the-dangers-of-trans-broken-arm-syndrome/.

56. stef m. shuster, "Punctuating Accountability: How Discursive Aggression Regulates Transgender People," *Gender & Society* 31, no. 4 (2017): 481–502.

57. Talia Mae Bettcher, "Evil Deceivers and Make-Believers: On Transphobic Violence and the Politics of Illusion," *Hypatia* 22, no. 3 (2007): 43–65; Spade, "Mutilating Gender."

58. For example, see Dwight B. Billings and Thomas Urban, "The Sociomedical Construction of Transsexualism: An Interpretation and Critique," *Social Problems* 29, no. 3 (1982): 266–82.
59. Spade, "Mutilating Gender," 317.
60. Davis, Dewey, and Murphy, "Giving Sex."

CONCLUSION

1. Pierrette Hondagneu-Sotelo and Michael A. Messner, "Gender Displays and Men's Power: The 'New Man' and the Mexican Immigrant Man," in *Theorizing Masculinities*, ed. Harry Brod and Michael Kaufman (Thousand Oaks, Calif.: Sage Publications, 1994), 200–218.
2. Dorothy E. Smith, *The Everyday World as Problematic: A Feminist Sociology* (Boston: Northeastern University Press, 1987); Erving Goffman, *The Presentation of Self in Everyday Life* (Woodstock, N.Y.: Overlook Press, 1973); Harold Garfinkel, *Studies in Ethnomethodology* (Englewood Cliffs, N.J.: Prentice-Hall, 1967).
3. Candace West and Don H. Zimmerman, "Doing Gender," *Gender & Society* 1 (1987): 125–51.
4. Judith Butler, *Gender Trouble: Feminism and the Subversion of Identity* (New York: Routledge, 1990).
5. Gayatri Gopinath's analysis of region, rurality and lesbian lives in India could be a start for further developing transnational regional analysis. "Queer Regions: Locating Lesbians in Sancharram," in *A Companion to Lesbian, Gay, Bisexual, Transgender, and Queer Studies*, ed. George E. Haggerty and Molly McGarry (Malden, Mass.: Wiley, 2007), 341–54. See also Mary L. Gray, Colin R. Johnson, and Brian Joseph Gilley, *Queering the Countryside: New Frontiers in Rural Queer Studies* (New York: New York University Press, 2016).
6. This also holds true with changes between men interviewed in the 1990s, e.g., Jason Cromwell, *Transmen and FTMs: Identities, Bodies, Genders, and Sexualities* (Chicago: University of Illinois Press, 1999); Aaron Devor, *FTM: Female to Male Transsexuals in Society* (Bloomington: Indiana University Press, 1997); those interviewed in the early to mid-2000s, e.g., Kristen Schilt, *Just One of the Guys? Transgender Men and the Persistence of Gender Inequality* (Chicago: University of Chicago Press, 2010); Raine Dozier, "Beards, Breasts, and Bodies: Doing Sex in a Gendered World," *Gender & Society* 19, no. 3 (2005): 297–316; and these interviews in the first half of the 2010s. Time will tell the long-term effects of the most recent and significant changes.
7. Dean Spade, *Normal Life: Administrative Violence, Critical Trans Politics, and the Limits of Law* (New York: South End Press, 2011), 33.
8. David Valentine, "The Calculus of Pain: Violence, Narrative, and the

Self," in *Imagining Transgender: An Ethnography of a Category* (Durham, N.C.: Duke University Press, 2007), 204–30.

9. Spade, *Normal Life*.

10. Christina B. Hanhardt, "Butterflies, Whistles, and Fists: Gay Safe Streets Patrols and the New Gay Ghetto, 1976–1981," *Radical History Review*, no. 100 (2008): 61–85; Katherine Whitlock, "In a Time of Broken Bones: A Call to Dialogue on Hate Violence and the Limitations of Hate Crimes Legislation" (Philadelphia: American Friends Service Committee, 2001).

11. Lisa Duggan, *The Twilight of Equality? Neoliberalism, Cultural Politics, and the Attack on Democracy* (Boston: Beacon Press, 2003).

12. Kimberlé Crenshaw, "Demarginalizing the Intersection of Race and Sex: A Black Feminist Critique of Antidiscrimination Doctrine, Feminist Theory and Antiracist Politics," *University of Chicago Legal Forum*, no. 1 (1989): 139.

13. Andrea Smith, "Heteropatriarchy and the Three Pillars of White Supremacy: Rethinking Women of Color Organizing," in *The Color of Violence: The Incite! Anthology* (Boston: South End Press, 2006), 66–73; Spade, *Normal Life*.

14. StormMiguel Florez, "Dear Austin Special Needs Bathroom," in *Gender Outlaws: The Next Generation*, ed. Kate Borenstein and S. Bear Bergman (Berkeley, Calif.: Seal Press, 2010), 52–53.

15. Indeed, Yve Laris Cohen points out that an abolitionist approach would demand all gender designations be removed from gender-segregated spaces. Kai Lumumba Barrow et al., "Models of Futurity: Roundtable," in *Trap Door: Trans Cultural Production and the Politics of Visibility* (Cambridge, Mass.: MIT Press, 2017), 321–37.

16. Alison Kafer, *Feminist, Queer, Crip* (Bloomington: Indiana University Press, 2013), 156–57.

17. Tristan Bridges and C. J. Pascoe, "Hybrid Masculinities: New Directions in the Sociology of Men and Masculinities," *Sociology Compass* 8, no. 3 (2014): 246–58.

18. Eric Anderson, *Inclusive Masculinity* (New York: Routledge, 2009).

19. Raewyn Connell and James W. Messerschmidt, "Hegemonic Masculinity: Rethinking the Concept," *Gender & Society* 19, no. 6 (2005): 829–59.

20. Bridges and Pascoe, "Hybrid Masculinities"; Michael A. Messner, "The Masculinity of the Governator," *Gender & Society* 21, no. 4 (2007): 461–80.

21. Connell and Messerschmidt, "Hegemonic Masculinity"; Bridges and Pascoe, "Hybrid Masculinities."

22. Paul J. Cloke, "Rurality and Racialized Others," in *Handbook of Rural Studies*, ed. Paul J. Cloke, Terry Marsden, and Patrick H. Mooney (London: Sage Publications, 2006), 379–87.

APPENDIX B

1. Lori Watson's discussion of being a woman who is constantly misgendered and the ways those experiences have shaped her life and political commitments to trans people resonate in many ways with my own experiences. "The Woman Question," *TSQ: Transgender Studies Quarterly* 3, no. 1–2 (May 1, 2016): 246–53.

2. Jack Halberstam and C. Jacob Hale outline these borderland tensions in "Butch/FTM Border Wars: A Note on Collaboration," *GLQ: A Journal of Lesbian and Gay Studies* 4, no. 2 (1998): 283–85. For another overview of these debates, see Carla A. Pfeffer, *Queering Families: The Postmodern Partnerships of Cisgender Women and Transgender Men* (New York: Oxford University Press, 2017).

3. Viviane K. Namaste, *Invisible Lives: The Erasure of Transsexual and Transgendered People* (Chicago: University of Chicago Press, 2000).

4. Jacob C. Hale, "Suggested Rules for Non-transsexuals Writing about Transsexuals, Transsexuality, Transsexualism, or Trans-," Sandy Stone website, last updated November 18, 2009, http://sandystone.com/hale.rules.html.

5. Kathy Charmaz, *Constructing Grounded Theory: A Practical Guide through Qualitative Analysis* (Los Angeles: Sage, 2006).

6. Emily Kayzak suggested this since it had been effective in finding interviewees for her work on rural Midwest gays and lesbians. Personal communication with author, 2012.

7. Most recent estimates posit that transgender individuals make up about .06 percent of the U.S. adult population or approximately 1.4 million people. Andrew R. Flores et al., "How Many Adults Identify as Transgender in the United States?" (Los Angeles: Williams Institute, 2016), https://williamsinstitute.law.ucla.edu/wp-content/uploads/How-Many-Adults-Identify-as-Transgender-in-the-United-States.pdf.

Index

adolescents, transition into men, 196. *See also* puberty
affect: bodily sensations of, 96–97; change in transition, 92; emotion and, 92, 238n9; in the humanities, 91–92; queer understanding of, 21–22; in testosterone therapy, 121–22, 123
aggression: biological/social explanations for, 104; in private space, 104; progressive men's rejection of, 54; relabeling of, 110–13; testosterone therapy and, 94, 101–4
Ahmed, Sarah, 91
Alexander, Michelle, 38
American Pie (film), sexual urges in, 114
amplified sites, defined, 156
Anderson, Eric, 17
anger: acceptable expression of, 108–11; versus assertiveness, 112; control strategies for, 108–9; in cultural imagination, 239n20; gendered expression of, 239n20; in hypermasculinity, 105; internalized, 110; legitimizing of, 110–11; among rednecks, 36; testosterone, due to, 95–96, 101–4, 110; white men's, 31, 110–11
antidiscrimination laws, transgender, 200–201
Appalachia: gendered violence in, 145; hegemonic masculinity in, 18; transition services in, 177
artisans, heroic, 228n13

authenticity: in expression of self, 62; in social recognition, 61–62
authenticity, gender: of cisgender men, 87; confirmation of, 85; family recognition of, 66; racialized, 87; recognition of, 86–87; transformative language in, 72; trans men's, 62, 69, 85
authority, medical, 173; gender difference in, 190; in informed-consent models, 175; over trans patients, 183–84. *See also* healthcare; medical institution; patients, trans

bathrooms. *See* public bathrooms
Bear communities, 235n34; assumption of heterosexuality in, 85; male bodies in, 72–73; queer space of, 236n35
behavior, human: backstage, 78, 79–82, 236n44; in public space, 127; situational, 5; sociocultural explanations for, 94
Bell, Shannon, 18
Bender-Baird, Kyla, 159
Bettcher, Talia Mae, 232n4, 243n22
Billings, Dwight, 13
Black Lives Matter movement, 154
black men: anger at racism, 111; angry image of, 113; assumptions of criminality concerning, 38, 83; faggy, 43; gender knowledges concerning, 83; lynching of, 38; perceptions of competence

|| 253

concerning, 83; police harassment of, 128, 196; police killing of, 1, 25, 27, 39; poor, 107; in prison–industrial complex, 38; professional, 236n48; in public space, 5; in rural space, 204; scrutiny of, 81–82; therapy for, 107; as threat, 1, 25, 37–38, 84, 152; as thugs, 39–40; trans, 1–3, 40–41. *See also* masculinity, black; trans men, black

Blackmon, Douglas, 38

blackness, and urban criminality, 38, 83

black persons, coded language describing, 38–39

Black Trans Lives Matter movement, 154

black women: feminist, 7–8; geographies of, 20; racialized violence against, 39; thug image and, 230n57

black women, trans: memorialization of, 129. *See also* trans women of color

Bland, Sandra, 39

bodily control, spatially based, 101

Bonilla-Silva, Eduardo, 235n21

borderlands, 216, 251n2

Boys Don't Cry (film), 131

Braun, Yvonne, 18

breasts: in heterosexual desire, 73; naming of, 232n1; sexual desire for, 115. *See also* chest reconstruction

Bridges, Tristan, 17–18, 56; on fluid masculinity, 57; on gender relations, 204

Brown, Michael, 25; police killing of, 39

Browne, Kath, 162

Brownlow, Alec, 134

Brown-Saracino, Japonica, 11

brutes, 37–38; media portrayals of, 38. *See also* thugs, urban

Bundy, Cliven, 25

Bundy family, 36

Butler, Judith, 13, 233n6; *Gender Trouble*, 9

caballerismo, 50

capitalism, effect on regional differences, 220n9

Cavanagh, Sheila, 159

census, U.S.: urban versus rural space in, 19

chest reconstruction, 59, 144; in expansive gender knowledge, 72, 73; in gender recognition, 70–74; media depiction of, 71. *See also* breasts

chests: exposure of, 71; gendered ideals of, 71; in gender knowledge, 70–74, 87; in public/private spaces, 71; role in social recognition, 71–72

cisgender men: authenticity of, 87; effect of testosterone on, 93; experience of puberty, 240n32; heterosexual, 46; narratives of emotion, 122; nonnormative bodies of, 63; social recognition for, 195–96; strangers' perceptions of, 150; suburban normality of, 243n23; support for, 106–7

cisgender persons: normative presentation by, 234n16; trans coworkers of, 237n50

cissexism: at medical institutions, 174; microprocesses creating, 171

class: in gender recognition, 81; multiplicity in, 7; place and, 10; reproduction in interaction, 8; in rural space, 149; space and,

10–11, 149, 197; in spatial masculinity, 28; in U.S. masculinity, 5; among white supremacists, 35
Coates, Ta-Nehisi, 112–13
Cohen, Cathy, 84
Cohen, Yve Laris, 250n15
Collins, Patricia Hill, 7; on brutes, 37–38; on controlling images, 26
Confederate flag, 111–12; white racial project of, 34
Connell, Raewyn, 13, 17–18; on embodiment, 233n5; on gender knowledge, 61, 63; on gender relations, 204; on hegemonic masculinity, 18, 226n75; on masculinity practices, 14–15, 16; on multiple masculinities, 39; on transition, 64
conservatism, gender-segregated bathrooms and, 157–58, 159
controlling images: of faggy men, 26, 47, 121, 166; hypermasculine, 98, 128; of marginalized groups, 26–27; of rednecks, 26, 33, 35, 43, 55, 164, 194; of thugs, 26, 40–41, 43, 48, 55, 127, 128, 194
Corn Belt, masculine ideal of, 30
country music, as lowbrow, 230n55
cowboys, 25; fantasy of, 29; white, 28, 29
Crenshaw, Kimberlé, 7; intersectionality theory of, 201
Creswell, Tim, 11, 233n6
criminal justice: neoliberal policies on, 201; spatial context of, 142
critical race theory, 200
crying, 97–101; appropriate, 97–98, 99–100; feminine, 98, 99; in public space, 101; in southern masculinity, 97–98; testosterone therapy and, 101; as weakness, 100

dandy, masculine aesthetic of, 45
Davidson, Lewis, III, 157
Devine, Phillip, 154
disability: masculinities and, 236n43; medical issues in, 182; in public bathrooms, 170
domestic space, norms of, 10
dominance, 5; in hypermasculinity, 105; relations of, 12, 197
domination: in gender recognition, 86; in gender-segregated bathrooms, 161; inequality in, 23; by institutions, 155–56; interlocking systems of, 7; intersectional analysis of, 203; role of fear in, 200; sexual assault as, 116; trans men's participation in, 151, 152; violent, 23
Duggan, Lisa, 201

effeminacy: gay mockery of, 45; gay stereotypes of, 235n34; radical faerie, 46; regular guys' distance from, 52. *See also* faggy men
emotion: affect and, 92, 238n9; captured in language, 111; cultural politics of, 91; disavowal of, 118; economies of sympathy in, 240n33; faggy men's, 98; feminine, 91, 98, 99, 102; gendered, 102; in gender recognition, 97; geographic understanding of, 91; in private space, 99, 100; queer understanding of, 21–22; racialized, 102; over racist imagery, 111; self-regulation of, 100; sites for contestation, 111; social constitution of, 91, 92; spatially appropriate, 195; stereotypes of, 91
emotion, masculine: appropriate, 89–93; effect of testosterone on, 93–97; expectations for, 101;

versus feminine, 91; rational, 22, 91
emotional control: in family space, 110; following transition, 98–99; gender identity and, 100; in Goldilocks masculinity, 22, 92–93, 102, 105, 114, 115; hypermasculinities in, 22, 122; inequality and, 92; learned, 104; masculine ideal of, 92; normative ideal of, 123; in power, 123; role of testosterone in, 93–97, 99, 117; of romantic emotions, 121; of sexual desire, 114–17, 122; across spaces, 108; spatially based, 100, 102; during transition, 89, 92, 93, 95–97; trans men's, 89–90
emotional expression: crying, 97–101; in families, 107; feminine, 98, 99, 102; with partners, 90; for powerful men, 91; weakness in, 90, 100
emotional subject, self-disciplining, 93, 107–8, 110–13, 123
Eng, David, 164
Equal Rights Amendment, 158

facial feminization surgery, 70
faggy men, 21, 43–47; black, 43; camp humor of, 46; in construction of gay masculinity, 45; controlling image of, 26, 47, 121, 166; in definition of normative masculinity, 46; effeminacy of, 46, 133–34; emotions of, 98; flamboyancy of, 44; gendered/sexual project of, 46–47; homophobia and, 43; misogynistic, 46; racialized ideals of, 47; regional masculinity of, 55; as ridiculous, 44, 45; in rural spaces, 45; as sexual threat, 43, 196; in urban spaces, 45; as victims of violence, 195
families: advice to trans men, 76; emotional expression in, 107, 110; gender binaries in, 67; gender recognition in, 66–67; knowledge of transition experiences, 67; normative formations of, 66–67; queer, 16; restrictive gender knowledges in, 75; role in transition, 16
farmers, 30; masculinity of, 31; white, 28
fear: effect on masculinities, 22–23, 127; enforcement of norms, 191; gendered, 127, 128; "geographies" of, 134; in Goldilocks masculinity, 134; institutional reproduction of, 191; at medical institutions, 155, 172–88; role in social domination, 200; of sexual assault, 125–26; of transgender violence, 129–31; trans men's relationship to, 126–27; trans men's resistance to, 153–54; of transphobia, 130
fear, spatially based, 124, 133, 137–40; conformity under, 151; gender presentation in, 147; lack of control in, 195; in locker rooms, 161, 167; in Midwest, 139–44; nuances of, 144; in public bathrooms, 150, 155, 160, 161–67, 171; in public space, 125–26; of racism, 145–46; in Southeast, 144–46, 148; urban, 134; in West, 135–39
Fellows, Mary Louise, 130
femininities: emotional expression of, 98, 99, 102; male practice of, 15; separation of regular guys from, 50

feminism: critique of misogyny, 105; on masculinities, 5; theories of violence, 241n1
feminism, women of color, 223n36, 227n4; intersectional perspectives of, 7–8, 216
Foucault, Michel, 10; on disciplinary power, 155

gangsta rap, thug image in, 41
Garfield, James A., 87
Garfinkel, Harold, 197
gay communities, urban, 11–12
gay men: body language of, 3–4; effeminacy stereotypes of, 235n34; "masc4masc" dating ads, 51; practice of masculinity, 44; in rural spaces, 45; straight-acting, 51
gender: amplified sites of, 156, 171, 180, 187, 188, 190, 191, 195; assignment at birth, 14–15, 63, 78; co-constitution with race, 221n19; cultural scripts of, 9; embodiment of, 71, 233n5; as form of categorization, 10; global order of, 17; hormone therapy and, 94; in ideas of place, 194; on identification documents, 233n12; institutional spaces of, 155; legal classification of, 233n12; in medical authority, 190; performance of, 60, 75–78; in places, 10, 70, 86, 194; race/class/sexuality interactions, 20, 194; regional meanings of, 8, 19; repetitive nature of, 198; reproduction in interaction, 8–9, 10; self-determination of, 187; shifts in expectations, 236n45; social construction of, 14, 75; spatial norms of, 197, 233n6

gender binaries, 232n3; in families, 67; heterosexual/homosexual, 10; knowledge of, 62–63; in public bathrooms, 169, 190
gender difference: amplified sites of, 191; creation in public bathrooms, 171; enforcement on trans patients, 190; in medical institutions, 187, 190
gender expectations: normative, 9; in urban space, 147; in women's bathrooms, 165–66, 190
gender inequality: in South, 54; subordinated practices in, 18. *See also* inequality
gender knowledge, 61–64; of appropriate masculinities, 75; concerning black men, 83; binary understanding of, 62–63; as common sense, 63; institutional, 63; men's chests in, 70–74, 87; norms of, 62; rednecks', 59–60, 87; self-knowledge, 69; spatial, 63, 67–70, 196; trans peoples', 60
gender knowledge, expansive: acceptance through, 66; chest reconstruction in, 72, 73; in queer space, 73, 85
gender knowledge, restrictive, 68; chest appearance in, 72; in families, 75; place in, 70
gender nonconformity: in gender-segregated bathrooms, 162, 202; in healthcare, 188; policing of women's bathrooms, 164–65; in public space, 169; in rural space, 163; sexual nonconformity and, 196; violence marking, 171
gender recognition, 61–64, 97; assumption of competence in, 82–83; assumption of knowledge in, 82; in backstage behavior, 78,

79–82; chest reconstruction in, 70–74; class in, 81; competing knowledges in, 63; conflicts of, 74–75; contexts of, 64–74; domination in, 86; expansive, 63, 65; in families, 66–67; formal rights in, 86; gendered embodiment and, 71; inequality and, 78; interactional effects of, 78–85; in interactional spaces, 67–70; knowledges involved in, 234n12; legal recognition of, 86; male privilege in, 85–86; narrow, 63; in organizations, 64–66; physical space in, 81; place-based, 86; practical, 64; race in, 69, 77, 81; respect in, 80–82; self-knowledge in, 86; sexual attractions in, 83–85; sexuality in, 78; social aspects of, 78–79, 86; spatially based, 69; by strangers, 67–70, 75, 79. *See also* identity, gender

gender relations: effect of industry on, 18; egalitarian, 204; hybrid masculinity and, 93; in trans men's lives, 19
gender theory, trans people in, 13
genital reconstruction surgery, 70
Gerson, Kathleen, 49
Gilmore, Ruth Wilson, 9
Glenn, Evelyn Nakano: *Unequal Freedom*, 8
Goffman, Erving, 197; on gender differentiation, 158–59
good old boys: southern, 30–31; white, 28
Gopinath, Gayatri, 249n5
Gore, Al, 91
Gould, Deborah, 91–92
Grant, Oscar: police killing of, 1, 39
Gray, Mary, 11, 243n29

gynecomastia, among male-assigned people, 71

habitus: fecal, 158; male-socialized, 168–69
Halberstam, Jack, 11; on bathroom problem, 159; "Butch/FTM Border Wars," 251n2; on trans vulnerability, 128
Hale, C. Jacob, 217; "Butch/FTM Border Wars," 251n2
Hames-García, Michael, 7
Han, C. Walter, "No Fats, Femmes, or Asians," 45
Hanhardt, Christina, 153
Haritaworn, Jin, 14
hate crimes, legal reform for, 200–201
healthcare, transgender, 172–88; avoidance of, 186; body-altering, 178–79; gender-confirming, 234n16; gendered assumptions concerning, 187; normative bodies in, 180–81; patients' access to, 174–77, 181, 188, 199; policy, 223n43; psychological injuries in, 174, 182; punishment of gender nonconformity, 188; racial disparities in, 186; search for, 186; standards for, 174, 247n44; support networks for, 181; transphobic violence in, 196. *See also* authority, medical; medical institutions; patients, trans
hegemony: Gramscian, 17; masculine, 16–18, 203, 226n75
heteronormativity, 84–85; backstage talk in, 79–80; emotional relationships in, 121; middle-class white, 21
heterosexism: in gender-segregated bathrooms, 156; in men's

bathrooms, 161, 171, 188, 195, 197; microprocesses creating, 171; in social relations, 203
heterosexuality: compulsory, 114; emotional relationships and, 121; heteronormative approval for, 84–85; intimacy and, 122; presumption for trans men, 84, 85; regular guys', 51; social relations of, 86; trans men's, 76–77
Hines, Sally, 240n35
Hoberman, John, 94
Hochshild, Arlie, 108
Hollander, Jocelyn, 127
Holt, Melvin, 157
Hom, Alice, 164
homophobia: concerning gender-segregated bathrooms, 156–57, 165–66; faggy men and, 43; hybrid masculinities and, 17; hypermasculinity in, 51; of men's bathrooms, 165, 168–69, 203; in Midwest, 142–44; racist, 149; in rural space, 146; in social relations, 203; spatially based, 142–46; in trans vulnerability, 134; violent, 135, 146–49, 156–57
Hondagneu-Sotelo, Pierrette, 101, 194
hormone therapies: colloquial reports of, 240n29. *See also* testosterone
Houston, Willie, 156, 170; murder of, 157, 189
Howard Brown clinic (Chicago), transgender healthcare at, 181
hypereffeminacies, 21; classed images of, 56; of faggy men, 43
hypermasculinities, 26; anger in, 105; association with the poor, 52; classed, 33, 106, 108; controlling image of, 98, 128; discursive distancing from, 42–43; emotional control in, 22, 122; in homophobia, 51; lack of control in, 104–8, 116; moving away from, 109; racialized, 21, 33, 39, 55, 56, 106, 108, 128, 194; redneck, 37, 147; reduced legitimacy of, 57; regular guys and, 49; rigidity in, 50; rural, 27, 39, 133; sexual dominance in, 105; sexualized, 33; spatially produced, 32–43; of thug men, 39, 40; of trans men, 32–33; in urban space, 133; violence in, 95–96, 106, 127, 164

identity: breadth of, 223n41; collective nature of, 233n8; intersectional understanding of, 7; nonbinary, 70, 197, 219n1, 223n40; questions establishing, 220n13; social achievement of, 233n8; spatially created, 11
identity, gender: affirmation of, 74–75; discrimination based on, 135; emotional control and, 100; institutional contexts of, 62; misrecognition of, 77, 234n18; passing in, 137, 232n4; in rural space, 11; spatial concepts of, 62. *See also* gender recognition
identity, male: essentialist understanding of, 62–63; social assessment of, 60
identity, racial: in organization of resources, 27–28; recognition of, 68–69
Industrial Belt, masculine ideal of, 30
inequality: contemporary understandings of, 23; emotional control and, 92; in gender recognition, 78; institutional, 7,

189, 191; in interaction, 8–10; intersectional study of, 197; masculinities and, 17, 56, 203–6; persistence of, 203; place and, 10–12; production in social life, 189; re-creation of, 8; role of hybrid masculinities in, 203; in social domination, 23; spatial, 10–12, 196–99; structural, 201
Inglis, David, 158
innocence: moves to, 130–31, 133, 154; narratives of, 125-34; of racist violence, 242n17; regular guys', 195; white, 130
institutional space, 23; interactional rules of, 154; population control in, 155; power formations of, 155; production of violence, 156; reinforcing processes of, 156
intersectionality, 7–8, 21, 201, 220n11; analysis of power relations, 203; in male experience, 6; perspective on trans men, 14; racial formation and, 221n19, 227n4; in study of inequality, 197; in understanding of identity, 7; in women of color feminism, 216
interviews: age of interviewees, 20; gender identities in, 218; grounded theory approach to, 20; in Midwest, 213; power dynamics of, 215; recruitment for, 217–18; in South, 212; in West, 211. See also narratives, trans men's

Jackman, Mary, 240n1, 248n49
Jackson, Janet: chest exposure of, 235n27
Jarosz, Lucy, 34
Johnson, E. Patrick, 11
Johnson, Marsha P., 200

Kafer, Alison, 202
Kandaswamy, Priya, 221n19; on racial formation, 227n4
Key, Keegan-Michael, 239n27

Lacan, Jacques: on public restrooms, 158
Lamble, Sarah, 130
Latinx men: assumptions of criminality concerning, 83; gendered division of labor, 50–51; intersectional framework for, 232n72; scrutiny of, 81–82; as threat, 37, 39
Lawson, Victoria, 34
lesbians: affirmation of trans men's identity, 85; male mistrust of, 216; relationships with trans men, 225n53; transnational regional analysis of, 249n5; urban communities, 11–12
LGBT people: antiviolence work of, 153; outside coastal cities, 199; safe spaces for, 141
locker rooms: fear of violence in, 161, 167, 171; genitals in, 168; privacy in, 190; spatial rules of, 167–68; trans men's use of, 167–69
Longhurst, Robyn, 71

machismo, 50
MacKaye, Ian, 53
Madríz, Esther, 127
Malheur National Wildlife Refuge, occupiers of, 36
man: bodies subsumed under, 195; distinction from masculinities, 15; social categories of, 21–22; as unstable category, 14. See also men; trans men
marginalization: class/race/sexual, 128; multiple forms of, 201, 205; of trans patients, 183

marginalized groups: controlling images of, 26–27; effect of activism on, 200; normative social ideals of, 133; participation in domination, 150; reinforcement of their status, 130–31
marriage, heterosexual: dynamics of, 50
masculine balance, 47, 98
masculinities, 14–18; assumed competence in, 79; balance in, 47; changes to, 17–18, 21; contested, 87; continuum of, 194–95; disability and, 236n43; distancing from homosexuality, 43; dominant narratives of, 117; embodied aspects of, 71, 119, 194; emotional control and, 89–92; factors in production of, 18; fears affecting, 22–23, 127; feminist scholars on, 5; gay men's, 44, 45; hegemonic, 16–18, 203, 226n75; heroic, 29; hierarchy of, 16; hip-hop, 15, 42; historic ideals of, 28; inequality and, 17, 56, 203–6; Israeli, 231n66; left/right, 237n57; male behavior and, 14–15; meanings in U.S., 1–4; nonhegemonic, 6; patterns of practice, 6, 14–15, 16; performance of, 152–53; physical ability and, 78–79; political, 196; raced/classed/sexualized, 105; regional, 8, 18, 26, 225n53; relational model of, 6; self-discipline in, 92; shift in, 6; social/historical context of, 15; social recognition of, 21, 123; spectrum of, 26–28, 32; subordinated, 34, 44, 46, 203; subsets of, 15; sustaining of society, 14; symbolic representations of, 27; textually appropriate, 75; toxic, 16–17, 32; trans men's, 4, 12–19, 75–78; twenty-first-century, 193–94; working-class, 34
masculinities, hybrid, 17; feminist challenges to, 51; gender relations and, 93; of Goldilocks masculinity, 6, 121, 123; in less progressive places, 204; on masculine spectrum, 27; meanings of, 203; of regular guys, 48; spatial dimensions of, 24, 204–5; in understanding of social inequity, 203
masculinities, rural: performance of, 60, 149; regional variants in, 31; versus urban, 26. *See also* rednecks
masculinities, spatial, 18–19, 20, 24, 25–59; class in, 28; faggy men's, 43–47; hybrid, 24, 204–5; hypermasculinities of, 32–43; locally situated, 18–19; in Midwest, 28, 29–30, 55; progressive men's, 52–55; race in, 28; rednecks', 31, 33–37; regular guys', 47–52; in South, 28, 30–31, 54, 55, 97–98; thugs', 37–43; transnational, 18; in West, 28, 29, 55; West Coast, 135; white, 28–29
masculinities, urban: versus rural, 26; thugs, 37–43; varieties of, 37. *See also* thugs, urban
masculinities literature: patterns of practice in, 6; trans men in, 5
masculinities studies, critical, 14
masculinity, black: policing of, 229n42; relationship to urban thugs, 40–42, 230n56. *See also* black men
masculinity, Goldilocks, 21, 219n3; avoidance of victimization, 186, 188; balance in, 98; calmness in, 97; effect on gender order, 57;

embodiment of, 101; emotional control in, 22, 92–93, 102, 105, 114, 115; fear in, 134; hybridity of, 6, 121, 123; hyperlocal contexts of, 57; "just right," 47; in masculine spectrum, 27; in medical settings, 188, 189; as normative, 203; positive traits of, 194–95; racialized, 113; of regular guys, 47–48, 51, 55, 127, 194; response to social movements, 56; spatially based control of, 110; testosterone therapy and, 95; trans maintenance of, 151

McDonald, CeCe: assault on, 140–41, 142

McIntosh, Mary: queer scholarship of, 10

McKittrick, Katherine, 20

medical institutions: abuse of trans patients, 176, 180–84, 201; abuse of trans patients' families, 185–86; authority of, 173, 183–84, 190; blocking of transition-related care, 174–79; cissexism at, 174; gender difference in, 187, 190; gendered work in, 190; Goldilocks masculinity in, 188, 189; power formations in, 155; rural, 176–77; surveillance by, 184; trans men's negotiations with, 179–82; trans men's vulnerability in, 172–88; transphobia in, 174, 177–78, 182, 184–85, 188; urban, 186; violence against trans men in, 156, 172–88, 189, 200, 248n49. *See also* authority, medical; healthcare, trans; patients, trans

men: assumption of competence for, 82–83; backstage/frontstage behavior, 78, 79–82, 236n44; disciplinary body of, 122–23; idealized emotional life, 89; physical space for, 81; in political life, 22; "real," 87; reluctance to dance, 236n40; self-identified, 74; self-presentation of, 78; social experience of, 60, 78–79. *See also* man; trans men

Messerschmidt, James, 16, 17; on fluid masculinity, 57; on gender relations, 204; on hegemonic masculinity, 18, 226n75

Messner, Michael, 91, 194; on crying, 101

Midwest: displays of affection in, 148; homophobia in, 142–44; interviews in, 213; passing in, 137; regular guys in, 48; spatially based fear in, 139–44; spatial masculinities of, 28, 29–30, 55; tolerance in, 135, 142–43; trans safety in, 139–44, 145; in U.S. imagination, 29

militants, white, 25, 27

misogyny, 79–80; faggy men's, 46; feminist critique of, 105; in hypermasculinity, 105; social relations of, 86

Mohanty, Chandra Talpade: *Feminism without Borders*, 8; on racial recognition, 68–69

Moore, Justin: "Bait a Hook," 36

Moore, Kayla, 39

mud bogging, 33, 229n31

Muhammad, Khalil Gibran, 38

multiplicity: in gender/race/class/sexuality, 7; of transgender violence, 202; in trans men's experiences, 197; of trans men's voices, 24

Namaste, Vivian, 13, 174, 216

narratives, trans men's, 4, 24, 27; affect in, 92, 121–22; agency in, 200; aggression in, 101–4; anger in, 101–4, 108–10, 112; on backstage talk, 80; black men's, 40–41; combatting of masculine privilege in, 205; comparative analysis of, 194; on competence, 82–83; crying in, 97–101; on degrees of safety, 142–45; emotion in, 89–90, 92, 101, 107–8, 121–23; the everyday in, 197, 205; as evidence, 217–18; faggy men in, 43–47, 227n1; fear expressed in, 22–23; feminine emotion in, 102; forms of intolerance in, 149; gender affirmation in, 74–75; gender flexibility in, 77; gender knowledges of, 62, 63; gender queer, 169–70; gender recognition in, 63–64, 67–68, 69, 78–79, 85–86; gender-segregated bathrooms in, 160, 161–65, 188, 189, 202; on healthcare access, 175–76, 177; heterosexual attraction in, 83–85; homophobia in, 204; hypermasculinity in, 32, 40, 42, 104–5; inequality in, 200; innocence in, 125–34, 154; institutional spaces in, 155; locker rooms in, 167–68; masculine compensation in, 106; masculine control in, 113; masculine ideals in, 26; medical abuse in, 180–86; on medical institutions, 172–73, 202; on medical surveillance, 184; men's bathrooms in, 165–67; normalized bodies in, 72–73; on passing, 137; performance of gender in, 75–78; of place, 19–20; progressive men in, 53, 54; race in, 20, 150, 197; racial difference, 150; racial justice in, 111–12; rednecks in, 33, 36–37, 227n1; regular guys in, 48–51, 55; resistance in, 206; on respect, 80–82; romantic emotion in, 117–21; rural migration in, 137–38; rural–urban distribution of, 20; self-interpretations in, 24; sexual assault in, 125–26; sexual desire in, 113–17; spatial hybridity in, 205; spatially based fears of, 137–50; spatially based ideals of, 26; Brandon Teena in, 131, 132–33, 146–47, 152, 153, 154; testosterone therapy in, 93–99, 102–4, 123; on thugs, 37, 40–41, 42, 227n1; transgender possibilities in, 138–39; transition services in, 177–78; trans safety in, 136; urban masculinities in, 40; violence in, 110, 132, 140–41, 148–49, 200; vulnerability in, 125–34, 154; white men's, 42; whiteness in, 150. *See also* interviews; trans men

Nash, Catherine Jean, 233n6

Native Americans: cowboy contact with, 29; dispossession of, 30, 31

NORMA (journal), on trans masculinities, 15

norms: disciplinary power of, 155; enforcement by fear, 191; reinforcement of, 23; spatial, 10, 197, 233n6

North Carolina, HB 2 law (2016), 159, 245n20

Obama, Barack: avoidance of anger, 112–13, 239n27; transgender support under, 199

Omi, Michael: on Confederate flag, 34; on race/class/gender relationships, 227n4; *Racial Formation*, 9; on racial identity, 27

Pain, Rachel, 127
Pascoe, C. J., 17–18, 56; on dominance practices, 57; on fag

discourse, 43, 44, 77; on gender relations, 204
passing, in gender identity, 137, 232n4. *See also* gender recognition
Pat (*Saturday Night Live* character), 220n13
patients, ideal, 174, 179
patients, trans: abuse of, 176, 180–84, 201; access to healthcare, 174–77, 181, 188, 199; avoidance of victimization, 186, 189; caregiver training for, 183, 187; disability-related medical care, 182; disempowerment of, 190; exposure of bodies, 187; gender-conforming, 174; harassment of, 182; healthcare centers for, 199; ideal model of, 179; invasive questioning of, 183; marginalization of, 183; medical authority over, 183–84; microaggressions against, 183; as model patients, 174–75; with nontrans issues, 183–84; powerlessness of, 183; psychological injuries of, 174, 182; psychotherapy for, 175; punishment in medical systems, 172–73; resistance to violence, 187; search for competent healthcare, 186; surveillance of, 184; travel for services, 181; unequal power relations of, 187, 188; vulnerability of, 172–88. *See also* authority, medical; healthcare, trans; medical institutions
patriarchy, legitimization of, 203
Peele, Jordan, 239n27
Pfeffer, Carla, 16
place: collective ideas about, 198; embodiment of masculinity in, 194; gender/race/class/sexuality in, 10; in gender recognition, 86; and inequality, 10–12; narratives of, 19–20; in restricted gender knowledge, 70; in rural sociology, 11. *See also* regions; space
Plemons, Eric, 70
Plummer, Ken: queer scholarship of, 10
politics, transgender: law-and-order tactics of, 23–24, 153, 201
power: disciplinary, 155; emotional control in, 123; in emotional expression, 91; production in social life, 189; spatial changes to, 204; of whiteness, 113
power relations: controlling images of, 26; intersectional analysis of, 203; rural/urban differences in, 204; spatial creation of, 206
prison–industrial complex, black people in, 38
private space: aggression in, 104; chests in, 71; emotion in, 99, 100; gender-segregated bathrooms in, 160; sexual desire in, 115–16
progressive men, 26, 52–55; backstage talk and, 80; commitment to social justice, 205; expression of masculinity, 52–55; feminine aspects of, 54–55; ideal of, 52–53, 56; as new age, 52; normative masculinities and, 55; profeminist, 52–53; racial justice concerns, 54; rejection of aggression, 54; transformative project of, 53–54; transitions of, 53
Prosser, Jay, 13
puberty: sexual desire in, 114–15, 116; trans men's empathy with, 115, 116, 117, 122
public bathrooms, 158–61; disability in, 159–60, 163, 170;

interactional function of, 158; in Jim Crow era, 198; origins of, 158; promotion of hygiene, 158; racial segregation of, 158, 198; reinforcement of sexuality/race/class, 159; as site for coalition building, 202; surveillance function of, 159; transgender/disability interaction in, 159–60
public bathrooms, gender-segregated: avoidance of, 163; conservatism and, 157–58, 159; debates over, 189–90; decisions concerning, 164; domination systems of, 161; enforcement of bodily conformity, 160; everyday experiences of, 215; gender conformity in, 170, 189; gender nonconformity in, 162, 202; health issues in, 163; heterosexism in, 156; homophobic violence concerning, 156–57, 165–66; identification for, 164; institutional arrangements of, 188; institutional fear in, 160, 161–65; interactional rules of, 23, 156, 158–59, 165–70, 188; multiuser, 160, 202; power formations in, 155; privacy in, 190; in private space, 160; race/gender/sexuality issues in, 164; reduction of fear in, 172; in rural space, 162–63; single-occupancy, 202; social domination in, 171; in South, 163–64; spatially based violence in, 162–63; state legislation on, 159, 199, 245n20; symbolic importance of, 190; trans men in, 160, 161–65, 188, 189, 202; trans people in, 5, 233n12; trans people's access to, 156–72, 202

public bathrooms, men's: fear of violence in, 161, 165–67, 168, 188; genderqueer men in, 170; heterosexism in, 161, 171, 188, 195, 197; homoerotic space of, 166; homophobic rules of, 165, 168–69, 203; interactional rituals of, 170; maintenance of heterosexuality in, 165–66; recognition as men in, 169; sexual logic of, 166
public bathrooms, women's: gender-nonconformity policing in, 161, 164–65, 171, 188; interactional rules of, 170; normative gender in, 165–66, 190; trans men's harassment in, 161–62, 165, 168, 170–71
public space: assault in, 126; black men in, 5, 125–26; gender nonconformity in, 169; genderqueer people in, 169–70; norms of, 10; private acts in, 160; sexual assault in, 127; sexual desire in, 115–16; trans men in, 1–3, 9; violence in, 152; women's behavior in, 127
Pyke, Karen, 16; on heterosexual marriage, 50

queer communities: safety in, 138; of San Francisco Bay Area, 216
queer people: of color, 12, 223n36; cultural experience of, 215; rural, 11, 22, 198, 243n29; as white, 12, 243n29
queer space: Bear, 236n35; expansive gender knowledge in, 73, 85; gender fluidity in, 235n33
queer theory: development, 223n36; race in, 12; trans people in, 12

race: as category, 9; co-constitution with gender, 221n19; cultural scripts of, 9; as fixed marker of difference, 150; as form of categorization, 10; gender/class/sexuality interactions, 20, 194; gender perspective on, 221n14; in gender recognition, 69, 77, 81; in ideas of place, 194; markers of difference in, 150; in queer theory, 12; regional meanings of, 8; reproduction in interaction, 8, 10; in rural communities, 149; spatially shaped, 196, 197; in spatial masculinity, 28; as system of meaning, 9; in U.S. masculinity, 5

racial formation theory, 9, 194, 221n19, 227n4

racial recognition, 68–69; social status and, 235n22

racism: anger at, 111; homophobic, 149; production of vulnerability, 9; redneck, 34; in rural space, 146, 194, 243n29; sexuality/class intersections of, 243n29; social relations of, 86; spatially based fear of, 145–46

radical faerie gatherings, effeminacy of, 46

rape, cultural narrative of, 116

rap music, as lowbrow, 230n55

rationality: distance from emotions in, 122; versus emotion, 91; raced/classed/gendered concept of, 99; of trans men, 99, 100

Raymond, Janice, 13, 223n43

Razack, Sherene, 130

Redneck Revolt (activist group), 37

rednecks, 21; connections with thugs, 135, 230n56; controlling image of, 26, 33, 35, 43, 55, 164, 194; discursive distancing from, 43; gendered knowledge of, 59–60, 87; history of term, 33; hypercontrolled emotions of, 107; hypermasculinity of, 37, 147; lack of control, 106; obsolescence of, 35; opposition to gay men, 45; patriotic anger among, 36; in popular culture, 35–36; protection of women, 163; race/gender/sexual projects of, 205; racial projects of, 34; racist, 141; reclamation of, 37; regional masculinity of, 55; rural, 31, 33–37, 40, 127; self-sufficiency of, 36; stereotypes of, 42; transregional, 33; violent, 132, 135, 200; white, 33–34, 42. *See also* masculinities, rural

regions: masculinities of, 8, 18, 26, 225n53; shared meanings in, 19–20. *See also* masculinities, spatial; place; space

regular guys, 22, 26, 47–52; adaptability of, 57; calmness of, 97; distance from effeminacy, 52; emotional control of, 195; flexibility of, 195; gender division of labor among, 49, 50; gentlemanly manners of, 50; Goldilocks masculinity of, 47–48, 51, 55, 127, 194; heterosexuality of, 51; husbands and fathers, 49–50; hybrid masculinities of, 48; ideals across regions, 56; masculine ideal of, 93; middle-class, 48, 51, 55–56; midwestern, 48; narratives of innocence, 195; normalized masculinity of, 27; protection of women, 163; role in family, 50, 51; in rural South, 49; self-control of, 95; separation from femininity, 50; separation from hypermasculinity, 49; suburban normality of, 50; trans men as, 138; treatment of women, 48; white, 48

researcher positionality, 24, 215
respectability, 41, 51, 133, 151, 152–53; dynamics of, 242n17
Rice, Tamir: police killing of, 39
Riggs, Marlon, 43, 44
romantic emotions: emotional control of, 121; in heterosexual dyads, 203; sexual desire and, 114, 117–21; after transition, 117–21
Rubin, Henry, 15, 237n56
rural space: as backward, 151; class in, 149; economic production in, 28; effect of capitalism on, 31, 35; electoral politics of, 140; fear of violence in, 146–51; gay men in, 45; gendered identity in, 11; gender nonconformity in, 163; gender-segregated bathrooms in, 162–63; gentrification of, 140; geographic imaginaries of, 152; homophobic violence in, 148; hypermasculinity in, 27, 39, 133; masculine ideals of, 31; masculine presentations in, 243n24; men of color in, 204; normative masculinity in, 146–47; performance of masculinities in, 60, 149; poor whites of, 35; pride in, 35, 36; queer life in, 11, 22, 198, 243n29; racism in, 194, 243n29; rednecks in, 31, 33–37, 40, 127; safety/violence in, 132, 136, 139, 140, 145, 146–51; sexuality in, 149; threats to masculinity in, 26; transition care in, 177; trans men in, 12, 59–60, 137–38, 232n2; trans people in, 22, 198–99; versus urban space, 18, 19

San Francisco Bay Area: geography of safety, 135–37; masculinities of, 136; queer communities of, 216; transition-related care in, 177; trans recognition in, 137
Sapolsky, Robert, 94
Schilt, Kristen, 16, 236n42; *Just One of the Guys?*, 225n58; on male competence, 82
scholarship, black feminist: on race/gender/sexuality, 7–8
Schrock, Douglas, 78
Schwalbe, Michael, 78
self, internal sense of, 62
sex, biological criteria of, 232n3
sexual assault: by acquaintances, 127; as domination, 116; fear of, 125–26; in public space, 127
sexual desire: emotional control of, 114–17, 122; homosexual, 117–21; in private space, 115–16; in puberty, 114–15; in public space, 115–16; romantic emotions and, 114, 117–21
sexuality: affective changes in, 113–17, 118; amplified sites of, 156, 180, 188; essentialist discourse of, 122; family and, 121; formation in interaction, 10; gender/class/race interactions, 20, 194; gendered notions of, 118; in gender recognition, 78; in ideas of place, 194; in postslavery era, 229n42; reproduction in interaction, 8, 10; in rural space, 149; spatially based knowledge of, 196; in U.S. masculinity, 5
sexual space, 10–11; institutional, 155; trans men in, 5
Shakur, Tupac: thug image of, 41
Shields, Stephanie, 90
Smith, Dorothy, 197
snap queens, 44
Snorton, C. Riley, 154; *Black on Both Sides*, 14

South: acceptable masculinities of, 60; degrees of safety in, 143; faggy men in, 45; gender inequality in, 54; gender-segregated bathrooms in, 163–64; geography of violence in, 139; interviews in, 212; intolerance in, 143; male interactions in, 60; racial inequality in, 54; racial knowledges of, 83; racism in, 30; regular guys in, 49; spatial masculinities of, 28, 30–31, 54, 55, 97–98; tolerance levels in, 135; transition-related care in, 181; trans safety in, 136; in U.S. imagination, 30

Southeast: intolerance in, 135; spatially based fear in, 144–46, 148; tolerant areas of, 144–45; transition-related care in, 181–82; trans men's vulnerability in, 145–46

space: abolition of gender segregation in, 250n15; amplified, 23; collective ideas about, 198; differing experiences in, 6; disciplinary mechanisms of, 198; embodiment of masculinity in, 194; in formation of sexual communities, 11; gender categorization in, 67–70; gender dynamics of, 48; gender/race/class/sexuality in, 10–11; in gender recognition, 81; identities created in, 11; inequality and, 10–12, 196–99; in interaction, 196–99; in rural sociology, 11; safety and, 135. *See also* fear, spatially based; masculinities, spatial; *specific types of space*

Spade, Dean, 153; on critical race theory, 200; on gender self-determination, 187; on legal equality, 199; on trans medical care, 174

Stone, Amy, 235n33, 236n35

Strong Families Trans Day of Resilience campaign, 244n35

strongman regimes, social inequality under, 57

suburban space: normative male fantasies in, 138–39; safety in, 138

support groups, transgender, 65

Teena, Brandon, 151, 152, 200; murder of, 128; in trans men's narratives, 131, 132–33, 146–47, 153, 154

testosterone, 92; adjustment to, 103–4; anger associated with, 95–96, 101–4, 110; crying and, 101; cultural scripts about, 102, 105, 196; as "cure" for homosexuality, 240n34; difficulty obtaining, 177–78; effect on cisgender men, 93; effect on emotion, 93–95; Goldilocks masculinity and, 95; heightening properties of, 105; material effects of, 123; permissive effects of, 117, 123; physical changes from, 94, 123; 'roid rage in, 105; role in transition, 93–121, 177–78; sexual desire in, 113–17, 239n38; virilizing effects of, 119

testosterone therapy: affect in, 121–22, 123; aggression and, 94; calm following, 95–96, 97, 110, 122; emotional control in, 93–97, 99, 117; homosexual desire following, 119–20; negotiation for, 179

thugs, urban, 21, 37–43; aesthetic of, 41–42; black men, 39–40; connections with rednecks, 230n56; discursive distancing from, 43; fear of assault by, 126;

hypermasculinity of, 40; lack of control, 106; liberationist potential of, 41; and middle-class propriety, 41; poverty of, 41; race/class/masculinity ideals of, 152; race/gender/sexual projects of, 205; racialized hypermasculinity of, 39; regional masculinity of, 55; in relation to black masculinity, 40–42, 230n56

trans communities: empowerment of, 129; hierarchies of, 65, 234n16

transgender, as umbrella term, 13

Transgender Day of Remembrance (TDOR), 129–31, 153, 200, 242nn12,18; increased scope of, 201; memorialization of Willie Houston, 156; stories of violence in, 140; vulnerability produced at, 129, 130; white innocence at, 130

transition, 13, 32–33, 53; affective change in, 92; Appalachian services for, 177; blocking of access to, 174–79; casual sex in, 119–20; celebration of, 176; confidence following, 112; emotional control in, 89, 92, 93, 95–99; families' knowledge of, 67; fear of public bathrooms in, 161; gatekeeping in, 176, 177; "growing up" in, 109; medical abuse during, 176; medical guidelines for, 248n47; medical intervention during, 174; performance of masculinity in, 76; physical aspects of, 92; recognition in, 64–65; role of family in, 16; romantic emotions following, 117–21; sexual desire in, 113–17, 120; social changes of, 97; testosterone therapy in, 93–121, 177–78; in trans men's narratives, 59, 76; uneven privileges of, 237n54

trans men: acceptance of, 65; access to resources, 136; affective sexual changes to, 113–17; affirmation by lesbian women, 85; antiracist practice of, 205; authenticity of, 62, 85; avoidance of victimization, 151; binary categorization of, 137; breasts of, 59–60, 65–66; cisgender bias and, 195; cisgender coworkers of, 237n50; comfort with femininity, 77; commitment to change, 205; comparative study of, 19; complicity with white supremacy, 152; conforming practices of, 151, 152–53; connection to past, 70; definition of, 219n2; disciplinary power affecting, 155; discussion of masculinity, 21; emotional control of, 89–90, 92; emotional friendships of, 120; emotional relationships with women, 120; empathy with puberty, 115, 116, 117, 122; experiences of embodiment, 73; experiences of violence, 23, 110, 126; families' advice to, 76; firing of, 65; flexible gender expression of, 77; gendered identification for, 164; gender-nonconforming appearances of, 169; genderqueer, 169–70; in gender-segregated bathrooms, 160, 161–65, 188, 189, 202; geographic imaginaries of, 19, 55; harassment in women's bathrooms, 161–62, 165, 168, 170–71; heterosexual interracial relationships of, 84–85; heterosexuality of, 76–77; heterosexuals' attraction to, 83–85; hypermasculinity of, 32–33; insights into masculinity, 13; intersectional perspective on, 14; knowledge of their lives, 217; legal recognition of, 86; locker room use, 167–69; male pronouns for, 137; in masculine space, 82; in masculinities literature, 5; masculinities of, 4, 12–19, 75–78; as men, 12, 13, 69–70, 148–49, 219n1; midwestern safety for, 139–44, 145; misrecognition of, 65, 66, 69, 101, 162, 196, 215, 234n18; multiple voices of, 24; normalization of bodies, 72; normative fantasies of, 138–39; normative masculine practices of, 75–78; participation in domination, 151, 152; partners of, 16; perception as gay men, 196; presumption of heterosexuality for, 84, 85; prior knowledge concerning, 86; as progressive men, 55; in public spaces, 1–3, 9; rationality of, 99, 100; as regular guy, 138; relationship to fear, 126–27; relationships with lesbians, 225n53; relationships with women, 83–85, 120, 240n35; relations with queer women, 85; respectability for, 152; in rural space, 12, 59–60, 137–38, 232n2; self-identity of, 4; self-knowledge of, 237n56; in sexual space, 5; situational behavior of, 5; social recognition for, 195–96; spatially based knowledge of, 86; strangers' categorization of, 67–70, 75, 79; surveillance of, 142; without testosterone therapy, 94–95; in Texas, 225n53; thug men and, 39, 40–41; undocumented immigrants, 164; unrecognized, 137; use of backstage talk, 80; white working-class, 149; workplace experiences of, 16. *See also* narratives, trans men's; patients, trans

trans men, black, 40–41; gay, 1–3; police harassment of, 126, 153, 201; as threat, 125–27

trans people: access to bathrooms, 156–72, 202; advice websites for, 76; backlash against, 199; classed/racialized visibility of, 243n22; as deceptive, 184–85, 232n4; diverse lives of, 199; everyday lives of, 217; gendered knowledge of, 60; in gender-segregated spaces, 233n12; in gender theory, 13; legal rights of, 86, 189, 199–200; marginalized, 130, 183; medical knowledge of, 174; as mentally unstable, 184–85; in military service, 199; in multiple locations, 202; murder of, 241n1; nonbinary, 70, 219n1; numbers in U.S., 251n7; pathologizing of, 175; police attention to, 201; protection from hate crimes, 200; in queer theory, 12; relationship with researchers, 217; rethinking of possibilities for, 14; rural, 22, 198; scientific studies of, 13; self-understanding of, 13; structural inequality experiences, 183; as subjects/objects, 13, 224n45; in urban areas, 5; varying resources for, 248n48; violence against, 23, 110, 126, 140, 233n4, 234n15; visibility of, 199

transphobia: among medical providers, 174, 177–78, 182, 184–85, 188; fear of, 130; in rural space, 146; violent, 148–49, 196

trans women: black, 129; queer research on, 224n44

trans women of color: in criminal justice system, 142; violence against, 140; vulnerability of, 244nn34–35
Trump, Donald: masculine practices of, 56–57; reversal of trans rights, 199; use of anger, 113

Urban, Thomas, 13
urban space: access to healthcare in, 186; black poor men in, 127; faggy men in, 45; fear in, 134; flexible gender expectations in, 147; gay identity in, 11; geographic imaginaries of, 152; geography of safety in, 139; heterogeneity of, 204; hypermasculinity in, 133; lesbian identity in, 11; marginalized communities of, 26; racialized ideals of, 42; versus rural space, 18, 19; safety in, 139; surveillance in, 142; violence in, 133, 141–42; western, 136

Valentine, Gill, 127, 134
victimization: blaming of victims for, 130, 151; characteristics leading to, 133–34; trans men's avoidance of, 151; trans patients' avoidance of, 186, 189
violence: blaming of victims for, 130; classed, 134; conservatism and, 144; disciplinary, 22, 152; discursive distancing from, 239n21; emotional components of, 124; enforcement of norms, 191; feminist theorists on, 241n1; gendered, 126, 128; homophobic, 135, 146–49; in hypermasculinities, 95–96, 106, 127, 164; institutional, 154, 191; male victims of, 128; marking gender nonconformity, 171; masculine, 95–96, 106, 127; racialized, 25, 39, 126, 134; redneck, 132, 135, 200; reforms countering, 200–201; in social domination, 23; spectacular, 128, 132, 140–41, 152, 242n18; structural explanations for, 122, 153; white heterosexual, 147; against women, 39, 104, 106, 125
violence, spatially based, 124, 125, 131–46; in gender-segregated bathrooms, 162–63, 165–66; in public places, 152; in rural space, 132, 136, 139, 140, 145, 146-51; in urban space, 133, 141–42
violence, transgender, 23, 110, 126, 199–203, 233n4, 234n15; common sources of, 201; denial of healthcare as, 176–79; against faggy men, 195; fear of, 129–31, 161; geographic imaginaries of, 135; individual responsibility for, 200; in institutional space, 156; law-and-order politics of, 201; in medical institutions, 156, 172–88, 189, 200, 249n49; multiple forms of, 202; patients' resistance to, 187; public bathrooms and, 155–57, 161–63, 165–66; in rural space, 132, 136, 139, 140, 145, 146–51; transphobic, 148–49, 196; vulnerability to, 151–52; white men's safety from, 150–51
vulnerability: discourse of, 131, 152; gendered, 127; production by racism, 9; rituals of, 129–30, 132, 200; to trans violence, 151–52; of women, 125, 127
vulnerability, trans men's, 125–34; discourses of, 128–29, 131–32,

153; displays of, 153; fear of homophobia, 134; in medical institutions, 172–88; in Southeast, 145–46; spatial, 132

vulnerability, trans peoples', 126, 127–29; at TDOR events, 129, 130

Wang, Jackie, 154
Ward, Jane: on giving gender, 74; on str8-identified men, 120–21
Watson, Lori, 251n1
West: interviews in, 211; spatially based fear in, 135–39; spatial masculinities of, 28, 29, 55; urban men in, 29; urban parts of, 136; in U.S. imagination, 29; white militants of, 25, 27. *See also* San Francisco Bay Area
West, Candace, 9, 13; on gender expectations, 198; on sex/gender distinction, 232n3
West Coast: masculinities of, 135; transition-related care in, 181
Westbrook, Laurel, 128, 237n49; on trans vulnerability, 128–29
white men: anger of, 31, 110–11; racial politics of, 25; regular guys, 48; respect for, 81; rural, 25, 31, 152, 240n36
white men, trans, 42; acceptance of, 150–51, 232n2; in gender-segregated bathrooms, 162; safety from violence, 150–51; working-class, 149
whiteness: in acceptance of trans men, 232n2; construction of, 9; power of, 113; rationality and, 99; rural, 25, 31, 152
white supremacy, 150; rewards of, 131; trans men's complicity with, 152; across urban/rural lines, 35
white womanhood, perceived threats to, 38
Whitlock, Kay, 153
Wilkins, Amy, 111
Winant, Howard: on Confederate flag, 34; on race/class/gender relationships, 227n4; *Racial Formation*, 9; on racial identity, 27
Wingfield, Adia Harvey, 112, 236n48
women: attraction to trans men, 83–85; censorship around, 80; fear of assault, 126; flexible gender expectations for, 147; male dominance over, 5; misogynistic talk about, 79–80; queer, 85; regular guys' treatment of, 48; relationships with trans men, 120; violence toward, 39, 104, 106, 125; vulnerability of, 125, 127. *See also* black women; lesbians; trans women
workers, ideal: separate spheres ideology of, 231n69

Young, Kathryne, 47

Zimmerman, Don, 9, 13; on gender expectations, 198; on sex/gender distinction, 232n3

Miriam J. Abelson is assistant professor of women, gender, and sexuality studies at Portland State University.

CPSIA information can be obtained
at www.ICGtesting.com
Printed in the USA
BVHW072030200819
556350BV00008B/63/P